Latinx and Latin American Profiles

Frederick Luis Aldama, Editor

Aquí and Allá

Transnational Dominican Theater and Performance

Camilla Stevens

University of Pittsburgh Press

Published by the University of Pittsburgh Press, Pittsburgh, Pa., 15260

Manufactured in the United States of America
Printed on acid-free paper
10 9 8 7 6 5 4 3 2 1

Cataloging-in-Publication data is available from the Library of Congress

ISBN 13: 978-0-8229-4586-4
ISBN 10: 0-8229-4586-X

Cover art: Susanna Guzmán and Ismael Cruz Córdova in *La luz de un cigarillo*. Photographed by Anthony Ruiz, ARuizphotography. Josefina Báez in *Dominicanish*. Photographed by Jorge Vismara.
Cover design: Melissa Dias-Mandoly

Contents

Acknowledgments

The origins of this book trace back to a 2005 roundtable discussion on current debates in Caribbean studies at a conference held in Santo Domingo hosted by the Caribbean Studies Association. As we reflected on recently published books in the field, including my own, *Family and Identity in Contemporary Cuban and Puerto Rican Drama* (2004), the distinguished scholar Silvio Torres-Saillant unsurprisingly inquired why my study excluded the Dominican Republic. Although I was prepared to answer that question, I walked away from the event knowing that my next project would address the lacuna in scholarship on Dominican literary and cultural studies, specifically in the field of theater and performance.

I spent the next few years developing curricula that remedied the underrepresentation of Dominican literature and culture in the courses I regularly teach at Rutgers, the state university of New Jersey. It was a collaborative effort and I am indebted to all my students, especially to Lorgia García-Peña and my other Dominican students, for their cultural insights, personal stories, and willingness to take courses with me. In particular, I would like to thank my research assistants, Elizabeth Sahner and Melissa Widdis, for helping me to think through and organize a largely unexplored corpus of materials I brought back from my visits to theaters, libraries, and book fairs in New York City, Santo Domingo, and Havana.

I would also like to acknowledge my Latin American theater and performance studies colleagues Laurietz Seda (University of Connecticut) and Jacqueline Bixler (Virginia Tech) and their organizational teams for their Herculean efforts in hosting the sixth and seventh iterations of the Latin American Theatre Today Festival and Symposium. At these events, I was able to see Claudio Mir's *Mondongo Scam* for the first time and to meet Frank Disla, who kindly gave me a copy of his play *Un búfalo de El Paso, Texas*. These New Jersey-based Dominican artists inspired me to develop a transnational vision inclusive of cultural production both *aquí* and *allá*. To my delight, many Dominican theater practitioners have generously shared play manuscripts, video recordings, and photographs with me, a North American scholar they hardly knew. I am grateful for their trust. It is my hope that documenting the plays and performances of the Dominican theater practitioners in this book brings their valuable work greater visibility and opens doors for further research.

In my journey to complete this book, I have received support in myriad ways. My conference posse (you know who you are) offered sound advice and needed respite from the daily grind. I wish to thank Gail Bulman, Stuart Day, Paola Hernández, Lillian Manzor, Priscilla Meléndez, Sarah Misemer, Beatriz Rizk, and Brenda Werth for organizing conference panels and edited collections where I rehearsed the ideas of this book. Many thanks as well to my long-standing mentors, Vicky Unruh and Yolanda Martínez-San Miguel, for their unfailingly thoughtful responses to my doubts. Selma Cohen, Cynthia Hill, and my anonymous readers at the University of Pittsburgh Press provided critical feedback and editing that has enriched my work. At Rutgers, numerous deans and colleagues made it possible for me to spread my intellectual wings in an ethnic studies curriculum, which had a decisive impact on the development of this monograph. In addition, current and former chairs from both of my departments—Marcy Schwartz (Spanish and Portuguese), Tom Stephens (Spanish and Portuguese), Carlos Decena (Latino and Caribbean Studies), and Nelson Maldonado-Torres (Latino and Caribbean Studies)—provided just the kind of encouragement I needed to finish this endeavor. I thank the Rutgers School of Arts and Sciences dean's office for supporting my work through a sabbatical and research funds, and I am grateful for the Rutgers Office of Research and Sponsored Programs for a research council grant to cover the costs incurred in the preparation of the manuscript. In all phases of the process of transforming the manuscript into a book, the University of Pittsburgh Press Latinx and Latin American Profiles series editor Frederick Luis Aldama, senior acquisitions editor Joshua Shanholtzer, editorial and production director Alex Wolfe, and managing editor Amy Sherman have been very helpful.

Finally, I would like to express my deepest gratitude to the loving support of my family. In the midst of our incredibly busy lives you helped me find a way to make the time and space necessary to complete this project. Michael Witt selflessly sacrificed our home office and kept the computer (and my mental stability) humming. In exchange for the happiness they bring to me, I hope that my sons, Sam and Oscar, have learned a lesson in perseverance by observing the many years their mother spent laboring to accomplish a singular goal. I dedicate this book to my beloved father, Bill Stevens, who, along with my late mother, Deborah Dyar Stevens, introduced me to the marvelous world of the theater.

For permission to reprint material that appeared in earlier forms, I am grateful to several publishers. A portion of chapter 2 appeared as "Performing Dominican Transnationalism in *P.A.R.G.O.: Los pecados permitidos* by Waddys Jáquez," *Symposium: A Quarterly Journal in Modern Literatures* 61, no. 4 (Winter 2008): 255–65. Shorter versions of chapters 4, 5, and 6 appeared as "'Home Is Where Theatre Is': Dominican Stories of Return Migration," *Latin American Theatre Review* 44, no. 1 (Fall 2010): 29–48; "'Get up, Stand up, Stand up for your Rights': Transnational Belonging and Rights of Citizenship in Dominican Theater," *Imagining Human Rights in Twenty-First Century Theater: Global Perspectives* (Palgrave Macmillan, 2013), edited by Florian Becker, Paola Hernández, and Brenda Werth; and "The Aesthetics of Minor Transnationalism in the Theater of Frank Disla," *Chasqui: Revista de literatura latinoamericana* 45, no. 2 (2016): 186–99, respectively.

Aquí and Allá

Introduction

Dominican Migration on Center Stage

In *Chicken Cordon Blue* (1997), a play by the Dominican author Frank Disla, the initial stage directions warn: "El espectador acostumbrado al colorido y oropeles tendrá que irse con su música a otra parte, porque lo que veremos aquí será la imagen de cuatro emigrantes que nada tiene que ver con *The King and I* o *Cats*, triste admitirlo, pero es la verdad cruda como la vida de estos personajes" ("The spectator used to bright colors and glitter will have to find their entertainment elsewhere, because the image of four immigrants we will see has nothing to do with *The King and I* or *Cats*, sad to say, but it is crude reality, like the lives of these characters"; 30).[1] The play is composed of four monologues voiced by actors playing the roles of Puerto Rican, Mexican, Dominican, and Cuban immigrants and performed on a bare stage—a minimalist style, the stage directions suggest, that departs from the typical theatrical fare offered in mainstream Santo Domingo auditoriums. In a similar fashion, the actor characters in *Paradise* (2006), a piece by Disla's compatriot Pedro Antonio Valdez, question the commitment of local theatergoers: "El público de esta ciudad no viene al teatro bajo la lluvia. ¡Cretinos! como si el agua los fuera a derretir" ("The audience in this city does not come to the theater if it is raining. Cretins! As if the rain would melt them"; 13). Despite the anticipated absence of an audience, however, the members of the theater troupe in *Paradise* opt to stay and to hone their craft through improvisation: "¿Por qué no hacemos un juego con la historia de Adán y Eva? Una versión libre . . . algo improvisado y atrevido" ("Let's experiment with the story of Adam and Eve. A free version . . . something improvised and daring"; 14). The troupe then imagines an Adam and Eve story of migration to a dubious US "paradise," experimenting in each scene with different genres such as *teatro de cámara* (chamber theater), *novela rosa* (romance novel), and film noir. In my view, the search for a new audience, new stories, and new aesthetics in these plays is emblematic of a dialogue transnational Dominican theater practitioners have begun with the national "script" for Dominican culture and identity. From the vantage point of the diaspora, prominent Dominican researchers from various academic disciplines such as the literature scholars Silvio Torres-Saillant and Daisy Cocco De Filippis, the sociologist Ramona Hernández, and the historian Frank Moya Pons initiated a rich debate on approaches to Dominican history and culture and the impact of migration on the changing character of Dominican identity during the latter half of the twentieth century that, more recently, has been taken up by a new generation of interdisciplinary scholars including, among others, Carlos Decena, Lorgia García-Peña, and Dixa Ramírez. The objective of this book is, first, to examine how theater and performance studies intervene in this interdisciplinary discussion and to examine a corpus of Dominican plays about migration that rehearse an expanding repertoire of *dominicanidad* (Dominicanness). Second, I contend that Dominican theater about the diaspora represents a unique site for producing a democratizing force on conceptions of collective belonging. By looking across and beyond the nation-state, I adopt a transnational framework to document how plays from *aquí* (here) and *allá* (there) foreground a bifocal vision that engages both the diaspora and the homeland. Throughout the book I argue that Dominican theatrical performance produces a transnational public that recognizes the linkages as well as the differentiations that characterize a multi-local Dominican nation. Finally, I suggest that the creative practices of transnational theater artists examined in this study compel us to complicate the national and ethnic categories that have defined Latin American and US Latino theater traditions. In what follows, I provide some brief historical context for Dominican migration and review what researchers have identified as its transnational qualities. I then discuss how diasporic literature and culture has contested exclusionary constructions of Dominican national identity and provide an overview of the development of Dominican literature and theater in the United States. In the subsequent six chapters I analyze the intersections of race, class, gender, and sexuality with different facets of the transnational migration experience, such as the journey itself, arrival and adaptation, assimilation and the second generation, return migration, and undocumented migration in over a dozen Dominican theater and performance pieces.

Transnational Migration between the Dominican Republic and the United States

In response to over a half century of political authoritarianism, economic insecurity, and chronic social immobility, over a million Dominicans have emigrated—primarily to the United States, the chief destination examined in this book—but also to Puerto Rico, Curaçao, Argentina, Venezuela, Italy, Spain, and the Netherlands. Broadly viewed, US-bound migration from the Dominican Republic forms part of a wave of post–World War II immigration in which Latin America, Africa, and Asia replaced Europe as the major sending states. This migration, the legacy of decolonization and the globalization of capitalism, marks a second major phase of global labor movement. As Nicholas Van Hear remarks in his study of today's "new diasporas," migration has "long been a feature of the world stage, a manifestation of wide disparities in socio-economic circumstances, perceived life-chances and human security" (2).[2] However, during the previous period of globalization, roughly 1880–1914, labor migrants faced "little or no restrictions in most states" as they spanned the globe in search of work in regions undergoing industrialization (Glick Schiller 19). By contrast, in today's restructured, postindustrial economy, capital and technology flow freely and, while there is great human mobility as well, most migrants encounter barriers erected by nation-states that attempt to limit entry. In the contemporary world, growing socioeconomic inequities encourages economic migration, but migrant receiving markets have become less absorptive of labor, and the negative perceptions of the political, socioeconomic, and security impacts of opening borders to migrants have intensified, creating "a potent cocktail of increased pressure to migrate set against hardening barriers to immigration" (Van Hear 3).

Regionally and historically specific political and economic processes such as neocolonialism also inform migration from the Hispanic Caribbean to the United States. In *Blurred Borders: Transnational Migration between the Hispanic Caribbean and the United States*, the anthropologist Jorge Duany writes, "Since the 1950s Hispanic Caribbean people have moved abroad en masse in response to changes in the global economy and their local repercussions. This exodus has deepened the region's dependence on the United States" (32).[3] Duany argues that employing a transnational lens to examine Dominican, Puerto Rican, and Cuban migration provides a comprehensive picture of Hispanic Caribbean migration because it illuminates the commonalities and, conversely, the particularities of the three migration experiences. For Duany, "the form, frequency, and intensity of transnationalism largely hinges on the nature of the relationship between sending and receiving countries" (*Blurred Borders* 7). By historically contextualizing migration from the region and comparing factors such as the sending and receiving country's policy toward emigration/immigration, recognition of dual citizenship and voting rights, relationship with the United States, immigrants' legal status upon arrival, context of reception, class and racial composition, mode of labor incorporation, type of migration, degree of transnational ties with country of origin, and level of remittances, Duany documents the varying nature and degree of the connections between points of origin and destination in Hispanic Caribbean migration (*Blurred Borders* 230). In large part, *Blurred Borders* reaffirms the continued strong homeland attachments fomented by economic remittances and the Dominican government, leading Duany to characterize the Dominican Republic a "transnational nation-state," whereas his research on Puerto Rico and Cuba challenges previously held assumptions about the ties between their insular and diasporic communities. Duany's research on the Puerto Rican Farm Labor Program of the 1950s–1970s and on Puerto Rican migration to Orlando, Florida, since the 1990s reveals numerous features of transnationalism that lead Duany to label Puerto Rico a "transnational colonial state," and although the historically antagonistic relationship between Cuba and its overseas migrants define Cuba as a "disinterested and denouncing state," since the end of the Cold War this tense relationship has softened due to strengthening ties between the Cuban American community and its homeland through a rise in telephone communication and social media use, economic remittances, and return visits to the island by Cubans living abroad. Thus, while Duany shows that Dominican migration may still be seen as the "classic" example of contemporary transnationalism, using a transnational methodology yields fresh insight on migration processes across the region. Consistent with Duany's transnational approach, in my study of Dominican theater and performance I aim to blur the borders of a national theater canon by reading together plays written and performed back home (the island, for some) and in the diaspora (now home, for others) and proposing instead a multilingual and multi-sited transnational Dominican theater practice that has developed over the past twenty-five years.

Significant numbers of Dominicans began migrating in the second half of the 1960s, with a marked increase in the 1980s and 1990s. Macrostructural historical conditions created a push-pull dynamic that motivated the massive migration to the United States. On the one hand, changing US policies, such as the Immigration and Nationality Act of 1965, increased the quota of Caribbean migrants who could legally enter the country each year. On the other hand, the economic and political woes under president Dr. Joaquín Balaguer pushed Dominicans to leave their homeland. Balaguer rose to power after the military dictator Rafael Leónidas Trujillo was assassinated in 1961, ending his three decades in power. The dismantling of the Trujillo regime was followed by five years of political instability that concluded with an American military intervention in 1965 to halt a civil war and to ensure that elected left-wing leader Juan Bosch would not regain power after being overthrown by a right-wing military coup. The candidate supported by the US government, Balaguer, was elected president, and his first period in office, 1966–1978, was characterized by heavy repression of the political opposition. During this period, many dissidents who opposed Balaguer sought exile, a move that was facilitated by the US government in the interest of easing the political conflicts in the Dominican Republic.

From the 1980s on, however, periodic economic crises and failed development policies have mainly driven Dominican migration (Hernández, *Mobility* 33).[4] Like in most developing countries, industrialization has encouraged internal migration as Dominicans seek alternatives to agriculture to power their economy. In the context of Latin America, the Dominican Republic underwent this transformation relatively late, after the demise of Trujillo. Balaguer's administration embarked on urban industrialization and modernization projects during his first regime, which lured thousands of Dominicans from the countryside to the capital, Santo Domingo, in search of better life opportunities. In the city, however, rather than enjoying social and economic mobility, many found themselves among new and growing masses of the urban poor. Without the passport and visa restrictions that tightly controlled the international movement of Dominicans during Trujillo's leadership, a second wave of migration developed, this time mainly to New York City.[5] There, a network of Dominican immigrants established in the 1960s provided the infrastructure that facilitated large-scale migration in the 1980s and 1990s, which served as a pipeline for the surplus of laborers produced by Balaguer's socioeconomic policies (Hernández, *Mobility* 8–9). The expulsion of workers was a safety valve for the Dominican government, but it did not correspond with labor demands in the US economy. As Ramona Hernández has demonstrated, Dominicans encountered a US labor market in the process of restructuring, leading most Dominican migrants to "find dead-end, low-paying, and undesirable blue-collar jobs, if not outright unemployment" (14). In pointing out the racialization experienced by Dominican workers, Hernández, in blunt terms, further details their vulnerability and marginalization in the receiving society:

> The majority of those who come are dark-skinned, and women predominate over men. These are facts. It is also factual that Dominicans came to a society that was undergoing a transformation process, which has left the economy without the kinds of jobs most of these new immigrants were equipped to do. To make matters worse, they came into a racially stratified society, where blacks and other dark people were marginalized, and where, since the very beginning, poor Dominicans were not needed nor wanted as workers. (85)

Despite the socioeconomic challenges identified by Hernández, tightening US immigration policies, and rising anti-immigrant rhetoric, in the

1980s and 1990s more Dominicans arrived in New York City than from any other nation (Ricourt 3). Based on the 2010 US Census and the 2012 American Community Survey data, it is estimated that 1.7 million people who were either born in the Dominican Republic or who report Dominican origin live in the United States, making them the fifth largest Hispanic group, just behind Mexicans, Puerto Ricans, Cubans, and Salvadorans (Nwosu and Batalova). Put another way, over 15 percent of the Dominican population lives in the United States—a reality that has impacted all facets of national life and has made it impossible to conceive of Dominican economics, politics, and culture without including the diasporic population.[6] In line with many scholars of Dominican migration, Duany claims that "the Dominican diaspora has reshaped practically every aspect of daily life in the homeland, from family structures and business enterprises to political ideology and religious affiliation. . . . It has also transformed the physical and cultural landscape of several American neighborhoods, cities, and states" ("Países" 29). The households, social webs, economic ventures, political activities, and cultural tastes of Dominicans both *aquí* and *allá* link and mutually constitute and influence one another. As we will see, Dominican theater and performance represents a site and an activity where a collective identity that transcends territorial boundaries is embodied onstage.

The theoretical lens most employed in analyzing the lives and identifications of today's migrants who move in networks that span nation-states is transnationalism.[7] Moreover, the sociologist José Itzigsohn, along with his co-researchers in the United States and the Dominican Republic, assert the confluence of Dominican migration and the development of this new line of inquiry in migration studies: "The large size of the migration flows, and the relatively short period time in which they occurred caused a large transformation in Dominican society, making the Dominican case a paradigmatic one for the study of the rise of transnationalism" (Itzigsohn et al. 318). Unlike the straight-line assimilation expectations for immigrants in the United States during the first half of the twentieth century or the melting pot theories of cultural pluralism developed in the 1960s, transnational migration studies came together as a field in the 1990s, just as mass Dominican migration to the United States was reaching a peak.[8] Different from the past, Dominicans, along with other migratory groups across the globe, tend to settle in host societies without severing ties to the homeland. These "transmigrants" cultivate multiple cross-border ties, creating networks that connect home and host societies and facilitate the movement of people, capital, and culture. Transnationalism as a framework of analysis developed in response to the need to investigate such migratory processes that connect nation-states, blurring their borders even as governments endeavor to make their boundaries more impermeable (Duany, *Blurred Borders* 1–2).[9] As noted previously, Dominicans entered the US labor market as unwanted surplus workers, and, consequently faced economic hardship and difficulty securing a social, economic, or political foothold in American society. This marginalization has encouraged immigrants to retain ties with their home societies so as to create social and economic stability for their families. The strategies they develop exemplify transnationalism "from below"—that is, they represent local resistances such as small businesses and informal economic activities, ethnic nationalism, and grassroots activism in contrast to what is known as transnationalism "from above"—the forces of transnational capital, global media, and supranational political and financial institutions (Guarnizo and Smith 3). In transnationalism "from below," writes Itzigsohn et. al, "immigrants use their social relations from their place of origin and their place of migration to build economic enterprises that operate across borders. A central characteristic of these enterprises is that their existence is dependent on the continuation of the transnational linkage" (318). Different from the diasporas generated by earlier global labor movements, today's transnational connections are more intense and reciprocal due to the ease of access to airline travel, telecommunications, the internet, and satellite technology. At the same time, Dominican enclaves in areas such as New York City, Boston, Providence, and San Juan constitute spaces where many aspects of "home" have been replicated. Migration and incorporation is enabled by ethnic neighborhoods that connect overseas Dominicans to the homeland through the familiar sounds of the Spanish language and bachata and merengue music, national dishes served in restaurants, style trends observable in Dominican beauty salons and retail stores, and easily accessible news from the Dominican Republic through online sources, print media, and cable television shows. As the anthropologist Ulf Hannerz explains in *Transnational Connections: Culture, People, Places*, the ethnic neighborhood in the diaspora changes how we understand "the local": "And if somehow these characteristic features of local life become differently distributed in the social organization of space, so that for example everyday life is less confined, or those 'real' experiences with a full range of senses are spread out more equally over some number of places which thus approach the qualities of 'home,' then the one and only local would appear to be a rather less privileged site of cultural process" (27–28). Acknowledging that in New York City, Miami, and San Juan—among other numerous other metropolitan areas—the diaspora from the Hispanic Caribbean has reproduced the Puerto Rican, Cuban, and Dominican "local" beyond the geographical confines of the nation-state represents a challenge to narratives of identity that privilege the insular identity as primordial, autochthonous, and authentic.

As with any new conceptual model, there have been fruitful discussions problematizing the novelty and usefulness of the category of transnational in migration studies. In an article engaging with the emerging field published in 1998, the eminent anthropologist Sydney Mintz pointedly observed that "the world has now become a macrocosm of what the Caribbean region was, in the 16th century" (120) and that the "new theories of transnationalism and globalization are not respectful enough of history, especially of the history of exploration, conquest and the global division of labor" (131). Mintz is on target in reminding us that globalization is not new and that transnational processes have long characterized Caribbean history. But the scope of his article does not cover what might be considered a subfield of transnationalism, transnational migration studies, which boasts a body of work strongly rooted in the regional specificity of the Caribbean. For instance, as mentioned earlier, research on Dominican migration facilitated the rise of transnational migration studies; in addition, in an overview of new directions in the field, Nina Glick Schiller counters Mintz's critique by drawing attention to numerous scholars who have built upon Caribbean history and research in their work on contemporary transnationalism (37).[10] She writes:

> The Caribbean experience provided an important conceptual base that allowed both scholars and political actors to think beyond a concept of bounded culture, because from the moment of conquest, Caribbean culture was openly hybrid, and its trans-border connections were apparent. Repeatedly, Caribbean researchers described migrations that connected people across borders and sought to conceptualize culture flows. At various times, Caribbean ethnographies and discussions of Caribbean life spoke of transculturation, creolization, circular migration, remittance societies and return migration. (22)

Both today's and yesterday's imperial projects create powerful economic asymmetries that ignite global labor migration. As the anthropological work of Caribbean-focused scholars such as Glick Schiller, Georges Fouron, Peggy Levitt, and Jorge Duany, among others, has demonstrated, transnationalism is a useful conceptual tool for approaching global migration patterns that complicate the model of the unidirectional sojourner and for interrogating conventional equations between territory, identity, and citizenship. Similarly, in the field of literary and cultural studies, scholars such as Vanessa Pérez Rosario (*Hispanic Caribbean Literature of Migration: Narratives of Displacement*) and Yolanda Martínez-San Miguel (*Caribe Two Ways: Cultura de la migración en el Caribe insular hispánico*) have shown that alongside canonical national literatures in the Hispanic Caribbean exists artistic production comprising a culture of migration that counters homogenous constructions of the nation. The bilingual traffic metaphor *Caribe Two Ways* is evocative of the impact of the diaspora on both *aquí* and *allá* and of the transnational connections that permit movement between these localities. In short, Caribbean transnational migration studies makes new uses of old concepts, it is grounded in historically specific processes, and it productively describes sociocultural, economic, and political relations that are qualitatively different from those of the past.

The development of transnational scholarship in the 1990s, however, was met with caution by scholars who maintained that the transnational paradigm runs the risk of overlooking the processes that empower the Dominican American community settled abroad. In 2000 Silvio Torres-Saillant, a key figure in establishing Dominican studies in the United States, suggested that there are researchers, including himself, committed to advocacy and community building who approach Dominican migration as a diasporic formation "invested in laying a solid foundation to assert its permanence here as an ethnic minority" ("Diasporic Disquisitions" 25). Torres-Saillant sets up a problematic dichotomy between the intellectual projects and the national origins of scholars who examine Dominican migration. According to Torres-Saillant, one side is "oriented by the corrective impulse typical of ethnic studies undertakings and the other satisfying itself with merely observing any trends deemed worth of scholarly explication. The perspective of those non-Dominican scholars who persist in locating the focus of their inquiry away from the community-building dynamics and toward the examination of unencumbered transnational mobility seems inevitably fated to appose the scholarship of their Dominican counterparts" (7). I sympathize with an urgent need for academics to include Dominicans in Latino studies scholarship—a field that has been dominated by research on Mexican, Cuban, and Puerto Rican communities—but Torres-Saillant's position is overly divisive and fortunately has been mitigated by subsequent research that examines the concepts of diaspora and transnationalism as overlapping and mutually enriching.[11] Definitions of *diaspora* commonly reference the following: diasporas are both ancient and modern; etymologically the word conveys "sowing" or "scattering" "through" or "across" space; the movement away from the ancestral homeland is mainly an involuntary exodus; and members of the diaspora often retain strong ties to their countries of origin.[12] For Torres-Saillant, the Dominican diasporic experience is both an experience of uprooting and a process of becoming rooted in a new host society (31). He is more interested in examining the struggle in developing a strong ethnic group consciousness in a society hostile to minority communities than analyzing the economic, political, social, and cultural bonds that link the Dominicans who migrated and those who remained behind. By contrast, scholars with a transnational orientation train their analytical lenses on the networks that maintain such ties. Irrespective of these differing orientations, there are enough conceptual commonalities that Jorge Duany uses the terms *diasporic* and *transnational* interchangeably (*Blurred Borders* 171). Similarly, in his cultural study on return migration in the Hispanic Caribbean, *The Diaspora Strikes Back: Caribeño Tales of Learning and Turning*, Juan Flores notes that "diasporas are by definition transnational, resisting both the jurisdictional confines of the nationally bounded polity and the territorial rootedness to a single location" (18).

In addition, despite the transnational turn in migration studies, transnational approaches do not eclipse the discourses surrounding Dominican migration. Scholars have responded to Torres Saillant's call for inquiry focused on the enfranchisement of the Dominican community in the United States.[13] For example, in 2002 Milagros Ricourt published *Dominicans in New York City*, a study that documents "the process of community formation from four interrelated perspectives: ethnic identity formation, community development, the politics of incorporation, and gender relations" (10). Ricourt argues that new immigrants, established immigrants, and Dominican Americans engage differently with community building and local politics. Her analysis emphasizes the key role of Dominican social services agencies in promoting a politics of incorporation into the receiving society.[14] Likewise, in *Dominican-Americans and the Politics of Empowerment*, Ana Aparicio argues that, over time, Dominican "organizers have altered the geopolitical focus of their efforts. That is, they have moved from sole emphasis on 'homeland politics,' or the transnational sphere, to include organizing to confront local issues in the city of New York" (3). Both Ricourt and Aparicio address how, for Dominicans, in particular the second generation, becoming part of American society has involved coalitions with other people of color and the development of new racial and panethnic identifications. Finally, José Itzigsohn's study of Dominican immigrant incorporation in Providence, Rhode Island, presents perhaps the most balanced approach to Dominican migration because he compares the range and degree of transnational identities and practices among the first and second generation, the type of community that evolves out of transnational linkages, and the relationship between transnationalism and incorporation in American society (140). His findings suggest that transnational involvement and incorporation are not mutually exclusive, but "simultaneous and complementary processes" (40), and that while both the first and second generation adopt a transnational framework in the construction of identity, the level of participation in transnational practices decreases (164).[15] Itzigsohn concludes: "For all their transnational involvement, the main efforts of first- and second-generation Dominicans are oriented toward local community building and empowerment" (165). Even so, numerous studies show that Dominicans in the United States continue to engage more frequently than most other Latinos in transnational practices such as calling, sending money and traveling home, as well as attending cultural events, belonging to hometown associations, and voting in their country of origin.[16] Looking at the interrelationship of transnationalism and incorporation into the host society enables us to temper the competing camps established by Torres-Saillant. Moreover, it reveals that transnationalism changes over time but is not a phase that disappears with the second generation.

In fact, at the same time Dominicans have been carving a niche in American society, back-and-forth migration between the Dominican Republic and the United States has persisted. Transnational political and economic projects solidifying the links between the sending and receiving states increased in the 1990s and beyond. State policies toward the migrant community shifted in the 1990s due to "the convergence of national economic dependence on the money that emigrants send home and the emergence of political competition" (Itzigsohn 144). The former Dominican president Leonel Fernández (1996–2000; 2004–2012), who grew up in Washington Heights and received strong support from the overseas Dominican community in his presidential campaigns, encouraged open-border neoliberal economic policies along with a new, twenty-first-century national imaginary that "embraces the migrant communities as part of a transnational nation" (Itzigsohn 145). Pamela Graham shows that what might appear to be local political processes, such as the creation of a Dominican voting district in New York City, and the amendment of the Dominican constitution to allow for dual citizenship and the right of overseas Dominicans to vote in national elections, involved transnational political mobilization in both countries. On the one hand, "the ongoing remittance of capital and goods to the Dominican Republic has legitimated migrating Dominicans within their country of origin and formed the basis of an argument concerning their access to the political system" (117). On the other hand, "The districting and campaign for a Dominican-born city council member also reflected ongoing ties to the Dominican Republic. The crossover of activists working on both issues . . . and the importance of Dominican identity to the districting and electoral processes revealed how a seemingly local, territorial issue can have transnational dimensions" (119). By allowing dual citizenship, Dominicans living in the United States are more likely to become naturalized American citizens, which increases their socioeconomic mobility and encourages their incorporation into the US body politic. At the same time, through dual citizenship the Dominican state is promoting the preservation of its national culture and the continued flow of economic remittances. This process, which Graham highlights as the alignment of "legal definitions of citizenship, nationality, and political rights with the material realities of a migration-oriented society" (119) results in the strengthening of "the relationship between state (as a territorial administrative apparatus) and nation (as a cultural and social construct less connected to territorial borders)" (119). In essence, Dominicans are far from occupying a "limitless mobility" that Torres-Saillant accuses scholars of transnationalism of celebrating; rather, nationalism becomes a multi-local process that binds migrants to both origin and receiving states.[17] The literature on transnationalism repeatedly demonstrates the presence of the state in shaping, regulating, and influencing the cross-national field linking Dominicans *aquí* and *allá*. Both the concrete geographical and symbolic, imagined contours of Dominican lives may have expanded, but far from becoming free floating agents, they remain grounded by the regulatory forces of two states.

It is with good reason, then, that Guarnizo and Smith pose the question of whether transnationalism "from below" produces inherently subversive or counter-hegemonic subject positions. They suggest that they do not, yet they assert that the identities of transnational migrants "are different from hegemonic identities imposed from above. The process of a subaltern identity formation is a process of constant struggle—a struggle in which discursive communities produce narratives of belonging, resistance, or escape. In these grand narratives of personal meaning, the spaces available for forming non-essentialist identities, while not entirely absent, are interstitial—i.e., they open up between such dominant discursive venues as the 'nation-state,' the 'local community,' and the 'ethno-racial community'" (23). The authors observe that being "interstitial" is not necessarily subaltern, but an in-between positioning does offer a fluid identity category that moves between and combines to differing degrees national, local, and ethnic identities. This obliges us to employ new ways of thinking about collective belonging and citizenship that is inclusive of Dominicans across borders.

The social, economic, and political research on Dominican transnationalism has opened Torres Saillant's oppositional framing of the field, allowing for different entry points into the analysis of Dominican migration. As a literature and ethnic studies scholar, my interest is in charting how the stories enacted in plays and performances about migration register a changing Dominican identity politics that is variably nationalist, ethnic, or transnational. I argue that Dominican theater artists have developed a dialogic and bifocal point of view that yields new insight into the lasting cultural connections of migrants to their homelands. By analyzing Dominican theater and performance, a cultural tradition that has received little attention, this book explores how the practices of theater might be seen as a transnational community-building activity.

Changing Conceptions of Dominican Literature, Culture, and Identity

As we have seen, economic and political factors have been central in developing migration patterns characterized as transnational. Along with bodies and capital, the ideas and cultural values that accompany the cross-border movements of transmigrants have become an important area of analysis. Transnationalism breaks with basic assumptions that formerly organized our understanding of culture and territory, such as the notion that "meanings and meaningful forms are distinctive to different human collectivities and that as a rule these collectivities belong in territories" (Hannerz 8). Territories cannot contain cultures when people move with their meanings. The Latino cultural studies scholar Juan Flores argues that it is precisely "in its cultural manifestations that diaspora life and return can be understood in its human, experiential qualities, and differentiated at more idiosyncratic levels" (8). Flores's focus on migrants who return to their homelands represents a transnational approach to diasporic studies since it blurs the borders of sending and receiving societies. In transnational migration, both poles send and receive migrants, creating a multidirectional and mutually influential flow of Dominican culture. Flores asks: "What can be said of cultural migrations between diasporas and homelands, and especially of the impact of return flows of people and their diaspora-forged cultural experiences and values?" (8). His study builds on the concept of "social remittances" developed in *The Transnational Villagers*, Peggy Levitt's anthropological study of the transnational connections between Miraflores, a town in the Dominican Republic and Dominicans in Jamaica Plain, a neighborhood in Boston. Levitt writes that global culture is diffused on a macro level through political and economic institutions, but that "ordinary people, at the local level, are also cultural creators and carriers. Migrants send or bring back the values and practices they have been exposed to and add these social remittances to the repertoire, both expanding and transforming it" (55). Levitt frequently references "global culture" in *Transnational Villagers*, but she does not address creative artistic expression among the features of social life that crosses borders. Flores aims to fill this gap by looking at what he calls "cultural remittances"—namely, expressive genres such as language, music, literature, and visual arts that transmit values and identities from the diaspora to the homeland (44–45). In my view, the collective endeavor of theatrical performance, in which actors play out stories for an audience, provides a unique laboratory for teasing out the idiosyncrasies of a collective identity. My interest lies in how the theater event provides a micro level, face-to-face interaction among "ordinary people." In the quintessentially local act of bringing artists and spectators together for the ephemeral performance event, theatrical performance rehearses expanding understandings of Dominican identity and becomes a site of transnational culture creation.

Characterizing the culture of the Dominican people as "transnational" is noteworthy because it de-links culture to territory and legitimates the cultural practices of Dominicans in the diaspora. The constant flow of material goods, styles, and ideologies through the movement of people and the global media exerts pressure to broaden conventional notions of Dominican identity. For Flores, there is oppositional potential in the "cultural remittances" sent to the homeland because they contain values and ideas that emanate "from poor, working-class and colonial diaspora communities or sectors" (46). Some of the lessons of the diaspora include an awareness of different arrangements of social power regarding class, race, gender, and sexual identity that might alter perceptions and behaviors of Dominicans both *aquí* and *allá*. The close readings of the plays and performances in this book will highlight how the *dominicanidad* imagined by artists, in large part, advocates for openness toward hybrid identities and cross-border cultures and affiliations.

This is significant, for in the Dominican Republic, beginning with its unique path to independence, the hegemonic and cultural homogenizing project of the nation-state has been markedly exclusive and authoritarian.[18] The island of Hispaniola was divided by French and Spanish colonizers, and, as a result, unlike any other country in Latin America, the Dominican Republic gained its independence from both a former French colony (Haiti) and Spain. Black revolutionaries in Saint Domingue overthrew French rule and proclaimed the independence of the Haitian republic in 1804. In 1822, in an attempt to unite Hispaniola under one flag, the Haitians invaded the eastern half of the island and occupied the Spanish colony of Santo Domingo for just over two decades. Accordingly, the Dominican independence movement developed a national discourse in opposition to Haiti, which ultimately created a sense of collective belonging among Dominican elites that rejected Haitian blackness.[19] Against a "barbarous," black African ancestry, the French-based Haitian Creole language, and the religious practice of voodoo, Dominican intellectual and political elites exalted a "civilized," white European heritage, the Spanish language, and Catholicism. In spite of popular expressions of Dominican identity that undermined the notion of the Haitian as "other," *Hispanicismo*, "the elevation of cultural norms and values associated with Spain and Spanish colonialism" (Mayes 19), developed into what Etienne Balibar would call a "fictive ethnicity," an invented ethnic uniformity of the community founded by the nation-state (96).[20] Anti-Haitian nationalism became an ideological tool that, to this day, has been mobilized by Dominican elites "at politically opportune moments in order to secure the domination of their class and direct attention from their exploitation of Dominicans in general" (Mayes 3).[21] Most recently, we have seen this strategy of managing national sovereignty rear its ugly head in 2013, when the Dominican Supreme Court ruled that descendants of undocumented Haitian migrants born after 1929 would be stripped of their citizenship, potentially leaving some 250,000 people stateless.

The anti-Haitian ideology and official state nationalism has been particularly effective in the Dominican Republic because, from the time of independence in 1844 to Balaguer's rise to power in 1966, a succession of Dominican leaders have imposed a prescriptive nationalist heritage through authoritarianism and state terror. The sociologist Ana Liberato writes that since the colonial era, the authoritarian character of Dominican leaders is evident "in terms of their monopolizing power, authority, and decision-making and manipulating mass participation" (44). Moreover, these strongman rulers "tended to keep control of the military, violate civil rights, intrude into the private sphere of the citizenry, pursue reelection, adopt clientelist and personalistic politics, and turn the state into a personal entity" (44). In the contemporary period, under Trujillo, Dominicans experienced one of the longest and most repressive regimes in Latin America between 1930 and 1961. This was followed by almost four decades of political dominance by his disciple, Balaguer, whose prolific writings and public discourses, "contributed to the stabilization of images of Dominican nationalism through pride in Spanish-Catholic ancestry and anti-black sentiment" more than any other politician during and after the Trujillo era (Liberato 63). Under both leaders, the project of the nation-state has been so thoroughly hegemonic, discriminatory, and culturally homogenizing that the literary scholar Néstor Rodríguez reads Dominican culture as internally colonized. He cites four examples that exemplify a symbolic form of colonial violence brought to bear by the racism and elitism of Eurocentrism. First, the fact that Dominicans elide their racial identity by self-identifying as *indio* (Indian), rather than using the categories of mulatto or black that realistically reflect the majority of the population. Second, celebrating the nation's Christian and Spanish roots by building in 1992, for the 500th anniversary Christopher Columbus's so-called discovery of the Americas, a massive mausoleum to house the purported remains of Columbus from which the symbol of the cross is projected into the sky. Third, the strong imprint of the ecclesiastical elite on the nation's newspapers. Fourth, the "demonization" of the overseas Dominican population by the island's intellectuals (6).

My analysis of the works by Dominican theater practitioners who stage stories of migration contributes to Rodríguez's latter point about the complex and sometimes difficult relationship between the diaspora and the homeland. The rapid exodus of Dominicans in the 1980s and 1990s and the frequent return travel to the island, whether to visit family, conduct business, or to permanently resettle, have resulted in a continuous cultural exchange. For Sagás and Molina, the cultural flows produced by the diaspora have had a salutary effect, for it has influenced Dominicans' "understanding and acceptance of the 'other' world. It is a means to alleviate the burden of strong, absolutist, oppressive cultural patterns and ideologies imposed on them" (8). In the diaspora, the hegemonic discourse of national identity is confronted by the cultural hybridity of the metropolis of New York City. In this urban space, Pedro Antonio Valdez, author of the play *Paradise*, recognizes an undeniable pluralism of peoples, cultures, and points of view: "New York, a diferencia de países como el nuestro, está integrado por una sociedad que asume su realidad multicultural, que no teme a las minorías ni a la mayoría democrática, no porque es una ciudad rica, sino porque sus parroquianos ven, y no pueden si no [*sic*] ver, la vida desde premisas plurales" ("New York, unlike countries such as ours, consists of a society that assumes its multicultural reality, that is not afraid of minorities or the democratic majority, not because it is a rich city, but because its parishioners see, and can only see, life from plural premises"; "Writing" 100–101). In the context of transnational migration, the nativist position that clings to a univocal discourse of collective identity and views the diaspora as an embodiment of corrupted national culture fails to hold sway, and *dominicanidad* undergoes transformations on both ends of the migratory circuit. Literature, and, as I argue, theater and performance, represent crucial cultural practices that register these permutations of Dominican culture and the shifting contours of Dominican identity.

In *Poemas del exilio y de otras inquietudes/Poems of Exile and Other Concerns* (1988), the first bilingual anthology of Dominican writings published in the United States, the poet and literary critic Daisy Cocco De Filippis affirms that "for Dominicans writing in the U.S., the written word has become the means to an existence, to mark their presence, 'de hacer constar,' as they would say. Language provides these writers with a biography by giving them the tools to record their lives both as witnesses and as witnesses of history in the making" (9).[22] Dominicans began to write themselves into the landscape of US culture and history in the 1980s in New York City. The literary historian, critic, publisher, and cultural administrator Franklin Gutiérrez signals his participation, along with Tomás Rivera Martínez, Fermín Cruz, Rafael Díaz, Juan Torres, and José Carvajal, in the literary workshop Rácata in 1982 as a foundational moment in the development of Dominican letters in the United States. During this decade, a literary infrastructure developed as Dominicans joined together in literary projects and created writing collectives, journals, publishing houses, and cultural centers.[23] The writer Viriato Sención recalls the excitement of the epoch:

> Era loco con los libros, la escritura y las actividades literarias. Para mí, fue la época más brillante de las artes de la diáspora dominicana de Nueva York. Lo hacíamos todo de gratis, la literatura por el gozo mismo de la literatura. Y fue, además, la etapa fundacional de todas las instituciones importantes de esa comunidad. Yo, personalmente, se lo debo todo a esa generación de la década de los ochenta de Washington Heights. ("Viriato")
>
> *I was crazy about books, writing, and literary activities. For me, it was the most brilliant period of Dominican diasporic art in New York. We did everything for free, literature for the joy of literature. Also, it was the foundational stage for all the important institutions in this community. Personally, I owe everything to this Washington Heights generation of the 1980s.*

Much of this literary work, however, did not gain significant traction in either the United States or Dominican publishing markets. Sención's 1992 *Los que falsificaron el nombre de dios* (*They Forged the Signature of God*), which caused a scandal because of its thinly veiled critique of the Balaguer regime, stands out as an exception. The novel was a bestseller and was translated into English and read by a wide Dominican audience. Similarly, prose by Julia Álvarez and Junot Díaz published in the 1990s enjoyed a widespread reception, though these authors wrote in English and Spanish translations followed.[24] Ironically, even though the vast majority of the writings by these and other Dominican American writers directly addresses questions of Dominican history and identity, the cultural establishment of the island has been slow to show interest in this literary production (Rodríguez 129). Valdez reports that Dominican writers in the United States were "sistemáticamente desdeñados" (systematically scorned) ("Writing" 100) by the homeland intelligentsia, which is confirmed by Gutiérrez, who makes the following comment in his role as former commissioner of the Dominican Commission of Culture in the United States:

> No es un secreto para la mayoría de los estudiosos de la literatura, que en la década de los 80 y parte de los 90, el escritor dominicano residente en el exterior era visto como una especie de despatriado, como una especie de traicionero que abandonó la patria, que estaba haciendo una literatura que no le interesaba mucho ni a la intelectualidad ni al mercado local. ("Dedican")
>
> *It is not a secret for most literature scholars that in the 1980s and part of the 1990s, the Dominican writer overseas was seen as a kind of expatriate, as a kind of a traitor who abandoned the fatherland and was producing literature that did not interest the local intelligentsia or the local market.*

In 1994 Cocco De Filippis boldly addressed the need for dialogue between island-based and overseas Dominican writers at a conference hosted at the City College of New York. Her opening remarks passionately advocate for an inclusive conception of Dominican literature. By her logic, joining forces can combat the marginalization of Dominican writers in world literature in general. She argues: "Las fronteras artificiales entre lo dominicano de aquí y lo dominicano de allá solo puede contribuir a nuestro aislamiento y marginación. Y a nuestro aislamiento y marginación ya es suficiente lo que contribuyen los demás. Los dominicanos de la diáspora y los de la isla son dos caras de la misma moneda" ("The artificial borders between what is Dominican here and what is Dominican there can only contribute to our isolation and marginalization. And it is already enough that others contribute to our isolation and marginalization. Dominicans of the diaspora and the island are two sides of the same coin"; "Palabras" 9). In De Filippis's estimation, Dominican writers should work together in combating the already peripheral status of the literary and cultural heritage of the Dominican Republic within both the Spanish-language world and the wider field of universal literature.[25] Moreover, De Filippis points out that the culture of exclusion in the Dominican Republic has marginalized intellectual production from its own people, which has been counterproductive in helping Dominican literature gain wider notice in the community of international readers. Finally, she suggests that the diaspora enriches Dominican literature by including new voices and experiences and by reaching new reading publics. This conference organized by Cocco De Filippis constitutes a call for recognition and collaboration across borders. It would appear that the new millennium, along with a shift in island politics, turned a new tide, yielding an increase in intellectual production dedicated to the study of the Dominican diaspora.[26] Some examples of recent intellectual activity related to the diaspora include *Desde la Orilla: hacia una nacionalidad sin desalojos* (From the Shore: Toward a Nationality without Evictions), edited by Silvio Torres-Saillant, Ramona Hernández, and Blas R. Jiménez (2004), which compiles essays presented in a collaborative, two-part symposium held in New York City and Santo Domingo in 2001, and inaugural Dominican book fairs in New York City and Lawrence, Massachusetts, in 2006. The 2005 national Feria del Libro in Santo Domingo marks another high point because for the first time it included and celebrated Dominican scholars and artists residing abroad.[27]

Thus, the late 1990s through the turn of the century were crucial years in asserting the presence of writers of the diaspora in the Dominican literary tradition. During this same period, researchers in the United States slowly began to integrate Dominicans in the field of Latino studies. Scholars such as Torres-Saillant have been critical of the fact that many Latino readers and anthologies overlooked Dominicans in their panoramas of Latino culture in the United States. Similar to the problem of internal colonization that locks Dominicans into a hierarchical understanding of national culture and identity proposed by Rodríguez, Torres-Saillant attributes the superficial treatment or absence of Dominicans in academic publications to an "intracolonial epistemological inequality that leaves Dominicans out of the master narrative of the Latino experience" ("Problematic Paradigms" 440). Among Latinos, there are "levels of marginality" due to questions of race, class, and citizenship status (440). In the United States, the double ascription of Dominicans as Latinos and blacks, and the discrimination and low social ranking that accompanies this process of ethno-racialization decreases their chances for upward mobility in a racially stratified American society, as does their incorporation into a labor market characterized by a growing low wage service economy and a declining manufacturing sector. In addition, Dominicans, along with other recently arrived immigrants from Latin America, suffer the disadvantage of facing increasingly stringent pathways to gaining citizenship. As Torres-Saillant indicates, it is not surprising that most authors and editors of collections of scholarly work on Latinos in the United States are from more politically and economically empowered Latino groups (439). Torres-Saillant suggests that consciously or subconsciously, these scholars reproduce colonialist relations because they tacitly concede that the knowledge produced by certain groups is unnecessary for understanding the Latino experience. Consequently, before scholarship on

Dominicans began to appear regularly in Latino studies publications, Dominicans first needed to forge a space for representing themselves as well as document this process.

The intention of this book is to celebrate the increasing visibility of Dominicans in Latino studies and to address the relative absence of theater and performance in Dominican literary and cultural studies; therefore, it is not possible to devote significant space to providing a detailed account of the genesis of Dominican studies.[28] Briefly, though, the field came into being in the early 1990s through the efforts of a small group of academics committed to stimulating academic research, teaching, and publishing that would serve the Dominican community and spotlight Dominicans as both subjects and producers of knowledge. In the arena of literary studies, the publication of translations of Dominican works, the appearance of English-language writers such as Álvarez and Díaz, and the work of anthologizing raised the profile of Dominican writers, as did academic conferences and the activism and institution-building efforts of faculty associated with the City College of New York—which culminated in 1992 with the founding of the Dominican Studies Institute, the first university research center dedicated to the people of Dominican descent.

Two decades later, the fruits of this labor are visible in the 2011 special issue of *Camino Real*, a journal of Latino studies published in Spain, dedicated to Dominican studies. In this issue, the Dominican Studies Institute librarian and researcher Sarah Aponte shows the "correlation between the length of time the Dominican population has been present in the United States and that population's increased presence in academia" (39). Her analysis of dissertations on Dominican topics published in the United States between 1939 and 2009 demonstrates a steady increase in dissertations on Dominican topics, and, more specifically, the rise in the 1980s of Dominican academics writing on Dominican topics in their dissertations (39).[29] In terms of specific themes, the late 1990s show an increase in dissertations about Dominicans in the United States and a growth in scholarship in literature, both of which are reflected in the selection of essays in *Camino Real.* One might argue, however, that a true boom in Dominican studies has taken place after 2009, beyond the time frame covered by Aponte's study. In recent years, monograph publications on Dominican topics by Ginetta Candelario, Carlos Decena, Lauren Derby, Lorgia García Peña, Maja Horn, April Mayes, Danny Méndez, and Dixa Ramírez to name just a few scholars, have immeasurably enriched Dominican studies with their analyses of the intersections of gender, sexuality, race, class, and authoritarianism, and they have generated enthusiasm for Dominican studies in the wider disciplines of Latin(o) American studies as well. Thus, while Torres-Saillant's concern about the underrepresentation of Dominicans Latino studies scholarship is valid, rather than continuing to draw attention to the many edited collections that overlook Dominicans, at this juncture it seems more fruitful to mention a handful of books that demonstrate the increasing incorporation of Dominican authors in Latino literary studies. For example, Dominican authors are included in *The Norton Anthology of Latino Literature* (2010), *Contemporary U.S. Latino/a Literary Criticism* (2007), and *Latino/a Literature in the Classroom* (2015), three collections that validate reading, teaching, and theorizing about Dominican literature. Still, deservedly popular writers, Díaz and Álvarez, followed by Angie Cruz, Nelly Rosario, and Loida Maritza Pérez, remain the main reference points for contemporary Dominican literature, while editors and publishers seem reticent to take a chance on showcasing lesser-known writers.

Transnational Dominican Theater and Performance

At the same time Dominican literary voices were emerging in the mid-1990s, artists associated with the performing arts were also exploring Dominican life experiences, and their work has gone largely unexplored. A survey of recent literature on Latino playwrights and performers might leave the impression that Dominicans have yet to make a home in the Latino theater community.[30] This is not the case, for there are many Dominican actors and playwrights who work in New York City today who simply have yet to be written into an historical account of the Dominican presence in Latino theater. This is partly so because Dominicans are involved in disperse theatrical activities and a movement has never coalesced around an exceptional individual or a stage of its own. At an earlier historical moment, foundational Mexican and Puerto Rican theater projects carved a space for Latino performing arts in the US cultural landscape, such as Luis Valdez's Teatro Campesino, established in 1965, and Miriam Colón-Valle's Puerto Rican Traveling Theater (PRTT), founded in 1967. These theater projects have shown the power of performance in confronting social issues and building community. However, I argue that "New Latinos,"—Colombians, Dominicans, Salvadorans—arriving in large numbers since the 1980s and 1990s, enter the US ethnic cultural space less apt to form a separate theater company rooted in national identifications.[31] Like their predecessors, these communities face difficult socioeconomic circumstances that postpone the investment of time and money in the arts. Moreover, the climate for municipal, state, and federal arts funding sources is even less generous than it was in the past. Thus, it is unlikely that a discrete, full-fledged theater movement—by which I mean a Dominican theater company with its own space—will develop.[32]

Furthermore, it must be noted that Dominicans in the diaspora did not bring with them a strong dramatic literature and theatergoing tradition. For years, the cultivation of a robust theater tradition in the Dominican Republic drama was doubly stymied. First, drama was neglected as a literary genre; plays were not included in many national literature anthologies and there were few opportunities to publish play texts. Second, scarce economic resources and political repression made it difficult for drama to come alive as staged productions. Additionally, the well-known novelist and enduring intellectual figure Marcio Veloz Maggiolo confirms a general lack of audience and interest in local playwrights: "La falta de un público, de un espectador consciente, siempre ha sido un escollo en la vida teatral de nuestro país. Esto, unido al ambiente político y la creencia de muchos directores de que toda pieza extranjera era mejor, atenuó la producción teatral llevándola casi a la nulidad" ("The lack of a public, of a conscious spectator, has always been an obstacle in the theatrical life of our country. This, together with the political environment and the belief of many directors that any foreign plays were best, diminished and almost nullified theatrical production"; 187). This is not to suggest, however, that Dominican theater did not exist.[33] Indeed, the intrepid Dominican researcher José Molinaza wrote over a thousand pages, a two-volume critical account of Dominican theater from its origins to 1930 that substantiates how Dominicans have employed theatrical modes of storytelling throughout the centuries.[34] Nevertheless, the critic asserts that his country lacks a true national theater tradition as a result of the political climate imposed by the Trujillo regime. Molinaza writes:

> El teatro dominicano representado en la era de Trujillo fue deficiente y pobre. Los antecedentes de esta circunstancia fueron la falta de identidad y representatividad, la descontextualización, la heterogeneidad, la infructuosa búsqueda de las raíces y, en consecuencia, la afirmación de la no tradición. . . . Entendemos por tradición la inexistencia de un teatro nacional en sentido estricto, donde la autoctonía juegue un papel predominante. ("1863–1987" 148)
>
> *Dominican theater staged during the Trujillo era was deficient and poor. The reasons for this situation were the lack of identity and representativeness, decontextualization, heterogeneity, the unsuccessful search for roots, and, as a result, the assertion of a non-tradition. . . . By this we mean the nonexistence of a national theater in the strict sense, in which the autochthonous plays a dominant role.*

It was not until the demise of the Trujillo regime and the cultivation of both experimental and popular, folkloric theatrical expression in the 1960s and 1970s that Dominican theater took the shape of a national movement and gained some measure of international recognition. Still, even in 2000, the editor Vivian Martínez Tabares notes the repeating theme of failure in her interviews with fifteen Dominican theater practitioners in a special issue of the Cuban theater journal *Conjunto*. I submit, however, that the work of these artists has yet to be fully investigated by researchers, and that new scholarship on the post-1960s era will no doubt identify noteworthy themes and practices in Dominican theater and performance. The exchanges with international companies since the advent of the International Theater Festival of Santo Domingo in 1997 has helped break Dominican theater out of its insularity, as have the transnational cultural flows from diaspora.[35] My objective with this brief outline of Dominican theater is not to lament a weak national tradition or the lack of theater movement in the diaspora, because there is still a great deal to be learned about Dominicans in the theater that I believe will qualify these claims. Rather, I hope to begin to characterize how spaces have been created for Dominican plays and performers in New York City, and I will conclude by describing the corpus of plays that comprises my study of Dominican plays about migration.

Dominican actors often appear in the casts of plays produced by established New York City Spanish-language and bilingual theaters such as Repertorio Español and PRTT. Beyond providing work for Dominican actors, since the 1990s these theater companies have played a crucial role in cultivating a Dominican audience. Repertorio Español invited the Dominican comedic actor Soraya María, popularly known as "La Cachita," to perform during the 1991–1992 season. The next year saw the first of various guest productions at Repertorio Español by the Dominican Republic's most prolific and lauded playwright, Franklin Domínguez. These performances likely attracted Dominican spectators from relatively privileged backgrounds who had exposure to drama in the homeland. Another strategy Repertorio Español has used to draw Dominicans to the theater is featuring plays on national topics such as the Trujillo regime. *La fiesta del chivo* (The Feast of the Goat) by Mario Vargas Llosa was performed between 2002 and 2011, and *En el tiempo de las mariposas* (In the Time of the Butterflies), an adaptation of Julia Álvarez's novel by Caridad Svich, has formed part of the company repertoire since 2011.[36] Similarly, PRTT staged *La bella alma de Don Damián* (The Beautiful Soul of Don Damián) in 1998, an adaptation of short stories by the revered Dominican prose writer and politician Juan Bosch. The production was included in the company's thirty-second tour of free plays performed in outdoor, public spaces, reaching audiences who are likely not regular theatergoers. Lastly, and by contrast with the smaller audiences reached by Spanish-language theaters, Puerto Rican Lin Manuel-Miranda's 2008 Tony Award–winning Broadway hit, *In the Heights*, while pan-Latino in scope, cast Dominican spaces and stories into the national spotlight.

Dominican actors formed part of the casts of all the aforementioned plays. In constructing a genealogy of Dominican performers in the United States, we might cite two contrasting female pioneers, María Montez (1912–1951) and Ilka Tanya Payán (1943–1996). The former, yet another "tropical bombshell" in the Latina performance tradition, Universal Picture's "Queen of Technicolor" and star of more than twenty adventure films—the latter, an actor-turned-lawyer and human rights activist killed by AIDS. Notable male figures include Rolando Barrera, who in the 1940s staged European classics in Spanish in New York City's Master's Auditorium, and Mateo Gó mez, who has worked in commercial stage and film vehicles since the 1970s (Torres-Saillant and Hernández, *Dominican Americans* 128).[37] In the independent theater scene, the performance poet, dancer, and director Josefina Báez has stood out since the 1980s for articulating a worldview that is both Dominicanyork and global. Báez is founder and director of Latinarte/Ay Ombe (1986), an art troupe that travels internationally conducting educational workshops and theater retreats that focus on creativity and spiritual and psychological well-being. Other lesser-known theater ventures directed by Dominicans include Teatro Experimental Comunitario (TEC), founded by the actor and director Luis Felipe Rodríguez in 1993. The mission of TEC is to create a professional Spanish-language theater in Washington Heights that promotes experimentation with contemporary techniques and the formation of new theater groups. Thus, TEC offers theater workshops, seminars, and lectures in addition to staging plays. As a reminder of the networks that connect Dominican theater transnationally, the island-based maestro Rafael Villalona, who has influenced generations of Dominican theater practitioners, offered workshops for artists in the diaspora during a six-week artistic residency in New York City at TEC. Young community organizer, actor, and Teatro las Tablas director Yolanny Rodríguez has also made an imprint in Latino independent theater. In a blog post entitled "Los ATI demostraron que vale la pena vernos también," (The ATI Showed that It's Worth Seeing Us as Well) Rodríguez documents how 2011 was a breakthrough year for Dominican theater activity and visibility. As an alternative to the longstanding Latin ACE awards presented by the Asociación de Espectáculos de Cronistas (Association of Theater Critics), the Premios ATI (Independent Theater Awards) have been awarded since 2011 to recognize independent

Spanish-language theater in New York City in a variety of innovative categories. For example, independent theater productions by companies without a venue stand as a category apart from productions associated with a permanent theater space, and there are acting categories for performers based in the United States and artists visiting from abroad. Dominicans figure prominently in the 2012 list of award recipients, highlighting the growing number of Dominican theater projects in New York City. During the 2011 season, Dominican themes and actors were seen in *The Brief Wondrous Life of Oscar Wao*, Teatrostage's adaptation of Junot Díaz's novel by the same name; *Sex on the Beach*, a solo piece by Roy Arias; and *La luz de un cigarillo*, an ensemble piece by Marco Antonio Rodríguez, staged at Teatro LATEA. Also in 2011, José Bonilla and the Dominican arts organization Casa de la Cultura Navarrete inaugurated an annual monologue festival with productions of eight monologues by the beloved Dominican playwright Iván García Guerra. The celebration of Guerra's legacy in the heart of the Dominican enclave community marks a noteworthy moment in Dominican theater in the United States.

There also has been transnational institutional support for developing Dominican theater in the United States. As mentioned earlier, in 2004 the Fernández government created the Dominican Commission of Culture in the United States, an organization dedicated to maintaining national values by supporting Dominican artists in the United States. Some of the cultural projects sponsored by the commission have the express purpose of educating second-generation Dominicans about their history and culture. For example, the commission funded projects such as the one headed by Yolanny Rodríguez of Las Tablas, which involved Dominican youths in creating a play about the republic's forefathers, as well as other educational programs promoting national folkloric dance and carnival traditions (Grant). The commission has also promoted artistic activity through its theater festivals and book fairs. Under commissioner Carlos Sánchez, who has a theater background, the Dominican Commission of Culture in the United States has brought performances to the Dominican community by hosting annual Hispanic theater festivals since 2010. While the contest is open to all Spanish-language theater groups based in the United States and Puerto Rico, the festival is largely a Dominican affair since it is hosted at the Dominican Commission of Culture in upper Manhattan and each year honors key figures in Dominican theater. Similarly, since 2006 the commission has sponsored an annual book fair that celebrates Dominican authors and draws an even larger number of participants than the theater festival. Festivals and fairs build community, and they offer cash prizes, productions and publications, and exposure for writers and performers. However, this state-supported activity also exposes some of the weaknesses that have plagued Dominican literary industry in the homeland and abroad. While the state has become more inclusive of its conception of Dominican literature—Editora Nacional, the Ministry of Culture's publishing house, has expanded its collections to include the Letras de Ultramar (Overseas Literature) series, and the Dominican Commission of Culture in the United States now has its own book series—there is a lack of publishing houses independent of the state's cultural apparatus, which ultimately allows politics to dictate publishing (and staging) trends.[38] The fairs and festivals are also under the auspices of the state, leading one to ask who makes up the juries that select the works for prizes and publication, and what future do the pieces not selected as winners have for publication, and, in the case of theater, staging? Shining the spotlight on one prizewinning work per genre during the time frame of the festival or fair does not seem sufficient to stimulate a healthy, consistent, and productive rhythm for promoting Dominican writers. In spite of these questions, there is no doubt that together, individual actors, independent theater endeavors, and state-sponsored institutions have forged a space for Dominican theater and performance in New York City.

The process of establishing Dominican theater in the United States, however, seems to be following a path that differs from earlier generations of Latino theater in the United States due to the continued transnational connections between the homeland and the diaspora, and the fact that a significant portion of Dominican writing in the diaspora is still strongly oriented toward a transnational Dominican audience. This is evident in the first anthology of plays by Dominican dramatists residing in the United States, *Máscaras errantes: Antología de dramaturgos dominicanos en los Estados Unidos* (Wandering Masks: Anthology of Dominican Dramatists in the United States edited by the US-based writer Dinorah Coronado and published in Santo Domingo by Editora Nacional (2011). Coronado situates the plays in the five-hundred-year history of Dominican theater and states that the objective of the anthology is: "Enriquecer el acervo bibliográfico de nuestra dramaturgia, para dejar huellas de nuestra presencia y compartir con teatristas de otros países y del propio suelo el legado cultural que envuelven estos textos" ("To enrich the bibliographic heritage of our dramaturgy, to leave traces of our presence and share with theater lovers from other countries and our own soil the cultural heritage embodied in these texts"; 13). Like Cocco De Filippis, who writes of the desire of Dominican authors in the United States to *hacer constar* (to register) the Dominican experience in writing, Coronado understands the urgency of preserving and disseminating the texts of little-known Dominican playwrights. However, Coronado frames these dramatists within the national theater, as well as the Spanish-language theater tradition, while Cocco De Filippis is more focused on Dominican writers making their mark in the context of literature produced by Latinos in the United States. For Cocco De Filippis, the "history in the making" these writers bear witness to is the experience of migration and adaptation. The task of documentation is especially urgent in the field of theater and performance, where critics and historians can counter the ephemeral nature of the theater event—though perhaps never capture it—by inscribing it into critical narratives. This book reasons that a transnational approach to Dominican performance reveals the presence of a wealth of theatrical activity that engages with Dominican-US migration in both the republic and the diaspora. Thus, my aim is not to recuperate a number of plays for the Dominican national tradition as much as it is to signal a transnational positioning that highlights how the texts are speaking to audiences in the Dominican Republic and abroad. I suggest that the works may be an extension of the tradition back home and representative of a new one in the United States. In sum, since the Dominican social and cultural unit is no longer territorially anchored, we must consider alternatives to the either/or logic that tends to place national and diasporic literatures in opposition.

Several concepts from transnational migration studies inform my reading of Dominican plays and performances. In this book, what I refer to as "transnational Dominican theater and performance" builds on the pioneering definition of transnationalism offered by the anthropologists Linda Basch, Nina Glick Schiller, and Cristina Szanton Blanc. They define transnationalism as

> the processes by which immigrants build social fields that link together their country of origin and their country of settlement. Immigrants who build such social fields are designated "transmigrants." Transmigrants develop and maintain multiple relations—familial, economic, social, organizational, religious, and political—that span borders. Transmigrants take actions, make decisions, and feel concerns, and develop identities within social networks that connect them to two or more societies simultaneously. (Basch et al., *Nations Unbound* 1–2)

The creative practices of transnational Dominican theater artists take place in a network of relationships that simultaneously links them to two nation-states. Similar to the characters in their plays who enact the social scenarios of migration, "transmigrant artists" and their artistic endeavors shift from one geopolitical space to another. Cultivating multiple cross-border ties enriches their art and increases their chances of having their works staged or published. A prime example is Waddys Jáquez, who has lived and worked in New York City since the 1990s, but has consistently returned to the Dominican Republic to premiere his artistic projects and to collaborate with artists on the island. In one interview, he simply states: "Soy un dominicano, punto, que vive en Nueva York, punto" ("I'm a Dominican, period, who lives in New York, period"; qtd. in Martínez Tabares, "Caribbean Bodies" 31). This transnational state of being evidently befuddled the jury of the Latin ACE Awards, who assumed that Jáquez did not live and work in the United States and named him *Actor Visitante Más Destacado* (Outstanding Visiting Actor) for his play *P.A.R.G.O.: Los Pecados Permitidos* in 2003. Jáquez's engagement with his resident country is functional in the sense that the United States is a source of job opportunities, creative freedom, and international exposure.[39] Studies of Dominican transnationalism show a pattern of transmigrants using the host nation-state as a resource while maintaining an emotive and cultural connection with the home country. They are not prone to adopt a "North American" identity and settle permanently in the United States and are therefore in constant dialogue with the discourses of identity in both locations. As demanding as the struggle for inclusion in two national imaginaries may be, the simultaneous access to the identity discourses of race, class, gender, and sexuality in different cultures nevertheless informs how Dominican transnationals articulate their concepts of self and society and opens up reductionist models of *dominicanidad*.[40]

The positive reception of Jáquez's work in different contexts—both within the Dominican Republic and the United States and beyond—speaks to his transnational method of producing theater and reflects the interest of multi-local national communities anxious to address issues of migration. I call *P.A.R.G.O.* and other plays included in this book, whether written or performed in the United States or the Dominican Republic, "transnational plays" because they have bifocal messages aimed at constituencies located in a social field that extends between the Dominican Republic and the United States. To categorize who and what kind of activity to consider transnational, Itzigsohn et. al envision a narrow to broad transnational continuum, distinguishing between the degrees of institutionalization, participation, and movement in transnational practices—in turn grouped as economic, political, civic-societal, and cultural— (324–25). Going to the theater is not a common cultural activity, and this is no exception for Dominicans whose everyday lives are informed by unstable economic conditions. Creating and attending theatrical performances might fall under the category of broad transnational activities, "a series of material and symbolic practices in which people engage that involve only sporadic physical movement between the two countries, a low level of institutionalization, or just occasional personal involvement, but nevertheless includes both countries as reference points" (323). The plays discussed in this book have enjoyed only sporadic productions in the United States and the Dominican Republic because of a lack of steady funding and institutional support for theater, though it is notable that transnational connections have enabled the production of the some of the plays in both places. Moreover, regardless of where the everyday lives of the theater makers and audiences take place, the stories they perform transform the stage into a field of Dominican symbolic references. In the transnational taxonomy discussed by Itzigsohn et al., the activity of theater would be regarded as "cultural," as it is a symbolic practice that helps form "identities, tastes, and values" (325). The authors note the mass media and the Center for Dominican Studies as examples of narrow cultural transnationalism because of their level of institutionalization and their continuous involvement in cultural production in both poles of the transnational sphere. In particular, the media allows for a constant connection, which "reinforces their identity as Dominicans, a feeling of being part of the national imagined community" (333).

By contrast, enjoying Dominican music, literature, and theatrical performance represents participating in transnationalism in broader terms, though these cultural practices similarly "refer to the definition and boundaries of 'being Dominican'" (335). To better understand the distinctiveness of theater in representing collective identities, we might juxtapose the narrow transnational practices of the media and the broad transnational practices of the theater and think about their aims and reach. Ulf Hannerz's analysis of culture in today's era of globalization offers insight for thinking about transnational theater. For example, he observes that different agents manage culture, "but with different motives and with varying degrees of deliberateness; some with relatively few reaching out through asymmetrical relationships to a great many others and a much greater number on the other hand reaching, through more symmetrical relationships to relatively few" (70). The media, controlled by relatively few, but powerful moguls, reaches mass audiences through an asymmetrical center-periphery relationship, whereas the projects and artifacts of a large number of cultural workers reach comparatively few people, but they do so through balanced and consensual relationships of power. Theatergoing is a deliberate and active practice—one must opt to attend and oftentimes purchase a ticket for a performance, whereas the relationship between the media and its mass audience is passive and can sometimes be described as accidental since it often reaches the viewer without their conscious consent. In addition, the global media is vast in scale, mediated, and experienced from a distance. By contrast, Hannerz's definition of the local is evocative of the experience of the theater: "People are in the local setting bodily, with all their senses, ready not only to look and listen but to touch, smell, and taste, without having their fields of attention restructured, pre-structured for them. There is a feeling of immediacy, even of immersion, of being surrounded. What is experienced is also extensively contextualized" (27). By these terms, we might claim that play performances create spaces and moments of locality. Theatrical performance frames and focuses the field of attention of the audience, creating an ephemeral community that experiences an embodied and sensorial event characterized by immediacy and historical contingency to the "real" world beyond the stage. It is owing to these local qualities that theatrical performance constitutes a powerful tool for exploring different ways of collective belonging.

Peggy Levitt and Nina Glick Schiller develop a differentiation between "ways of being" and "ways of belonging" in transnational social fields that can also be usefully linked to the art of the theater. On the one hand, a way of "being transnational" is simply moving in a social field in which every day practices and social relations cross borders (1010). These are lives shaped by transnational relationships and interactions, regardless of whether individuals migrate. On the other hand, "ways of belonging" involves action and awareness and refers to "practices that signal or enact an identity which demonstrates a conscious connection to a particular group" (1010). What I find intriguing for thinking about the theater is how performances enact and encourage ways of belonging. As I have suggested, the artists engage in cross-border social relations and practices to create their works, which in turn address experiences of migration. Theater might be seen as a catalyst for shifting transnational "ways of being" into transnational "ways of belonging." Levitt and Glick Schiller write that through "memory, nostalgia or imagination," individuals, who by virtue of occupying a transnational social field are already enacting a transnational way of being, can access ways of belonging (1011). By structuring a forum of collective address in which people interact through speech and gesture in the active roles of actors and observers, plays in performance do just this—they set in motion memory, nostalgia, and imagination, which serve to stimulate identifications. Furthermore, just as memory, nostalgia, and imagination are associated with different temporalities, the theater represents a multi-temporal locality; it is moored in the present, but the stories staged often serve to examine the past and as a laboratory for *as if*, the rehearsal of an alternative present or future. The stories performed thus encourage a consciousness of multiple time frames and places. On another level, in the performance event, spectators experience a similarly transnational consciousness of simultaneous temporalities and localities, of the present "here" of the real-world theater space, and the time frame of the "elsewhere" on stage. Likewise, from a transnational point of view, there is no contradiction in living in one place while simultaneously engaging in activities located elsewhere. The textual analyses that follow hypothesize that plays about the experience of migration in performance lead some spectators to access a transnational understanding of their collective belonging. Theatrical performance, then, has a unique role in facilitating the constitution of a Dominican transnational public sphere that encompasses both *aquí* and *allá*.

Overview of Chapters

Since the 1990s, Dominican playwrights and performers have produced a diverse corpus of performance texts addressing the experience of migration. The new, transnational subjectivities embodied in some of their texts and performances unsettle the relationship between nation and identity and challenge hegemonic notions of citizenship and national belonging. At the same time, their transnational perspectives and work methods challenge the paradigms that have organized how critics approach US Latino and Latin American drama. Global mobility constitutes an explicit theme in the plays included in this study, though the experiences of migration they depict are diverse. The plays tell different variations on that theme and comprise a variety of contemporary performance projects ranging from solo and dance performances, to one-act and full-length ensemble plays. This book treats performance as it relates to theater. I use terms such as *drama*, *play*, *theater work*, and *performance piece* to refer to stories told by actors in onstage spaces for an audience. And while the object of my inquiry is theater, I also engage with the notion of performance as a lens through which to view the world as it is used in the field of performance studies. Embodiment, the sense of occasion afforded by the performance event, and the reflexivity it encourages in all who participate in it is common to both theater and performance studies, whether the performance is framed by a stage space or takes place in everyday life. My analyses refer to the script, the "sole constant element in what goes on in the name of theater" (Issacharoff 4). However, as "the place of inscription of virtual performance" (4), my readings discuss the staged text, and, in most instances, my readings are informed by photographic images and having seen either a live or recorded performance of the work. All the pieces have received some level of public presentation, and a few have been fully staged in both the United States and the Dominican Republic. In addition, most of the pieces have been published, which recognizes their contribution to Dominican literary culture. I include new and established dramatists and performers, all of whom have lived transnationally and variously write in Spanish, English, or a mixture of both.[41] The plays are not discussed chronologically, though overall, the corpus of plays covers roughly twenty-five years, from the 1990s through 2015.

The organization of this book is guided by different facets of the migration experience. I begin with plays that portray the moment of departure and the physical journey of migration. Chapter 1 examines the biopolitical impetus for migration and the politics of representing perilous journeys in small boats called *yolas* in two ensemble dramas—*Miches: Ponle Esperanza* (Miches: Name it Hope) by Julissa Rivera Céspedes (2005) and *Yoleros* (Boatpeople) by Álex Vásquez Escaño (2008). I figure boat migrants as the disposable wreckage of the processes of the globalization, and I explore how theater intervenes in the stream of disturbing narratives and images of *yola* migration circulated in the mass media. Chapters 2, 3, and 4 present a range of nonnormative gender and sexual identities in stories of assimilation (or lack of), the second generation, and return migration. From the migrant boat people expelled from the national body politic, in chapter 2 I shift my attention to the "deviant" poses struck by male characters in a three solo performance pieces—*P.A.R.G.O.: Los pecados permitidos* (P.A.R.G.O.: Permitted Sins) by Waddys Jáquez (2001), *Ciudadano cero* (Citizen Zero) by Rey Emmanuel Andújar (2005), and *Cosa nostra dominicana* (Dominican Cosa Nostra) by Dió-genes Abréu (2011). I argue that the male characters in the plays adopt positions of marginality with respect to national identity and resist assimilation and stereotyped models of masculinity. In chapter 3 the exploration of nonnormative masculinities links the theater of Marco Antonio Rodríguez to the experimental solo pieces in chapter 2, but their context is markedly different: Rodríguez constructs a Dominican American world of long-settled immigrant parents and their children with dramatic realism in *La luz de un cigarillo* (*Ashes of Light*) (2011) and *Barceló con hielo* (*Barceló on the Rocks*) (2014). In both plays, the characters definitively live *aquí*, in the United States, but I argue that *allá*, the Dominican Republic, still weighs heavily on their lives through Dominican technologies of gender that have sustained a national culture of authoritarianism to this day. Both plays show a transnational orientation through the family's strong affective ties with the homeland and the enactment of the Dominican practice of silencing of marginalized sexualities. Chapter 4 also weighs in on the concept of assimilation, but in the context of return migration. In *Por hora y a* Piece-Work

(Hourly and Piece Work) by Elizabeth Ovalle (1994), *Ay Fefa, Where is the Wind?* by Zaida Corniel (1994), *Nuyor/Islas* (New York/Islands) by Chiqui Vicioso (2003), and *Dominicanish* (2000) by Josefina Báez, the female characters who return "home" are engaged in claiming and being claimed by two nation-states—a paradoxically vulnerable and empowering position that informs how they articulate their gendered concepts of self and society. In each story, the drama of return reflects different degrees of embracing or resisting dichotomist nativist/diasporic positions on *dominicanidad* and shows that for transnational migrants, "home" can be conceived of as pluri-local and mobile. Chapters 5 and 6 unpack the similar aesthetic strategies employed in representing both the undocumented migrant's quest for citizenship and the transnational playwright's quest for recognition. In chapter 5 I argue that *Mondongo Scam* by Claudio Mir (1994) and *Las viajeras* (The Women Travelers) by María Isabel Bosch (2003) exemplify how performance places spectators in the ethical position of having to adopt a stance on human rights and citizenship. The plays give voice to undocumented Dominican immigrants and place audiences in the ethical position of having to assume a stance on the topic of human rights and citizenship. Through their engagement with hybridity as a theme and an aesthetic strategy, Mir and Bosch not only explore new modes of political, personal, and artistic belonging, they also join people in public sites of conviviality that imagine a more accessible and expansive body politic. Chapter 6 rounds out this study by suggesting that the works of Fank Disla can be situated among Dominican artists who have developed their theater projects transnationally but also in a broader context of minority cultural formations produced within and across national boundaries. I maintain that the cosmopolitan and creolized sensibilities of Disla's theater about migration, its exploration of difference and exclusion, and its challenge to hegemonic forms of citizenship, is productively understood within the cultural orientations of what Françoise Lionnet and Shu-mei Shih call "minor transnationalism." By positioning Dominicans in a wider framework of global migration and insistently experimenting with different genres and strategies of metatheater and intertextuality, Disla develops an aesthetics of minor transnationalism useful for understanding a wide array of theater practitioners working across borders.

Framed by theories of theater and performance, culture and identity, and migration, the analysis of plays and performances in *Aquí and Allá: Transnational Dominican Theater and Performance* illuminates the dynamic and heretofore unrecognized role of theatrical performance in discipline-spanning debates on changing perceptions of *dominicanidad* brought about by migration. I seek to offer insight on queries such as: What are recurrent motifs in the stories staged about Dominican migration? To what degree do the characters on stage display a dual frame of reference or bifocality typical of transnationalism? How is the theatrical performance a strategic site for observing the production, negotiation, and social reproduction of transnational social identities? How do artists understand and portray a sense of collective belonging increasingly shaped by the interplay between Dominicans *aquí* and *allá*? And finally, how does transnational Dominican theater and performance challenge the categories that have organized our thinking about culture and national identity?

Chapter 1

The Drama of *Yola* Migration and the Biopolitics of Disposability

Puerto Rico queda cerca
Pero móntate en avión
Y si consigues la visa
No hay problemas en Inmigración

Pero no te vayas en yola,
No te llenes de ilusiones
Porque en el Canal de la Mona
Te comen los tiburones

—**Wilfrido Vargas**

A pervasive image of the Dominican migrant is the stereotypic Dominicanyork dressed in fashionable jeans, gold jewelry, and trendy athletic shoes. Further accessorized by the ubiquitous giant suitcases that mark their status as a person on the move, this migrant crisscrosses the Caribbean Sea by airplane, aptly described by the Puerto Rican writer Luis Rafael Sánchez as a *guagua aérea* (flying bus) to capture the easy mobility of Puerto Ricans between the island and New York City. Sanchez's homonymous essay depicts the cultural disconnect between the gringo flight crew and the Puerto Rican passengers and the conversations and camaraderie that arise among the commuters during a festive night flight from San Juan to New York City, underscoring a bicultural Puerto Rican identity and the tensions that characterize Puerto Rico's colonial relationship with the United States. Due to mass migration since the 1960s, frequent air travel between Hispaniola and the United States has added another flying bus route over the Caribbean Sea, making Dominicans similarly "at home" in the interstitial space of transnational migration. Unlike Puerto Ricans, however, they cannot count on possessing US citizenship to ease their arrival and integration. Lured by the dream of economic security and expelled by a state that has failed to provide the majority of its population with social and economic stability, Dominican migrants carry a great deal of "baggage" with them, as Silvio Torres-Saillant incisively explains:

> La sobrecarga en el equipaje de los dominicanos de Nueva York que viajan de regreso a su tierra natal podría verse como el peso social que ha caído en los hombros de los emigrados, quienes se han visto obligados a suplir las insuficiencias de su país. Además del envío en dólares de remesa multimillonarias cada año, la comunidad dominicana residente en el exterior ha debido echarse literalmente a cuestas los enseres, aparatos y productos requeridos por sus familiares y allegados en el país para satisfacer necesidades materiales. ("Retorno" 30)
>
> *The excessiveness of the luggage of New York Dominicans who travel back to their homeland could be seen as the social weight that has fallen on the shoulders of emigrants, who have been forced to compensate for the deficiencies of their country. In addition to sending remittances in dollars each year, the Dominican community living abroad has had to literally carry on their backs the belongings, appliances, and products required by their relatives and friends in the country to satisfy material needs.*

In addition to the onus of supporting family back home through economic remittances and return visit gifts, Dominican migrants bear the weight of the uncertainty of their citizenship status, their new identity as an ethnic minority in the United States, and the disdain of middle-class nonmigrant Dominicans who displace their own socioeconomic precariousness and inferiority complexes by marginalizing migrant Dominicans with distorted images of delinquency and subalternity (Torres-Saillant, "Retorno" 18–20).

From the image of migrants arriving and departing on airplanes with overstuffed suitcases, however, I would like to shift the focus in this chapter to migrants in the predawn darkness, with only a small plastic bag in hand, rapidly wading toward handmade wooden boats called *yolas*. This is a scene that has been repeated unabated since the first recorded illegal boat trip from the Dominican Republic to Puerto Rico in 1972. In open vessels ranging from twenty-five to fifty feet in size, illegal migrants pay, on average, \$500–\$4,000 to attempt to cross the Mona Passage, a strait that separates the islands of Hispaniola and Puerto Rico and connects the Atlantic Ocean to the Caribbean Sea. The trip, which usually takes a little over twenty-four hours, depending on the route and weather conditions, is known to be one of the trickiest passages in the Caribbean due to tidal currents and long sand banks on the coasts of both islands. The yolas, overloaded and considered unfit for the high seas by navy and Coast Guard standards, easily capsize in the large waves, leaving passengers to drown or be devoured by sharks. While these migrants are forced to travel light, their willingness to risk their lives to leave their homeland reveals that they carry the heaviest burden of the Dominican state's failure to support its citizenry on a most basic level by protecting human life. Nobody knows exactly how many Dominicans have migrated by yola, but US Coast Guard statistics indicate that between 1982 and 2009, over seventy thousand undocumented Dominicans have been intercepted at sea (Duany, *Blurred Borders* 59, 193).[1] Nor does anybody know how many have died en route, though media chronicles of the retrieval of dozens of corpses from the sea after each shipwreck would suggest that hundreds of Dominicans die annually in search of a better life. Yet, despite the perilousness of the journey, tightening state border control, and increasing criminal prosecution of illegal migrants, poor Dominicans repeatedly make death-defying attempts to arrive at Puerto Rican shores.

It goes without saying that migration by yola is dramatic—it is an extreme response to the economic inequities of global capitalism and it often has a tragic outcome. My interest here is to explore how theater intervenes in the constant stream of disturbing narratives and images of yola migration circulated in the Dominican Republic by the news media, public awareness campaigns, film, and music. In many ways, the stories performed in plays such as *Miches: Ponle Esperanza* (Miches: Name it Hope) by the island-based playwright Julissa Rivera Céspedes (2005) and *Yoleros* (Boatpeople) by the New York City-based playwright Álex Vásquez Escaño (2008) stage the same tragedies that have been countlessly depicted in the media.[2] A legitimate question is: Why repeat these real-life "ripped from the headlines" stories in the theater? I suggest that when audiences are invited to negotiate between the representations of the problem of illegal migration onstage and the representation of the same stories in the mass media, they engage with a thinking-through of relations of power, which, for the theater theorist Joe Kelleher, defines the relationship between theater and politics (3). The inherent political qualities of the theater, "its liveness and sociality, the simple fact that it happens and that it gathers people, who may well be strangers to each other around issues of disagreement but of common concern" (Kelleher 10) contrast with the passive, often solitary, and distant consumption of images of human suffering displayed in the global media. I submit that the fictions created in *Miches* and *Yoleros* have the potential to make a more profound political impact on spectators than the real-life tragedies depicted in the media because, through the live bodies of actors: "The theatre 'represents' us, both in the sense of showing us images of ourselves and in the sense of standing in and standing up for us, like a delegate or a substitute or—indeed—a political representative. Theatre represents our lives to us in ways that can persuade us to make judgments on the quality and fidelity of those representations and to make critical judgments too on the lives that are so represented" (Kelleher 10). Ephemeral theater events reach a far smaller number of citizens than the mass media, but the efficaciousness of the theater has significantly less to do with sending direct political messages than the thinking and feeling that is activated by encountering representations of ourselves. While *Miches* and *Yoleros* seem to simply echo narratives of tragedy with which Dominicans are already familiar, they bring into sharp relief that poor women of color bear the brunt of what Henry Giroux calls a "biopolitics of disposability" in which neoliberal states do away with the "baggage" of embarrassingly vulnerable populations.

Nation Castaways: Flotsam on a Sea of Global Capital

Pleasure cruisers beware—the beautiful Caribbean and Mediterranean seascapes have become dotted with the flotsam of shipwrecked yolas, *balsas*, and *pateras* built by migrants seeking to escape political oppression, human rights violations, and economic insecurity through clandestine sea crossings. This mainly northward sea migration has occurred throughout the twentieth and twenty-first centuries in waves. In the Mediterranean, 2.1 million African and western Asian migrants arrived in Europe between 2009 and 2018 via Morocco-to-Spain, Africa-to-Italy, and Turkey-to-Greece sea routes (Connor). This migration peaked around 2015, when tragic shipwrecks routinely made headlines, making evident an international humanitarian crisis. In the Caribbean, migratory flows are inextricably bound to US economic and political policies. "Rather than well-reasoned, proactive policies developed through consideration of the complexities—such as US labor demand and the global effects of neoliberalism—" Frank Graziano writes, "The United States has taken a simplified approach: to repel maritime migrants as far from the U.S. shores as possible and, that failing, to expedite their removal from the country" (*Undocumented* 171). The different treatment of Haitian, Cuban, and Dominican migrants has created "inconsistencies and even absurdities. Dominicans who enter the United States are detained and reported, for example, but Cubans who do the same are paroled and eventually granted lawful permanent residency" (171). Moreover, Haitian migration has been reductively understood an economic migration. In the 1970s, 1990s, and after the 2010 earthquake, hundreds of thousands of Haitians sought to escape political persecution, violence, and environmental and natural disasters (all of which have contributed to unrelenting poverty) by crossing the border to the Dominican Republic or undertaking a treacherous seven-hundred-mile sea journey in makeshift rafts to reach the southern shores of the United States.[3] The 1980 Mariel boatlift and the mid-1990s crisis of the "Special Period" in Cuba also motivated mass migration in small boats and homemade rafts. In the Cuban case, however, the *balseros* (rafters) were more likely to succeed in navigating the approximately ninety-mile sea route to Florida, and, until recently, were treated as political refugees and given asylum if they were interdicted at sea or reached land, whereas Haitian migrants have always been subject to immediate deportation.[4] Whether in the Mediterranean or the Caribbean Sea, images of floating debris—pieces of wood boats, plastic gasoline containers, clothing, and even corpses—are jarring reminders that for thousands of migrants never complete their journey and that the sea becomes their final resting place.

I argue, however, that perhaps even more worrisome to the sending and receiving states are the live bodies that comprise a floating population of migrant human flotsam. Mass migration from the Dominican Republic has long been caught up in the tides of globalization of the world economy. According to the sociologist Ramona Hernández, the Dominican exodus "developed in response to the socioeconomic policies implemented in the Dominican Republic after 1966" ("On the Age" 91). These policies, which mobilized the integration of the Dominican Republic into the global economy, were instituted when the US-backed strongman president Joaquín Balaguer shifted the agro-export economy, sustained by traditional products such as sugar, tobacco, coffee, and cocoa, to an import substitution model in the 1970s, an export model in the 1980s, and a neoliberal "new economic program" in the 1990s. By the time the nation's next caudillo, Leonel Fernández, arrived on the political scene as president in 1996, the Dominican Republic had become a service economy dominated by assembly export free-trade zones and tourism and was dependent on foreign investments and remittances from Dominicans living abroad. Over the years, neoliberal economic strategies have produced, intermittently, very strong economic periods of growth, but the price has been a gaping social deficit and an enormous foreign debt that allows the International Monetary Fund (IMF) and other international lenders to dictate national fiscal reforms. Reforms such as the implementation of fiscal austerity packages reducing social welfare spending and eliminating subsidies for electricity, propane, and food; the privatization of state-owned industries such as sugar, electrical power, and mining; and trade liberalizations have been the hallmarks of Fernández's neoliberal economic policies. These policies have maintained macroeconomic stability by serving the interests of the domestic oligarchy, the US government, and other foreign investors. At the same time, neoliberal economic strategies have weakened public institutions, social welfare, and civil society. Over half of all Dominicans live in poverty, 40 percent of the nation's wealth is concentrated in the hands of 10 percent of the population, and the country ranked third lowest in Latin America in social spending, which includes "health, education, drinking water provision, housing, sports and culture, sanitation, social security and welfare" ("Millennium").

In response to the chronic social immobility and pervasive poverty of the past fifty years, over a million Dominicans have emigrated—chiefly to the United States and Puerto Rico—but also to Curaçao, Venezuela, Italy, Spain, and the Netherlands. Torres-Saillant minces no words in characterizing the exodus as a forced economic emigration: "Sépase que la gente normalmente no abandona su tierra de manera voluntaria. Se desgaja de su cálido terruño, sus paisajes familiares, su lengua, su cultura y sus amores compelida por la urgencia material. Emigra quien no puede quedarse. Se van aquellos a quienes la economía nacional les ha cerrado las puertas" ("Know that people don't normally abandon their country voluntarily. They break away from their warm homeland, familiar landscapes, language, culture, and loved ones compelled by material urgency. Those who emigrate can't stay. Those who go are those for whom the doors of the national economy have closed"; "Retorno" 18). Similarly, Graziano explains, "Dominicans do not migrate because they are starving; they migrate to escape dead-end destitution that is maintained by forces—global economic structures, U.S. foreign policy, Dominican government indifference, incompetence, and corruption—beyond their control" ("Why" 2). Paradoxically, in their attempt to overcome poverty and to gain some control over the precariousness of their daily lives, the most vulnerable Dominicans are forced to embark on a journey that risks everything. Yola migration is a perilous undertaking that requires relinquishing one's fate to the elements and to the smugglers and yola captains who organize and pilot the trips. There are various outcomes to this gamble. A good number of Dominicans arrive safely and are able to integrate successfully into Puerto Rican, and, in some cases, US society; others drown when boats capsize or die by dehydration when outboard motors fail and the boats go adrift; some yolas are interdicted at sea and passengers are deported by the US Coast Guard and Customs and Border Protection or the Dominican navy; and, lastly, others survive an unsuccessful journey (perhaps engineered by the dishonest smuggler who set up the trip) and return home, only to attempt the journey again. Most narratives surrounding the yola experience, including the two plays analyzed in this chapter, highlight failure and death. It is this population that has died or is caught in an unproductive cycle of repeating attempts to illegally migrate that has become the flotsam, the human wreckage of global capitalism.

Dominican boat people adrift in the Caribbean Sea represent an unequivocal image of migrants as nation castaways expelled from the body politic. The reliance on the escape valve of migration—the alleviation of social and political pressures and the benefits of economic remittances from Dominicans abroad—makes patent the Dominican government's reneging of its social contract with its citizens and its willingness to set an impoverished underclass afloat to fend for themselves. I read this situation as an example of what Henry Giroux calls a "biopolitcs of disposability." Although theorists such as Michel Foucault, Michael Hardt, Antonio Negri, and Giorgio Agamben work through the idea of biopolitics differently, they share, according to Giroux, a reformulation of "the meaning of politics and how it functions within the contemporary moment to regulate matters of life and death, and, in turn, how such issues are intimately related to both the articulation of community and the social, and the regulation, care and development of human life" (*Stormy Weather* 12). For Giroux, the aftermath of Hurricane Katrina exposed a biopolitics of disposability in the United States that has "largely given up on the sanctity of human life for those populations rendered 'at risk' by global neoliberal economies, and, instead, have embraced an emergent security state founded on cultural homogeneity" (11). The shocking images of dead bodies and reports of people left to die in the media coverage of Hurricane Katrina evinced the confluence of race and poverty in the communities most devastated by the disaster, and it made visible entire populations that have been excluded from a neoliberal agenda lacking in social obligation and civic responsibility. Moreover, in the era of globalization, as nation-states such as the Dominican Republic increasingly surrender "control of their economies and public policies to transnational structures of political and economic power, they have been faced with crises of governance that are by no means new—that of repressing populations *whose lives have become unsustainable*" (Gregory 244; emphasis mine). Social unrest and protest against the social exclusions and inequalities created by neoliberal restructuring of the Dominican economy, for example, have been "typically greeted with violent repression from Dominican security authorities" (244). In my view, the failure to deter undocumented maritime migration represents another form of violent repression and an exercise in biopower in which some of the most vulnerable citizens of the nation—those whose lives are no longer deemed sustainable by the state—are allowed to subsist on the margins of society or disappear into the sea.[5]

Beyond the brutal conditions that push people to migrate and the aggression exercised to stop them, migrants are also subject to the violence of the dangerous journey itself, which, as we will see, is orchestrated by human traffickers. In *Gore Capitalism*, Sayak Valencia examines how violence as paid work has become a strategy for operating within extreme neoliberal capitalism. In the US-Mexican border, and, as I argue, in the Caribbean maritime borderlands as well, Valencia identifies how new, monstrous, *endriago* subjects find agency in the neoliberal project "by means of *necroempowerment* and the fugitive, dystopian *necro-practices* of gore, as they . . . attempt to *legitimate* the processes of underground economies (black market, drug trafficking, weapons, bodies, etc.) through their reign of violence" (27; emphasis in original). On a smaller scale, this episteme of violence has also made its way to the Dominican Republic. In the industry of illegal boat migration, in which death is always a risk, men marginalized by low wages, poverty, and inequality in the hegemonic global economy become empowered by not only managing the lives of people (biopolitics) but also commodifying death (necropolitics). That is, they achieve a foothold in society via the potential death of others.

The state response to crack down on illegal migration is mostly an empty gesture that avoids the root causes of the problem; this response signals the growing tendency of governments operating in what Agamben calls "states of emergency" that suspend democratic principles and permit extra-judicial state violence to "protect" their populations. Similar to the post-9/11 focus on the War on Terror and border protection in the United States, in the Dominican Republic, rising drug-related violence and human rights violations against Haitians can be justified by a "state of exception" invoked in border wars against narcotrafficking and illegal Haitian migration. Not only does biopower function within global neoliberalism, it goes hand in hand with the rise of security states structured around cultural and racial homogeneity. Just as Dominican migrants in Puerto Rico and the United States, Haitians in the Dominican Republic, driven from their country by poverty, find a place in the labor market doing exploitative work rejected by many nationals. In both cases, in spite of the push-pull factors at play—that is, the inevitability of masses of people moving across borders in sync with global labor demands—the receiving societies' rejection and resultant persecution of the migrants is motivated in great part by racism and xenophobia. In line with Giroux's understanding of biopolitics, borders, for Joseph Nevins, whether they be the long frontier between Mexico and the United States or the liminal space of the sea between North Africa and Europe or the Caribbean and the United States, represent "the connections and divisions between those granted life and those assigned to the realm of death—and all the stations in between the extremes of injustice" ("A Tale"). Those relegated to the realm of death are obviously most likely to be poor and of color. Invoking W. E. B. Du

Bois, Nevins cites an example of the global color line in parallel shipwrecks that took place in the winter of 2012. On the one hand, the *Costa Concordia* luxury cruise ship wreck off the coast of Italy on January 13, 2012, in which thirty-two people were confirmed to have died, had intense international media coverage, whereas the sinking of a yola and the loss of fifty-two lives off the coast of the Dominican Republic appeared in only one brief report on CNN. Nevins claims that "the attention afforded to the deaths of almost exclusively luxury tourists from Western Europe dwarfs that paid to the drowning of dozens of unauthorized Dominican migrants reproduces a world of profound inequality and injustice" ("A Tale").

Therefore, undocumented Dominican and Haitian migrants are victims of racialized state violence, whether through biopolitics, a strategy of marginalization and neglect, the necropolitical violence of the criminal underworld, or detention and deportation carried out by state authorities.[6] When yola migrants are intercepted at sea they are caught between two sovereignties, threatening each in different ways. On the one hand, Puerto Rico/the United States wishes to close its borders to illegal migrants, even though supporting "authoritarian regimes, labor exploitation, or the political and economic hegemony of a small elite, U.S. foreign policy is an indirect cause of the same migration U.S. border enforcement attempts to curtail" (Graziano, "Why" 6). On the other hand, if the stability of Dominican society depends on the safety valve of migration, then the reintegration of deportees with even fewer resources than when they left exacerbates the same social and economic problems that prompted them to leave.[7] Trapped between the two sovereignties, unwanted yola migrants futilely circulate in a militarized global frontier land managed by biopolitical states more invested in securing borders than in sustaining democratic values, social investment, and life itself.

While the media coverage of Hurricane Katrina was a sudden and shocking spotlight on poor and mainly black communities relegated to the margins and written out of the neoliberal agenda, the smaller catastrophes of yola migration are continually displayed in the Dominican media. On the radio, lively songs warning of the dangers of illegal migration play; on television, famous entertainers such as Juan Luis Guerra participate in public awareness campaigns such as "Los viajes ilegales son viajes a la muerte" ("Illegal Journeys are Trips to Death"), and in movie theaters films about dangerous boat migration such as *Paisaje de ida* (1988), *Viajeros* (2006), and *60 millas al este* (2008) have reached large audiences. Taking a different tack, the conceptual artists Ángel Rosario, Maurice Sánchez, and Miguel Canaán of the multidisciplinary creative design group Colectivo Shampoo have drawn attention to yola migration in a ludic fashion with their *D' La Mona Plaza* print and video project.[8] They imagine a giant commercial rest stop in the middle of the Mona Passage for weary yola travelers. Elegantly titled and supposedly built by the apocryphal Puerto Rican construction group Constructora Intranaútica del Caribe, the print and video show *yoleros* (boat people) envisioned as plump tourists in Lycra outfits strolling an ultramodern rest stop complete with a dry dock and marina for yolas, first aid, showers, internet access, fountains, grass, and trinket and snack sellers. Ironically, news of the floating rest stop/mall was picked up in the Dominican media and thought by some to be a real construction project. More savvy interpreters realized that the project was a satirical meditation on the American dream of modernity that lures Dominicans from the dire economic realities of their country.

In the news media, both national and international coverage tends to report on the tragic outcomes and exceptional stories, and it contains little analysis addressing the causes of the problem or the solutions that might help a disposable population become indispensable to the creation of a healthier economy.[9] For example, the danger of sharks referenced in the Wilfrido Vargas merengue lyrics in the epigraph recalls the 1987 Death's Head Beach incident in which as many as 70 of approximately 150 passengers packed on a yola were drowned or eaten by sharks when, just four miles out to sea, the boat's two outboard motors exploded. Military authorities failed to send rescue helicopters, and Eugenio Cabral, the director of civil defense, recounts watching in horror from a plane as the aquamarine sea turned red from the blood of over a dozen capsized boat people being devoured by sharks (Doerner).[10] The stories of shark-infested waters are no tall tales, nor are the survival stories involving the taboos such as adults breastfeeding and cannibalism. In 2001 Faustina Mercedes Mauricio was lauded as a national hero (and was compensated by the state) for nourishing seven women and nine men with her breast milk as their boat drifted at sea for nearly two weeks ("Faustina, la mujer"). In a less uplifting story, in 2004, after five days adrift, passengers attacked two lactating women and reportedly threw a third overboard who refused to cooperate ("Dominicans Saved"). One of the two women who helped over a dozen people later died, covered in bruises from being attacked by fellow passengers trying to access her body. In other stories of yolas gone adrift, survivors resorted to cannibalism.[11] Suspicions arise when survivors tell conflicting accounts of what happened on the high seas. In one instance, animosity between communities developed when families discovered that seventeen of eighteen passengers from Villa Altagracia were among the dead, whereas a good number of survivors hailed from Villa Riva. The sole survivor from Villa Altagracia, who had lied on the boat about where he was from, fled his village for fear he would be hunted down by survivors from Villa Riva if he disclosed what happened while the boat drifted at sea (Romero). Unlikely as it might seem, warring sea villages, Roman Charity, and cannibalism, tropes more common in classical literature, become the stuff of mainstream contemporary newscasts.

Less extreme and more common are the stories with headlines that detail the fluctuating number of injured, dead, and disappeared that dominate newspapers for weeks at a time as rescue efforts unfold. For example, in a film about yola migration I later discuss, radio news reports similarly enumerating these statistics are constantly heard in the background. The presence of death among the living has become disturbing quality of destitute beach towns impacted the greatest by yola migration. Death becomes a part of everyday life of these small coastal villages since shipwrecks impact what residents hear, see, smell, and feel for extended periods of time. In the Bahía de Samaná tragedy in February 2012, thirteen travelers were rescued, fifty-four were found dead, and at least a dozen were never found. As one news report shows, at times residents literally could not escape the stench of death: "Debido a la demanda, las mascarillas se agotaron en farmacias, el hospital y clínicas, porque todo el pueblo corrió a la playa y quería taparse las narices ante el hedor que expedían los cuerpos en descomposición" ("Due to high demand, face masks were sold out in pharmacies, the hospital, and clinics, because everyone in town ran to the beach and wanted to cover their noses from the stench emitted by the decomposing bodies"; Vega). Local medical facilities were overwhelmed, medical examiners lacked basic supplies such as rubber gloves, and photographs show bodies wrapped in blue plastic being hauled to be buried in mass graves. In what looks like a postmortem newspaper photograph, we see at least six semiclothed bodies are crammed together on the floor of a small building, but the caption—"Dos de los cadáveres"—may very well give the viewer pause, since it is impossible to discern which are live bodies and which are corpses ("Pocas"). Equally disturbing is not knowing the whereabouts of the deceased. In one photograph, a yola sits on the beach with photographs of the missing posted on the stern (G. Pérez). This gesture recalls the images of the disappeared in Argentina during military rule and the walls of photographs of the missing posted in New York City after the 9/11 attacks and places the tragedies of yola migration at the level of a national trauma that resists closure. However, the continual loss of life recounted in the media does not seem to constitute a national crisis that would join Dominicans in protesting the problem of illegal migration. In fact, the call for a national day of mourning after the Bahía de Samaná tragedy made by the newspaper *Diario Libre* was greeted with just as many blogger responses calling the migrants ignorant, suicidal, and unwilling to solve their financial problems as there were responses expressing empathy and anger toward the government's reluctance to confront the issue of illegal maritime migration ("Diario"). There is, in sum, the sense that the migrants lost at sea form an underclass already expelled from Dominican society and are, therefore, not worthy of being mourned. Thus, not only does the media depict the victims of violence as occupying "spaces considered *outside of* and therefore unworthy of attention," (Valencia 287; emphasis in original), it "contributes to venerating violence through spectacularization and endless coverage, while simultaneously neglecting to report on its real consequences" (291).

The US-based Dominican filmmaker Jorge Lendeborg's 2008 film, *60 millas al este*, by contrast, focuses on the living and tells the far more ordinary story of yola migrants who return home alive after failing in their attempt to reach Puerto Rico. Touted as the Dominican Republic's first "reality film," Lendeborg states that his intention was not to film a movie; rather, he sought to film reality as events unfold during a yola journey. The unscripted story played out by nonactors was praised by Dominican critics for the veracity with which it portrays the lives and emotions of Dominicans who see no other option than to risk everything to leave their country.[12] Since the trip is set up by Lendeborg—he locates a yola trip coordinator who is willing to be filmed—the claim "it's all real" is doubtful, but my interest here in briefly analyzing the film is not to untangle fact from fiction. In my view, *60 millas al este* stands out for capturing the routine, quotidian qualities of the yola smuggling trade, thereby offering a different perspective from the more sensational controversies and deviancies in the media reports discussed earlier.

Yola migration in *60 millas al este* is not portrayed as an exceptional tragedy; rather, it has come to form an ethnoscape, what Arjun Appadurai calls a "landscape of persons who constitute the shifting world in which we live: tourists, immigrants, refugees, exiles, guest workers, and other moving groups and individuals constitute an essential feature of the world and appear to affect the politics of (and between) nations to a hitherto unprecedented degree" (33). At the beginning of the film, Lendeborg inserts himself in this ethnoscape of mobility and films his arrival at the Aeropuerto de las Américas in Santo Domingo, making evident that he, too, is a Dominican migrant, though the legal means by which Lendeborg moves between countries makes him clearly more fortunate than the compatriots he has come to film. Juxtaposed with the scene of Lendeborg advancing through an orderly modern airport, we also see in the film's opening sequence a chaotic scene of a group of men carrying a casket surrounded by overwrought mourners through a bustling village. This less felicitous return and the failed trip that constitutes the main narrative in *60 millas al este* serve as cautionary tales about the dangers of the industry of illegal smuggling of people across national borders.

60 millas al este examines both the motivations for migrating and the operations that make it possible. One narrative shows the complete cast of characters involved in the yola trade: the *organizadores* who plan the trips, the *buscones* who recruit passengers, the *maestro constructores* who clandestinely build the yolas, and the fishermen who become the *capitanes* who pilot the trips, all of whom play a part in the informal economy of yola migration. The film's narratives foreground the passengers and their reasons for attempting undocumented entry into Puerto Rico and the sixty nautical miles of the boat journey itself. From the hustle of planning the trip, the story shifts to a drummed countdown from three hours to the final moments in which, under the cover of darkness, the twenty-eight travelers move through a mangrove and wade into the sea to board the small boat. All the activity and movement of the earlier scenes ceases, and the gravity of the uncertainties of being crammed in a small open vessel on the high seas settles in. With the exception of a few tense moments when tempers flare, such as when the captain announces to the suspicious passengers that the motor is damaged and that they must return home, much of the journey takes place in a numb silence. Lendeborg trains the camera on the expressionless faces of the travelers lulled by wind, sun, and waves. He shows extreme close-ups of seasick men and women vomiting overboard, and repeats shots of the Sisyphean effort of bailing the water that the newly constructed boat began to take on the moment the passengers boarded it. Despite the many individual close-up shots of the faces of the yoleros shown in *60 millas al este*, one gets the sense of the collective "being in the same boat"—that is to say, at the mercy of both the elements and the global economy.

Lendeborg uses brief flashback interviews to break up the slow journey and maintain the viewer's interest, and, more importantly, to give a voice and identity to the nameless and mainly silent passengers. Each flashback is titled with the interviewees name, occupation, and number of yola migration attempts. We see, for example, the impoverished environments in which Noelia, Fior, Chacha, María, all single mothers, live and struggle to feed their children, a beautiful Boca Chica beach where a *Sanky Panky* (male sex worker) lives off tourists, and a field where Molino, a Haitian *jornalero* (day laborer), cuts sugarcane. We learn that one mother cannot support her children with the wages she earns in a free-trade zone, and that Molino and his community of cane cutters had to work years to raise enough money to pay for a single yola passage that was to set off a chain of migration once he arrived in Puerto Rico and sent for the others. In all cases, the interviewees perceive their situation as sufficiently dire to risk death (and orphaning their children) in search of a better income. Furthermore, the vast majority have attempted to reach Puerto Rico on multiple occasions, this trip being the twelfth attempt for one young man.

Perhaps the "reality" Lendeborg best captures is the anxious monotony of sixteen hours at sea and the anticlimactic failure of a trip. The tragedy in this story is the vicious cycle of poverty in which poor Dominicans, motivated to feed themselves and their families, invest what little they have in repeat attempts to reach this goal. Also fueling this desire to reach Puerto Rican shores are the workings of global media, which "foster awareness of deprivation, propagate illusions of American opulence, fuel the fantasy of easy access to wealth, provide fictional role models, and enhance the desire—particularly among youth—for unaffordable name-brand products that an emerging identity requires" (Graziano, "Why" 8–9). The logos of American professional baseball, basketball, and football teams and the high-fashion English brand Burberry plaid seen decorating the travelers' baseball caps and T-shirts highlight the disjunctures produced by the ethnoscapes of moving culture and capital described by Appadurai. This apparel is suggestive of the idealized expectations that are soon frustrated by the realities of racial discrimination, unfamiliar and unwelcoming new laws, and limited opportunities the migrants confront upon arrival. The easily recognizable logos bobbing on the waves make a striking image of the human wreckage adrift in a sea of neoliberal global capitalism. Ironically, considered superfluous and disposable for their inability to be productive consumers, the boat people bear the very symbols that suggest the consumerist desires encouraged by globalization. The migrant bodies complicating today's seascapes signal what Iain Chambers would call an "interrogative presence" that forces us to question "conclusive framings of existing political, cultural, and historical narratives" (678). For example, bodies that have experienced modernity in different ways wash up on northern shores and interrupt "the facile evaluations of a linear mapping disciplined by landlocked desires of unilateral progress and a homogeneous modernity" (681). While from the north, the sea may be seen as a border, a barrier not to be crossed, for migrants from the south pulled by the forces of globalization, the sea is a passage that inevitably connects histories and cultures in a more fluid cartography of transnational belonging. In the following section, I argue that theater performances of the very same narratives of yola migration represented in the media offer a more productive space in which to develop an oppositional politics that counters the civic indifference that dominates the political economy of neoliberalism and gore capitalism.

The Drama of Yola Migration: *Miches: Ponle Esperanza* and *Yoleros*

During the same period Lendeborg filmed and screened *60 millas al este*, *Miches: Ponle Esperanza* by Julissa Céspedes Rivera and *Yoleros* by Álex Vásquez Escaño were performed in Santo Domingo and New York City.[13] Like Lendeborg's film, the yola boat journey comprises the central narrative of the plays, and nearly all the same topics in the media coverage on yola migration reappear not only in these two plays but also in several Dominican migration dramas I will include as precursors to the plays by Céspedes Rivera and Vásquez Escaño. What, then, do the fictions created by these plays contribute to the narratives that have long circulated about yola migration? What kind of relationship do the plays create with their audiences and what are their politics? Obviously, center staging the plight of poor Dominican migrants in the public institutional spaces of the theater is a political gesture. For Joe Kelleher, though, the efficacy of the theater has less to do with a play's message than the uniqueness and repeatability that define play performances. Theater is inherently repetitious, for a play performance is a representation of a script (which in turn is a representation of the reality of the world the play represents), actors brings characters alive through repeatedly rehearsing their lines, and productions play to audiences night after night. However, each theater event is unpredictable because of the many different variables that inform audience response before and after the performance—we cannot know what viewers will think and feel during the show, or what thoughts and emotions will remain with them after the performance (Kelleher 22). What happens when the yola migration story, which has been repeatedly played out in the mass media (music, film, newspapers) and in everyday life (oral traditions such as survivor tales and rumors) enters the representing machine of the theater? Important tension is derived in witnessing how the play repeats the story and represents onstage the world outside the theater. The thinking and feeling that is triggered from watching the performance obviously will not touch us in the same way as a real-life tragedy would, but it impacts our consciousness, "in that complex way the theatre specialises in, which has to do with the ones who are here, who are on the spot, standing in for the others who are not. The ones standing in are the actors and spectators, for example, who turned up this evening to participate in the show, but they are also the characters themselves, whose lives have been ruined, who are standing in for, or representing, all the other people whose lives have been changed in this way" (Kelleher 26). There is the immediacy of those "on the spot," as audience or performer in the event, who metonymically represent a wider population, a larger public sphere. Even though a small group is convened for only a brief period of time, there is awareness that the potential impact of the event transcends these limitations. Joining people together to awaken a sense of social responsibility about the issue of yola migration, by judging the characters and stories that are represented onstage and comparing them to real-life stories may change how people perceive and respond to the problem in the world outside of the theater. There are abundant images in the Dominican media of the rescue of moribund migrants and of the body bags of even less fortunate travelers. Valencia calls for the extrication of "the body from media discourses that spectralize it" (292). In my estimation, the embodied suffering in the plays about yola migration studied here constitute one way "to make sure that the death and the pain of an Other cause a shudder in all our bodies" (Valencia 292). For audiences accustomed to seeing images of bodies pulled from the sea, the theater offers a space where these bodies are brought back to life and given subjectivities that force viewers to engage, critically and ethically, in the role of witness rather than passive voyeurs to spectacles of suffering. Engaging in theatrical performance as a producer or a viewer, then, can be a powerful activity "to dismantle the illusion created by news media that artificially naturalizes the exercise of violence, rendering it invisible through the protective distance of the screen, which tells us that extreme non-consensual pain only happens to the bodies of Others" (Valencia 292–93). The narratives performed in the plays discussed shortly, in sum, are already familiar to Dominican audiences, but they are repeated with a difference because they not only resurrect a sector of society that the nation would prefer to forget, ironically, they present a much fuller and more nuanced story that official discourses would prefer to silence.

Since the 1990s Dominican theater has become an important site for engaging with, and often countering, negative representations of Dominican migrant identity. Many plays about Dominican migration center on the experience of transnationalism and explore stories of migrant characters adapting to life in the United States while remaining connected in various ways with their home country and, in some cases, moving back and forth between them. The journey itself to another country, however, does surface as a theme in several plays. In three wildly different pieces, brief mentions of yola migration preview some of the themes and techniques used in *Miches* and *Yoleros*. One of the most curious prizewinning plays anthologized in the Casa de Teatro volumes, Otto Caro's *"RR" Tragedia Musical* (1983), tells the story of a campesino who goes from laboring in the sugarcane fields to working as a prostitute in Puerto Rico and later as a drug dealer in New York City.[14] Caro's play stands out for its unusual diagrammatic script that presents speech and movement, sound effects and soundtrack, and lighting in three columns. *"RR" Tragedia Musical* is also memorable because it presents the outcome of illegal migration as tragic and highlights the vulnerability of migrants ensnared in criminal smuggling organizations. To my knowledge, the elaborate musical play was never produced, but the fact that it was awarded a prize and published tells us that the arts were not exempt from circulating negative representations of migration during a period in which the Dominican Republic was reeling from intense social and economic changes brought on by a sharp increase in migration. The downward spiral for the protagonist, identified as RR, begins when he is approached at a bar by men who tell him that they organize safe boat trips to Puerto Rico and that "con ochocientos pesos me llevaban sin tener documentos y que allá nos estarían esperando otros señores para darnos trabajo bien pagado" ("for eight hundred pesos they would take me without documents and that over there men would be waiting for us there to give us a well-paid job"; 354–55). According to stage directions, the journey by yola is reenacted with stormy audiovisual effects and a *danza trágica* with dancers surrounding the yola that later transforms into a *danza de búsqueda* in which sea officers search the coast for illegal migrants. Three well-dressed men emerge from the shadows to take RR to his new job, which, he soon learns, is selling his body. In this over-the-top spectacle, migration becomes a grotesque nightmare that can only lead to death.[15]

As we will see in chapter 4, the characters in Elizabeth Ovalle's realist social drama *Por hora y a* Piece-Work (1993), by contrast, have a certain degree of success in securing jobs in the exploitative New York City garment industry and in finding pathways toward gaining citizenship and receiving social services support. Ovalle does not stage the actual yola journey in her play, but in mentioning the physical and legal risks yoleros take to improve their station in life, *Por hora y a* Piece-Work echoes Caro's melodramatic musical. For example, the character Juana, a new worker at the factory, reveals that it was fortunate that the yola in which she travelled was interdicted by the authorities, since the high winds were about to capsize the vessel in the middle of the Canal de la Mona (250). After being picked up, she was incarcerated in the *preventiva* for six months, which evidently did not deter her from later reaching the United States. Ovalle's play also injects the theme of stigma that is attached to yola migration. The following factors—how long migrants have been in the United States, how they arrived, their regional origins, and whether they have papers—all contribute to creating social hierarchies among the factory workers. Juana, a campesina who has recently arrived and is undocumented, resorts to a derogatory phrase Dominicans use to refer to yola migration and lies about her mode of arrival when she feels threatened by her more experienced coworker from Santo Domingo nicknamed Capitaleña: "¿Y tú?, de seguro fuiste la que viniste en doble A, (agua por delante y agua por detrás), yo vine por Méjico, mi hija, en avión y tren" ("And you? Surely you were the one that came in first class double W, [water in front and water behind], I came from Mexico, my dear, by plane and train"; 253). The central characters in *Por hora y a* Piece-Work do not die tragically, but the narrative arc, which ends with Juana ultimately rejecting New York City and returning to the Dominican Republic, situates the play within the negative representations of migration that abounded in the 1980s and 1990s.

Paradise by Pedro Antonio Valdez (1997) is also a cautionary tale that depicts Dominican migrants caught up in the drug trade and ends with the protagonists, none other than Adán and Eva, returning to Santo Domingo, their *verdadero paraíso* (true paradise) (29). Using humor, however, the play presents a much more balanced view of migration. For instance, in the telenovela-esque final scene in which the protagonists are seated on a park bench cooing over their happy return, a striking mob comes upon them, demanding fair salaries, food, and electricity, suggesting that neither the Dominican Republic nor the United States constitute a paradise. Valdez, who writes each scene using a distinct theatrical style, titles Adán and Eva's yola journey "La yola de los locos" and labels the scene *teatro grotesco*. In keeping with the deformations that operate in the aesthetics of the grotesque, Valdez subverts the terror of being at the mercy of the elements on the high seas and turns the shipwreck scene into a comedy:

> ADÁN: (Achicando con una lata.) ¡Si esta vaina se hunde, nos va a llevar el diablo!
>
> EVA: (Maquillándose, usando de espejo el fondo de una lata.) El diablo es el capitán de la yola. ¿No ves, Adán?
>
> DEMONIO: ¡Achiquen! ¡Achiquen! ¡Dejen de hablar mierda y achiquen!
>
> ADÁN: Achica tú, buen maricón. Te pagué veinte mil pesos para que nos lleves a Puerto Rico, no para que nos pongas a botar agua. (14)
>
> *ADAM: (Bailing out water with a can.) If this thing sinks, we are going to hell!*
>
> *EVA: (Putting makeup on using the bottom of a can as a mirror.) The captain of the yola is the devil. Don't you see, Adam?*
>
> *THE DEVIL: Bail! Bail! Stop talking shit and bail!*

> *ADAM: You bail, faggot. I paid you twenty thousand pesos to take us to Puerto Rico, not for us to bail out water.*

Desperate to escape poverty, Dominicans are willing to put their lives in the hands of the devil, cast here as unsavory trip organizers and boat captains. In both *Paradise* and *"RR" Tragedia Musical*, agreeing to the terms set by these characters is akin to making a pact with the devil.[16] Even though in this scene Adán jokingly insults the devil-captain, in return for safe passage, little does he know that he has relinquished his autonomy and will become a puppet in the drug trade, just as in *"RR" Tragedia Musical*. The yola capsizes, not because of the stormy sea, but due to a tempestuous battle of the sexes that develops between Adán, Eva, and the Demonio. In the end, Eva, feeling insulted by both men, sinks the ship by ripping off its rudder. There is no tragic death, however, because in the next scene we find Adán being interviewed by a bureaucrat from the American consulate, which is amusingly and aptly played out in the style of theater of the absurd. While the theme of yola migration appears only briefly in these three plays, it is useful to include them in this analysis since, in addition to showing the dangers and stigma attached to yola migration and documenting artistic responses to the transformation of Dominican society at the end of the twentieth century, they help establish a yola "scenario" with certain narrative structures and assigned roles that are repeated and further developed in *Miches* and *Yoleros*.

The shipwreck, like Diana Taylor's example of the scenario of conquest, contains narrative and plot, milieux, and the embodied behaviors of social actors that are already known to us by the force of their repetition in cultural representations (28). From the Greeks, to the early modern European discovery and conquest of the New World, to today's desperate crossings across the Caribbean and Mediterranean Seas, the shipwreck scenario plays out within a set of conventions: the scene takes place on a boat or on a beach; the outcomes include reaching the coast, rescue, or death at sea; and the social actors include a captain and passengers often cast as archetypal characters. These familiar narratives are just as much a part of the repertoire as they are the archive, and reading them as a performance scenario "places spectators within its frame, implicating us in its ethics and politics" (Taylor 33), a positioning that differs from the voyeurism assigned to viewers in much contemporary media.[17] In the plays analyzed here, the bulk of the action takes place mainly in the intimate confines of a yola at sea, which casts the sun, waves, and sharks as enemies, and limits the action to passengers anxiously discussing how they found themselves in their present calamitous situation;

jumping ship or being thrown overboard; divvying up sources of nourishment and hydration; and slipping into delirium or death.

All of the aforementioned occurs in *Miches*, a tragedy on the high seas in which a yola with nine passengers from Miches, a fishing village in the province El Seibo on the northeast coast of the Dominican Republic, loses its motor, goes adrift, and capsizes. The yola scenes, which make up the greater part of the action, are framed by an auditory prologue in which the audience, in complete darkness, hears the sounds of nocturnal animals, lapping water, and the prayers and conversations of the travelers attempting to steal away in a yola, as well as two monologues by nontravelers. In the first monologue, Muchacha regrets being afflicted by seasickness and, consequently, her inability to commit to a yola journey. As she recounts the many reasons why the townspeople of Miches attempt to migrate, the monologue acquires an omniscient quality through the repetition of the phrase "los veo" (I see them) at the beginning of neighboring sentences describing her compatriots' migration experiences (197). By employing anaphora, Rivera Céspedes emphasizes themes and creates rhythm and a poetic tone to the numerous monologues that structure the play. In the second on-land monologue, Madre-Miches laments the slow death of a town so hypnotized by the sea that lures them to a new life that the town's raison d'etre is defined only by "los que se van y los que están en la lista de espera" ("those who leave and those who are on the waiting list"; 199). As I discuss in the final section of this chapter, figuring the town as a mother in turn anthropomorphizes the nation, posing questions about how illegal migration impacts the *madre patria* (motherland).

In *Yoleros* Máximo, Demecio, and Dinorah set off by yola in search of better opportunities from the coastal town Boca de Yuma; they fail to reach Puerto Rico, and only one of the three returns alive. Act 1 takes place on land and serves to introduce the three characters—the captain, a lottery ticket seller named Máximo; Demecio, a newspaper vendor; and Dinorah, a young mother—and to show the tense operations that set up the illegal trips. When act 2 opens with the question ¿Dónde estamos? (Where are we?), the characters have already been lost at sea for three days.

In comparison to *Miches*, apart from three brief metatheatrical scenes, *Yoleros* downplays lyricism and theatricality and relies instead upon spare dialogue to drive the action and develop the themes. One metaphorical twist that defines the play, however, is the notion of life as a game of lottery that very few people win. In contrast to Demecio, who sells newspapers filled with stories based on reality, Máximo's lottery tickets sell dreams. Defending his other occupation, his "nueva rifa" ("new raffle"; 78), Máximo tells

1.1. The cast of *Yoleros*. Photo credit: Gustavo Mirabile.

Demecio that he will hit the jackpot because, "no lo hago por dinero sino para el nuevo comienzo," ("I don't do it for money but for the new beginning"; 78). The numbers Máximo sells are lottery tickets for a space on his yola and the new beginnings he refers to is migration. In spite of his doubts, "¿Y qué tú quieres? ¿Qué dé dinero pa' una rifa sin saber si voy a ganar?" ("And what do you want? That I spend money on a raffle without knowing if I'll win?" 80), Demecio is desperate enough to take the risk. In both plays, it turns out that the only "winners" in the migration gamble are the male boat captains, because they survive the ill-fated trips. Nevertheless, each dread having to respond to the questions they will face upon return. *Yoleros* ends with Máximo asking himself: "¿Qué van a decir cuando me encuentren? ¿Van ellos a creer que viajé solo? ¿Me harán preguntas?" ("What will they say when they find me? Will they believe that I traveled alone? Will they ask questions?" 119), while the boat captain in *Miches* wishes he had died, because by returning "tiene que contar, tiene que explicar, tiene que responder. Tiene que recordar, aunque no quiera y sentirse culpable . . ." ("he has to tell, he has to explain, he has to answer. He has to remember, even if he does not want to and feel guilty . . ."; 237).

The representation of yola migration—what is said and what is left unsaid—not only becomes a theme in these plays, their very function is to show and to tell, to encourage the audience to question, and to remember. Both the oral tradition and the newspaper motifs in *Yoleros* remind us that the subject of yola migration is controversial. Demecio frets about the gossip that will circulate when the townspeople discover that he has gone; he fears gossip that will suggest that he has fled because he is hiding something or being judged for risking his life and seeking an "easy" route out of poverty. He is painfully aware of the perception that those who migrate by boat "son de la clase más baja del país" ("are from the lowest class in the country"; 93). Dinora is less preoccupied by *el qué dirán* (what people may say), and her doubts about joining the trip stem from the constant stream of media stories of sharks devouring yoleros. She asks Máximo: "¿Qué tú quieres si eso es todo lo que se lee? 'Se los comen los tiburones,' 'Yoleros son devorados,' y quién sabe qué más que yo no he leído" ("What do you expect if that's all you read? 'Eaten by sharks,' 'Yoleros are devoured,' and who knows what else I haven't read"; 86). Máximo points out that sensationalist narratives serve to sell newspapers, and that "los periódicos tienen un lindo juego: publicar una lista de los nombres de aquellos que no llegan. Siempre he querido que escriban una de esos que llegan" ("newspapers play a nice game: they publish a list of the names of those who don't arrive. I have always wanted them to write one of those who do arrive"; 102).[18] According to Máximo, the story of yola migration depicted in the media is always incomplete because it never highlights the success stories which might encourage more Dominicans to attempt illegal migration. The tales of yola migration circulated by the travelers themselves are also necessarily incomplete. In the midst of their suffering as the yola goes adrift, Demecio asks his travel companions if they have heard unpleasant stories from anyone who has returned from a yola trip (109). Nobody speaks of the traumas they face on the high seas, Máximo points out, "Ellos se guardan sus desgracias para ellos mismos" ("They keep their misfortunes to themselves"; 109). Thus, while the media seems to depict too much of the horror, the people themselves who lived the experience divulge too little. Revealing too much might have the effect of dissuading some would-be migrants whereas telling too little might encourage others to take their chances. The plays show that Dominicans, like the characters Demecio and Dinora, even when caught between knowing too much and wanting to know more, are willing to invest in the dream of a winning lottery ticket—safe passage to Puerto Rico and the chance to achieve economic stability.

One reason the stories imagined by Rivera Céspedes and Vásquez Escaño are so valuable is precisely that they help fill this knowledge gap. They serve the important function of telling a more complete story, one that is undoubtedly "ripped from the headlines," but through the development of

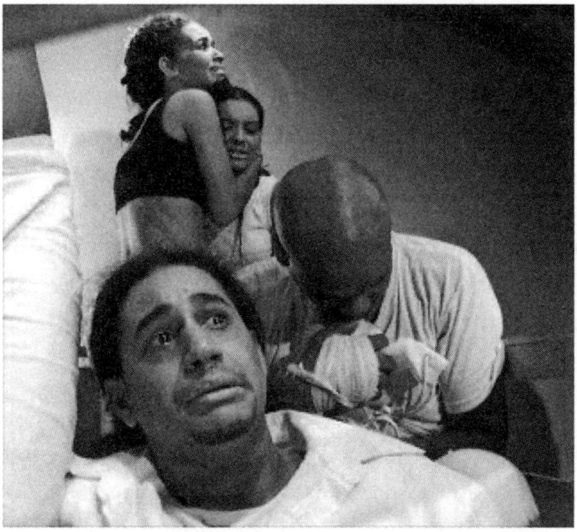

1.2. Cast members from *Al garete*, a stage version of *Miches: Ponle Esperanza*. Photo credit: La Cuarta Espacio Teatral. Courtesy of José Rafael Sosa.

character psychology and the communicative modes of monologue and dialogue, they exceed the one-note tenor of tragedy to include both humor and the grotesque. They offer audiences a compact yet nuanced analysis of a social problem that plagues their nation, inviting an emotional and intellectual engagement that differs greatly from a news report. Firstly, through the boat conversations of the characters, and especially a number of monologues that foreground how everyone has a voice and a story to tell, it becomes evident that the desire to escape from a situation experienced as unlivable is motivated not only by poverty but by other factors as well. Whereas *60 millas al este* captures the anxious silence of a yola journey and relies upon pre-trip interviews to offer minimalist backstories, in *Miches* the characters are engaged in constant conversation and storytelling. Rivera Céspedes uses archetype characters—Embarazada, La Rebelde, Loquita, Deportado, Maestro, Estudiante, Boricua, Capitán, and Ayudante—who, rather than conveying a sense of anonymity or generic simplification, present a far fuller array of motivations for wanting to leave the Dominican Republic.[19]

In the scene "historias de alta mar," (stories on the high seas) for example, we hear life stories, rather than stories of yola migration. Consequently, we gain insight into an existential awareness of an absurd lack of opportunities, and how identity categories such as sexuality and gender come into play in the decisions of Estudiante, Loquita, and Rebelde to migrate. In his monologue, Estudiante recounts how he came from a poor rural family to study architecture in Santo Domingo. However, once immersed in his studies in the capital, he realizes that rural to urban migration and education will not increase his chances for social and economic mobility. Observing engineers and lawyers who sacrificed greatly to earn their academic degrees *motoconchando* (working as motorcycle taxi drivers), Estudiante comes to understand "el sinsentido de estudiar, el sinsentido de existir en este último rincón del planeta" ("the absurdity of studying, the absurdity of living in the furthest corner of the planet"; 207). Instead of fomenting aspirations and providing a pathway to a productive career, going through the motions of being a student became a farce:

> Empecé sentirme ridículo con mi regla T prestada, de otro a quien se la prestó otro, quien también había dejado la carrera porque no daba . . . otros que no comprendieron que no eran ellos los que no daban, sino la carrera, la universidad, el país, el mundo. Otros que como yo no estaban dispuestos a dejar su sangre detrás de un título para bailar la bachata de la miseria. (208)

> *I started to feel ridiculous with my borrowed T square, borrowed from someone who borrowed it from someone else, who had also dropped out because it wasn't worth it . . . others who didn't understand that it wasn't they who weren't worth it, but the major, the university, the country, the world. Others like me weren't willing to give their blood for a degree to dance the bachata of poverty.*

Estudiante's existential crisis leads him to make the abrupt decision to abandon everything and to go to Puerto Rico by yola. By becoming a labor migrant and taking the risk of dangerous and illegal migration, Estudiante assumes he will be able to participate in the global economy in a way that his country—"este último rincón del planeta"—cannot offer. Loquita's desire to migrate, by contrast, is unrelated to material aspirations. Loquita, who contributes humor, camaraderie, and compassion to the mix of people on the boat, ventures on the yola journey because she lacks the relationships that would emotionally sustain her: "El caso es que estoy aquí porque . . . no tengo nada . . . Mis hermanos todos viven afuera, no vendiendo droga, porque todo el que está afuera no está vendiendo droga, pero están afuera. Más bien la que está fuera soy yo. Fuera de sus planes, fuera de sus vidas. Y aunque no me falta nada, comencé a sentirme muy sola" ("The fact is that I am here because . . . I have nothing . . . My siblings all live abroad, not selling drugs, because not everyone who lives abroad is selling drugs, but they are out. Rather, the one who is out is me. Out of their plans, out of their lives. And although I don't lack anything, I started to feel very lonely"; 227). Unlike most yola migrants, material reasons do not motivate Loquita's desire to leave the Dominican Republic. Loquita leaves because she is lonely. We might surmise that her loneliness stems in part as a consequence from the reconfigured households with transnational families living in separate locations. However, that Loquita is "out" of her brother's lives may very well also relate to her sexual orientation as an "outed" gay man. Rejected by her family and Dominican society, Loquita hopes living as a sexual minority in New York City can bring her some fulfillment. By Manuel Guzmán's terms, Loquita's migration could be viewed as a "sexile"—"the exile of those who have had to leave their nations of origin on account of their sexual orientation" (227).[20] Lastly, the character Rebelde constitutes an example of how gender intersects with migration. As the name would suggest, Rebelde stands out among her fellow travelers as a voice of social critique and a strong leader. She is painfully aware of the inequalities she faces due to her gender: "Ser mujer es como ser zurdo. El mundo está hecho para manejarlo con la otra mano" ("Being a woman is like being left-handed. The world is made to be handled with the other hand"; 231). Like so many other women around the world who migrate, Rebelde is a single parent forced to leave her children because she cannot adequately support them. She works in the globalized spaces of Dominican free-trade zones, where she suffers human rights abuses and earns a salary insufficient to feed and educate her children: "Maltratos, humillaciones, abusos, frío, de todo. El infierno tiene que ser como de zona" ("Mistreatment, humiliation, abuse, cold, everything. Hell must be like the free-trade zone"; 231). Yet, as she clings to the capsized yola, Rebelde tragically concludes that the terror of the silence and darkness of the sea far exceeds the suffering on land.

By comparison, in *Yoleros* the characters reveal much less about themselves and their motivations for migrating. While they all purport to be seeking new opportunities and a better life, Máximo pointedly asks, "¿Y por qué le huyes a tu realidad?" ("And why do you run away from your reality?" 110). Without divulging the characters' secrets other than discovering that Máximo's mother is dead and thus his performance of the role of a dutiful son is a sham, the play permits us to intuit that the lure of a new life might be motivated by a complex set of reasons, not solely the desire to escape poverty. Though *Yoleros* does not dwell on the character's life stories, Máximo transforms into a storyteller and ironically narrates the very ordeal many yola travelers keep to themselves that and that he and his fellow passengers are beginning to experience after spending six days lost at sea. Máximo is reluctant to speak of his previously unsuccessful yola outing, but Demecio insists: "Pero dinos . . . Por algo estás vivo . . . ¿Cómo lo hiciste?" ("But tell us . . . There must be a reason why you're alive . . . How did you do it?" 112), and Dinora adds "No pares por mí. Si quieres contar tu historia, pues cuéntala . . . ¡Como si yo nunca hubiera oído historias de yoleros!" ("Don't stop because of me. If you want to tell your story, go ahead . . . As if I had never heard stories of yoleros!" 112). Nevertheless, as Máximo narrates his story, Demecio and Dinora become overwhelmed with the knowledge that they will soon be facing whatever measures he and the handful of survivors took to survive for thirteen days at sea; in fact, the two narratives intersect when Máximo proposes that they might survive if Dinora would be as generous as the *comadres* (godmothers) on his previous trip and allowed them to breastfeed. This survival strategy is something that has been reported on in the press. Here, however, the intimate and collective space of the theater will certainly impact how spectators receive a story that undoubtedly makes people uncomfortable; moreover *Yoleros* shows how a woman grapples with the ugly realities of what this situation implies for her, which is quite a different than the whitewashed story of the mother-heroine that tends to appear in the media.

In the context of the theater, audiences desensitized by hyperbolic journalism might respond differently to actors performing live scenarios. Here, bodies lost at sea and stories silenced come back from the dead and confront audiences with the human wreckage of yola migration history. These stories, though often told, seem to fall on deaf ears, as Madre-Miches expresses in frustration: "Y yo sin saliva de repetir las historias que nadie quiere oír que nadie escucha" ("My mouth is dry from repeating stories that no one wants to hear, that nobody listens to"; 240). It is difficult not to listen, however, when the terrifying reality of taking to the sea in a small open vessel is depicted poetically. Muchacha, for example, muses, "Sólo de pensar en ese solazo, que se refleja en el agua, en la arena, en tus ojos, que se te mete como si fueran abejas calientes una por cada poro. Ese sol, ese sol que te deja ciego, que te pone loco, que te hace hablar disparates, llamar muertos, ver visiones" ("Just thinking about that scorching sun, reflected in the water, in the sand, in your eyes, that gets inside you pore by pore like hot bees. That sun, that sun that blinds you, that makes you crazy, that make you talk nonsense, call the dead, have visions"; 196). The stinging, blinding pain of the sun literally roasts the travelers alive, as Demecio complains in *Yoleros*:

> DEMECIO: (Con miedo). Puedo oler mi piel quemándose . . .
> MÁXIMO: ¿Piel quemada . . . Por un segundo oí que dijiste carne ahumada.
> DEMECIO: Dije quemada.
> DINORA: Yo aguanto las quemadas, lo que no aguanto es esta sed. (102)
>
> *DEMECIO: (Fearfully). I can smell my skin burning . . .*

> *MÁXIMO: Burned skin? . . . For a second, I though you said smoked meat.*
> *DEMECIO: I said burned.*
> *DINORA: I can endure the sunburns, what I can't bear is this thirst.*

The macabre notion of a human burning alive takes a grotesque turn when Máximo's misinterpretation of Demecio's complaint indirectly introduces the theme of cannibalism. It is likely that Máximo's hunger leads him to hear "smoked meat" rather than "burning skin," and that the reality of perceiving fellow passengers as eventual sustenance is not out of the question. In performance, this conversation likely comes off as laughably grotesque, as does the following reference to a different sort of cannibalism made by Madre-Miches, "Yo no como nada que venga del mar, nada, que en el Caribe deberían prohibir la pesca. Qué sabe uno a qué primo se está comiendo" ("I don't eat anything from the sea, nothing; in the Caribbean fishing should be forbidden. Who knows which cousin you could be eating"; 203). Certainly, Madre-Miches's colorful declaration gives spectators more pause than the continual lists of drowning victims reported in the newspapers.

Indeed, the use of dark humor in *Yoleros* and *Miches* is an important strategy in performing stories of yola migration that audiences will not only hear, but also listen to. In the theater, a passive response to the trauma of yola migration disasters is challenged through infectious and cathartic humor. In *Yoleros*, for instance, Máximo displays a dry sense of humor when they come upon an orange floating in the sea and Demecio wonders if compassionate cruise ship passengers threw it overboard. Máximo retorts that tourists have no interest in the plight of the poor in the Caribbean and sarcastically voices the perspective of a tourist: "Vamos a tirar unas cuantas naranjas al mar para darle a esos yoleros una ayudita para no sentirnos tan culpables de estar aquí arriba" ("Let's throw a few oranges into the sea to give those yoleros a little help so we don't feel so guilty about being up here"; 98). Similarly, when later Demecio notices a shirt floating in the water and wonders whether it came from a luxury ship, Máximo responds: "Sí, claro. No quiero ser el infeliz que está llorando porque perdió su camisa favorita" ("Yeah, right. I don't want to be the poor guy crying because he lost his favorite shirt"; 103). These comments might make audiences chuckle, but the unspoken thoughts about the human wreckage floating in the Caribbean Sea is unsettling. No one on the yola dares to point out that the debris they encounter is from another ill-fated yola. Suffering from dehydration, sunburn, and hunger, their hidden fears are made manifest in a series of delirious metatheatrical scenes in which Máximo plays multiple roles. As Richard Hornby has noted, in metatheater, when a character takes on another role, ironically, the role is often "closer to the character's true self than his every day, 'real' personality" (67). This is indeed the case with Máximo, who is cast in authoritarian and even menacing roles in the metatheatrical scenes: first as a Coast Guard officer, then a smooth-talking shark, and, finally, as a captain defending his cruise ship from attacking yoleros. Demecio's dream shows that Máximo has lied about his mother, Dinora's dream underscores her fear of sharks, and Máximo's dream shows his anxious desire to control Dinora and Demecio. These absurd scenes add psychological depth to the characters, and they contribute an uneasy mix of humor in a plot inexorably headed towards tragedy. By shifting tenors, the playwrights complicate and activate the role of the spectator in responding to the events unfolding onstage.

In *Miches* Boricua adds comic relief to the tragic story line, though it bears noting that his is the first monologue of the yola journey, a moment marked by hope and incipient camaraderie that soon fades as the catastrophic trip advances. Boricua's relentless optimism and naiveté is evocative of Balbuena, the humorously charming Dominican protagonist of Ángel Muñiz's film *Nueba Yol*. Unlike Balbuena, though, who confronts many hardships in New York City, Boricua's utopian migration fantasy is never debunked because the journey fails. Boricua has acquired his nickname for his repeat attempts to reach New York City via Puerto Rico, and for his mindless devotion to what he deems as superior American (and Puerto Rican, by virtue of its colonized status) culture. His opening declaration is amusing because it is one of his many categorical remarks that reflect popular attitudes carried to the extreme, and because we discover he has never even been to Puerto Rico or the United States: "El que muere sin ir a Nueva York se murió ciego. El norte es el norte y lo demás es parking, como dicen los boricuas, es decir, parqueo" ("He who dies without going to New York died blind. The north is the north, everything else is parking, as the Boricuas say, that is, a parking lot"; 204). According to Boricua, in the Dominican Republic, "uno no es nadie" ("you are nobody"; 204), "nada sirve" ("everything is worthless"; 204), and there are "tantos brutos" ("so many ignorant people"; 204) due to a diet heavy in plantains as opposed to the ostensibly superior corn flakes and turkey consumed by North Americans. Being Puerto Rican is desirable because "es como si fuera americano, es muy gente, en cierta forma son más gentes que uno" ("it's as if one were American, classy, somehow better than us"; 206). Boricua embraces and imitates the cultural codes of the United States and even racializes his inferiority complex when he insists that when Dominicans migrate, "se le ve el progreso, uno empieza a blanquear, se le ponen los cabellos buenos y uno como que coge un feeling" ("you can see progress, you start to get lighter, your hair gets straightened, and it's like you get a feeling"; 205). True to Frantz Fanon's psychoanalytical interpretation of the colonized black man adopting a white mask in order to become a colonial subject with some social mobility, Boricua understands that achieving social progress is predicated on racial disavowal and embracing white supremacy. Boricua's attempt to masquerade as a Puerto Rican, nevertheless, undermines him as an authority on the cultural codes of the United States and Puerto Rico. He takes great pride in his "costume," a faded hand-me-down American flag T-shirt he believes will help him pass as Puerto Rican. This is comic, first, because Boricua insists on the authenticity of the shirt, when in reality it appears to be a cheap knock-off with faulty graphics, "tenía sus cincuenta y dos estrellitas, yo se las conté . . . son cincuenta y dos por los cincuenta y dos estados" ("it had its fifty-two little stars, I counted them . . . they are fifty-two for the fifty-two states"; 205). Second, if Boricua does not know that there are fifty American states, it would follow that his knowledge of Puerto Rican culture may also be lacking. His assumption that Puerto Ricans are a US flag-loving people is humorous when one takes into account the ubiquity of the Puerto Rican flag on the island and in the diaspora as a key marker of Puerto Rican ethnonationalism that evokes an alternative to US colonialism. Finally, Boricua's tale reaches a comic climax when he admits that the one time he thought he had made it to Puerto Rico, he was swindled by the trip organizers and delivered to an unfamiliar area in the Dominican Republic that he mistook for Puerto Rico, even though everything looked very familiar. Boricua laughs at his humiliating mistake, and so will spectators, who undoubtedly will question his authority and become suspicious of overly Manichean cultural representations.

If we are to follow Lendeborg's example of a yola trip in which the motor, wind, and waves seem to numb the passengers and drown out most communication, the constant dialogue in the yola dramas seems unrealistic. However, we have seen that the artistic rendering of yola migration also allows for shifting between humor and the grotesque in search of connecting with audiences. In *Miches* in particular, the author uses dialogue to explore different views of migration and the changing nature of Dominican national culture. The constant stream of out-migration, legal and illegal, by airplane and by boat, represents a stress on the national psyche (and, at the same time, an economic relief). Rivera Céspedes includes these conversations not because they are likely to take place on the high seas in a small boat, but because they stage for the audience a sort of talking cure in which the characters reveal the personal and collective trauma of migration. Overall, *Yoleros* and *Miches* present a critical view of the impact migration has had on Dominican society. The character who covets American culture, Boricua, is parodied, and characters such as Muchacha mock the hybrid cultural forms they see evolving through their island's transnational relationship with the United States. Observing the townspeople of Miches, Muchacha says, "Veo a los que desde aquí se van dominiyorkan . . . Con sus pantalones exagerados, sus tenis horrorosos y las mentadas cadenas, que no les cabría otro nombre, que no podrían llamarse de mejor manera" ("I see those who leave becoming Dominicanyorks . . . With their exaggerated pants, horrendous sneakers, and famous gold chains, that's the only name for them, there's no better way to call them"; 197). As Muchacha observes, the fashion tastes of the youth of Miches who have gone nowhere at all are impacted by migration. The bidirectional transnational linkages between a tiny village and New York City allow for Dominicans to imitate Dominicanyork fashions even though they have never been there. Interestingly, of the many variations of the term *Dominicanyork* we see referenced in the plays and performances throughout this book, this one invents a verb form that spelled out completely would be *se van dominiyorkando* (they are becoming Dominicanyork). Muchacha thus emphasizes the inevitable and processual quality of becoming a hybrid subject; to the discomfort of some, Dominican culture is changing regardless of whether one migrates. Madre-Miches does not use strong adjectives denigrating Dominicanyorks, but one can sense her frustration in seeing well-made new clothes, nice shoes, and candy from the United States influence "los muchachos, y hasta gente vieja, dispuesta a todo por alcanzar el paraíso" ("kids and even old people willing to do anything to reach paradise"; 240) even though migration to "paradise" results in orphans and broken marriages. The characters project the nation's anxieties about the cultural changes brought about by migration onto the figure of the Dominicanyork. Unlike migration dramas that portray stories of migrant identities undergoing transculturation—with all the cultural exchange, loss, and adaptation that this experience implies—these plays show the starting point of the journey that precedes these experiences. Focusing on this moment of liminality allows the playwright to show the contradictory positions of characters whose desire for personal fulfillment and a better material future outweigh their present distaste and perhaps misunderstanding of a subject position they, too, may soon embody.

Staying Afloat, or the Survival of the Fittest

In this section, I shift my analysis to focus on how gender, family, and nation are enfolded in a politics of disposability in which women and the marginalized classes lose in the neoliberal game of the survival of the fittest. In each play, only the male figure of the captain survives the yola journey. This might not seem surprising given their familiarity with the sea; as the captain in *Miches* boasts, "Sé de agua y con una hebra de hilo, mirando el cielo, yo llego, ¡sin brújula!" ("I know about water and with a strand of thread, looking at the sky, I arrive, without a compass!" 235). All macho bravura fades, however, when both men dread having to account for the ill-fated outcome of their trips. Specifically, they fear having to respond to their mothers.[21] The mother and son relationships in both plays, as well as the pseudo familial relationships developed on the yolas, serve as an entrée for envisioning the yola dramas as metaphors for the nation. Indeed, *Yoleros* and *Miches* fit Nadine Holdsworth's definition of the state-of-the-nation play, which "deploys representations of personal events, family structures and social or political organisations as a microcosm of the nation-state to comment directly or indirectly on the ills befalling society, on key narratives of nationhood or on the state of the nation as it wrestles with changing circumstances" (39). As this book argues, the Dominican diaspora is rewriting narratives of Dominican nationhood, and the theater not only has the potential to reflect the state of the nation "but, via its discursive, imaginative and communal realm, to contribute to the creation of the nation through the cultural discourses it ignites, the representations it offers and the stories it chooses to tell" (Holdsworth 79–80).

In both plays, surviving the journey is met with the anxiety of having to explain to the mother(land) why the captains were the only survivors. In *Yoleros* Máximo's mother is dead, but he gives the impression that she is alive to support his illegal migration enterprise: potential travelers are more likely to entrust their lives with Máximo if they believe he is working to support his mother. Although the mother is never seen onstage, Máximo converses with her as though she were there or perhaps in another room. In these one-sided conversations, we intuit that Máximo feels guilty about something that happened to his brother and defends his decision to sell his brother's belongings. Responding to his absent mother Máximo says, "Si ya sé lo que me va decir ahora 'Y qué clase de hermano eres tú?'" ("I already know what you're going to say now 'What kind of brother are you?'" 75). *Yoleros* seems to posit this very question: what kind of brothers and sisters have Dominican citizens become? Máximo's admissions of guilt, shame, and desperation suggest that the sea survival story he must narrate to his mother will uncover an unflattering portrait of the national family.

The mother in *Miches* is more obviously figured as the motherland or the nation. In addition to her hyphenated name, Madre-Miches, the omniscient

1.3. Madre-Miches in *Al garete*, a stage version of *Miches: Ponle Esperanza*. Photo credit: La Cuarta Espacio Teatral. Courtesy of José Rafael Sosa.

quality of the opening monologues in *Yoleros*, in which she and Muchacha make observations about the impact of migration on the lives of the townspeople, serves as an important clue that Madre-Miches represents the *madre patria*. "Mamá piensa en todo, y en todos . . . piensa mucho, por eso sufre" ("Mom thinks about everything, and everyone . . . she thinks a lot, that's why she suffers"; 237) remarks the captain, aptly named Moisés. On a personal level, Madre is terrified of the sea since it threatens to rob her of what she loves most, her son. She waits anxiously at a window on terra firma for his return, ever convinced that each trip out to sea will be his last. At the same time she is Madre-Miches, the collective mother, aggrieved by the social and economic crisis that fuels illegal migration and the slow death of her town. *Miches* registers a strong critique of Dominican society through the mother's characterization of Miches as a dead ghost town. The failure of a community like Miches is symptomatic of a much larger collective decline in civic responsibility and democratic ideals:

> Antes quería que en Miches pusieran escuelas, que los comerciantes pusieran negocios, que algo le diera vida a este cementerio, pero ya no pido más. No quiero nada. El cura pidiendo la madera de la yola para unas puertas de la iglesia, el director de la escuela pidiéndola para hacer unos cursos. Al final, la guardia quemándola en escarmiento público. ¡Qué graciosos! ¿Por qué no queman los buenos miles que se embolsillan? (201)
>
> *I used to wish that in Miches they opened schools, that merchants would set up businesses, that something would give life to this cemetery, but I don't ask anymore. I don't want anything. The priest is asking for the wood from yolas for some church doors, the school principal is asking for it for some courses. In the end, the police burning it as a public warning. How funny! Why don't they burn the few thousands that they pocket?*

For Madre-Miches, it is too late to revive a town in which the very institutions which are to guide it have been contaminated by the illegal migration industry. The former "pillars" of society—the education system, the church, and law enforcement—are now physically and economically supported by the materials and cash generated by informal yola migration economy.

Thus, while the poor in Miches are surely attracted to the consumer lifestyles they have been exposed to through the globalized media and transnational networks of migrants, it is equally important to consider the "push" factor in abandoning the homeland. The corruption described by Madre-Miches is one sign of the disaffection and apathy that has been bred in the marginalized sectors. Deportado's explanation to his teacher as to why he never attended to the school flag ceremony also exemplifies this alienation:

> ¿Yo tengo patria?, le dije un día . . . que la respeten sus dueños, los dueños de todo. Qué graciosos, el país para ellos y la patria para nosotros. Así sí es bueno, yo, que respete la bandera. Y a mí, ¿quién me respeta? ¿Y mi hambre? Y mis sueños, y mis esperanzas . . . ¿quién me las respeta? Se cogen el país y a mí me dejan un trapo. Le dije a la maestra yo no tengo patria. (234)
>
> *Do I have a homeland? I told her one day . . . that its owners should respect it, the owners of everything. How funny, the country for them, the homeland for us. So yes, that's right, I should respect the flag. But, who respects me? How about my hunger? And my dreams and hopes . . . who respects them? They take the country and leave me with a rag. I told the teacher I don't have a homeland.*

Deportado has no allegiance to his flag because his nation has not honored the promise of providing rights, protection, and good government for all.

The powerful oligarchy owns the land and operates the economy while the marginalized sectors are handed empty patriotism. Deportado does not imagine himself part of the nation because he, and by extension, the poor population, has been effectively designated as "collateral damage in the construction of a neoliberal order" (Giroux, *Stormy Weather* 11). Deportado, like many of his compatriots, is thus pushed to fix his gaze outward to search for the economic and social security he is not afforded in his homeland.

The search for solutions abroad empties towns of productivity because everyday life becomes overtaken by desiring to leave, preparing to leave, and waiting for loved ones to return (who will likely leave again). Consequently, citizens cease to be engaged in productive activities: "En este pueblo nadie sabe hacer nada . . . Un oficio, costura, zapatero . . . la gente aquí . . . nadie se casa, nadie consigue un buen trabajo, no hace un negocio . . ." ("In this town nobody knows how to do anything . . . A trade, sewing, shoemaker . . . people here . . . nobody gets married, nobody gets a good job, nobody does business"; 199). While out-migration represents a passive antidote to the nation's social and economic woes, the fruitless circular migration that brings return migrants back to the Dominican Republic serves as a continual reminder that the same conditions that provoked their migration persist. *Miches*'s ending is ultimately very pessimistic, as Madre-Miches acknowledges that the nation has gone adrift in a sea of hunger and corruption: "Al garete va la tierra girando sin agua, sin comida. Convertida en tierra de nadie, en pastel de ocho o nueve mafiosos . . . que se las han arreglado para agarrar su salvavidas desde que la cosa se ponga fea, sin importarles que en este mar picado nos metieron ellos, despojándonos de todo, arrebatándonos todo" ("Adrift goes the land, spinning with no water or food. Converted in no-man's-land, in a prize for eight or nine gangsters . . . who have managed to grab their life jackets when things get ugly, not caring that they got us in this choppy water, stripping us of everything, snatching everything from us"; 241).

In the marginalized sectors set adrift, *Yoleros* and *Miches* show women as the most vulnerable participants in the collectivity of the yola, and, by extension, the nation. Just as Deportado articulated his lack of allegiance to the homeland, Maestro confirms that the survivors of the informal economy are not envisioned as full members of the nation: "Pero nosotros no vivimos en su mundo. Nos han dejado uno de tercera categoría para que nos acomodemos como podamos. Y en eso estamos, matándonos por el último poquito de comida y de agua. Acaparando, empujándonos unos a otros, a codazos como animales salvajes, echando a los tiburones a los más débiles para ganar algo de tiempo" ("But we don't live in their world. They have left us a space in third class to fit in it the best we can. And we are trying, killing each other for the last bit of food and water. Hoarding, pushing, elbowing each other like wild animals, throwing the weakest to the sharks to buy some time"; 226). In this dehumanizing drama of survival, only the male captains endure. The male-headed boat echoes the structure of a patriarchal family, complete with a mother figure since one of the passengers is a pregnant woman. Figuring the collectivity of the boat as a domestic, familial space, however, is contested. When Loquita, in an effort to build camaraderie, references the group as a family, in line with his earlier declarations of disassociation, Deportado retorts: "Yo no soy familia de nadie, así es que suspende la confianza" ("I'm not anyone's family, so cut the familiarity"; 214). Deportado, in turn, is put in his place by the Capitán-Father of the vessel: "¿Qué es lo que pasa? Así es que empiezan los problemas y los fracasos. Quiero que todo el mundo esté callado" ("What's going on? This is how problems and failures begin. I want everybody to be quiet"; 214). The captain maintains order on the boat, but he is unable to play the traditional part of the morally minded nineteenth-century maritime leader who followed the ethical code of attending to women and children first in life-threatening situations.[22] By contrast, in this context, women and children are the first to be thrown overboard when the yola goes adrift. Embarazada gives birth, aided by her fellow passengers who optimistically name the baby Esperanza (Hope). The small boat is covered in blood, however, and sharks circle. To the horror of Capitán, who frantically struggles to wash away the blood, Ayudante and Deportado take charge and toss both mother and baby overboard alive. Rebelde, who helped with the birth, is stripped of her blood-stained clothes and left naked. Ayudante confirms: "Parece cruel, pero ésta es la ley aquí. No hay amigo, no hay nada, cuando estás frente a un tiburón le das cualquier cosa menos tu pellejo . . ." ("It seems cruel, but this is the law here. There is no friend, there is nothing, when you face a shark you give it anything but your skin"; 224–25). In Giorgio Agamben's view of biopower, the raw image of women and children naked, bloodied, and tossed overboard captures the barest life reduced to *homo sacer*.[23]

The entire population of yola migrants might be envisioned as an underclass expunged from society, no longer valued as citizens, and tacitly sanctioned for sacrifice. For Foucault, "racism justifies the death-function in the economy of biopower" (258), while Giroux emphasizes the confluence of race and class inequalities with neoliberalism and state violence in "a new and dangerous version of biopolitics" (*Stormy Weather* 21). In *Yoleros* and *Miches* we see both forms of biopower operate, but the denouement of the shipwreck dramas draws special attention the gendered vulnerability of female yola migrants in the dehumanizing acts of survival. As I have previously noted, in illegal trafficking, the male boat captains have found a space for belonging and dissidence in extreme times of neoliberalism and have become "endriago subjects" empowered by the deaths of others. Given the outcomes of the stories, however, it would be difficult to interpret the actions of gore capitalism's endriago subjectivities as an effective form of resistance since they "preserve masculinist hierarchies" (Valencia 284) and their actions are "tied to a program that has been previously defined by a violent, hegemonic, capitalist, masculinist framework" (284). Valencia argues that these dystopian dissident subjectivities, however, point to the need for transfeminism, envisioned as "a social movement made up of women, but also as an epistemological category for the conception and creation of new, non-dystopian—feminine and masculine—identities" (273). The gender disobedience generated by transfeminism would most certainly reimagine the social construct of the family.

The boat passengers in Vásquez Escaño's *Yoleros* are also imagined as a family of sorts. Here, Dinora is forced to adopt a "familial" role when Máximo tells her "nuestra salvación está tus manos" ("our salvation is in your hands"; 116) and recounts how a lactating woman helped nine people survive on a previous journey. The audience realizes now that the captain selected Dinora for the trip precisely because he knew she was nursing; in their first onstage interaction, she had confessed that she was motivated to take the risky trip because of the powerful maternal love she feels while nursing her son (83). However, Dinora resists playing the role of mother as savior of the nation and pays for it with her life. By contrast, in a real-life case, Faustina Mercedes Mauricio, nicknamed Ángelita del mar (Little Angel of the Sea), saved sixteen passengers while their boat drifted at sea for nearly two weeks. As reported in the media, Faustina comforted her fellow passengers: "No tengan vergüenza, no nos vamos a morir, le dijo a sus compañeros. Y cada uno de ellos pasó entre dos o tres veces al día a tomar leche de su pecho. Fue un ritual desesperado que se extendió por cinco días hasta que los equipos de rescate de la Marina dominicana los encontró en las costas de Nisibón" ("Don't be ashamed, we're not going to die, she told her fellow travelers. And each one of them drank milk from her breast two or three times a day. It was a desperate ritual that lasted for five days until the Dominican navy rescue team found them on the shores of Nisibón"; "Faustina, la mujer"). To reward Faustina's extraordinary act of generosity, the Dominican government provided her a home and a job. Faustina's experience presents nursing as an instinct and ethical urge that fulfills her role as a mother of the nation.[24] This maternal representation helps society elide the unbearable reality of what takes place in desperate situations on yolas and it naturalizes women's subaltern status. Breast milk is a female resource, but Faustina and her fictional counterpart are forced, with no compensation from their fellow passengers, to become wet nurses for the boat. That is, not only are Dominican migrant women nourishing the nation through the remittances they send from abroad to support their own families, in the patriarchal space of the boat they are literally compelled to feed the nation. Máximo exerts his authority by telling Dinora that the women who refused to nurse the other travelers were thrown overboard, and after Demecio refuses to take advantage of her—he states that she reminds him of his sister—Máximo pushes him overboard (46). In desperation, Dinora appeals for Máximo to think of his own mother:

> MÁXIMO: ¿Mi mamá? Nada. ¡Ella está muerta!
> DINORA: ¿Ella no estaba enferma?
> MÁXIMO: Sí, lo estaba. Sólo quería tener un poco de compasión en este viaje . . .
> DINORA: Eres un animal.
> MÁXIMO: . . . que sabe sobrevivir . . . (Máximo trata de agarrarla)
> (Dinora se tira al mar). (119)
>
> *MÁXIMO: My mom? Nothing. She's dead!*
> *DINORA: Wasn't she sick?*
> *MÁXIMO: Yes, she was. I just wanted a little compassion on this trip . . .*
> *DINORA: You're an animal.*
> *MAXIMO: . . . Who knows how to survive . . . (Máximo tries to grab her)*
> *(Dinora throws herself into the sea).*

This scene imagines the terrible stories trip survivors rarely recount, and the stage serves as a laboratory for exploring a hypothetical scenario in which a group is stranded at sea in a small fishing boat. In the Ángelita del mar narrative, nursing an adult evokes Roman Charity, the iconic image of the selfless act of easing the suffering of hunger; in *Yoleros*, on the contrary, the idea of adults feeding on the mother is one taboo that evokes even more troubling ones: cannibalism and incest. In both plays, those with unsustainable lives in the neoliberal order are left to feed on each other, with only the strongest male surviving.

The yola scenarios imagined by Vásquez Escaño and Rivera Céspedes situate spectators in the middle of a (failed) journey of migration, while the following plays and performances explored in this book grapple with the transnational identities that develop in different stages of arrival, adaptation, and return. The impact of the yola migration plays is achieved by enabling theatergoers to witness what they already know, but that has not been brought into appearance in quite the same way the theatrical performance does. Although the stories of yola migration recounted in the press or dramatized onstage may be similar, in line with Kelleher's stance on theater and politics, staging the stories implicitly stands up for migrants by standing in for them. These plays raise consciousness of how some lives in the Dominican national family are valued more than others; Dominican boat people form a disposable population, which according to Giroux, "are already seen as dead within the global economic/political framework" (*Stormy Weather* 22). The theater event makes visible the subjectivities of migrants that have been relegated to spaces of invisibility and disposability and challenges the civic indifference to their plight. While both the media and the plays depict the dismemberment of the national family through illegal migration as tragic, representation in the theater event serves to re-member this collectivity. In an epoch in which "Democratic values, identities, and social relations along with public spaces, the common good, and the obligations of civic responsibility are slowly being overtaken by a market-based notion of freedom and civic indifference," writes Giroux, "it becomes more difficult to translate private woes into social issues and collective action or to insist on a language of the public good" ("Reading Hurricane Katrina" 186). Plays like *Miches: Ponle Esperanza* and *Yoleros* underscore the political relevancy of the theater in carrying out the urgent task of animating audiences to reconnect feelings and actions with the values of social obligation and civic responsibility.

Chapter 2

Alternate Belongings

Dominican Male Solo Performance

Irrespective of the phase of migration dramatized, the theatrical production examined in this book resists facile celebrations of the hybrid identities and interstitial spaces that have resulted from the increased global mobility of Dominicans. In the plays depicting boat journeys discussed in the previous chapter, the conversations among the passenger characters underscore how notions of collective identity have been complicated by mass migration. For example, the character Maestro in *Miches: Ponle Esperanza* suggests that migrants sacrifice any sense of belonging they may have felt as a rooted national: "Los ahogados en tierra, los ahogados en esta tierra en la que nunca estarán secos del todo. Los que perderán todo y se quedarán secos por dentro, para siempre, desterrados de dos mundos y de todos. Ni domini, ni yorkan, ni nada" ("The land drowned, the drowned on this land, where they will never be completely dry. Those who will lose everything and remain dry inside forever, exiled from two worlds and from all. Neither *domini* nor *yorkan*, nor anything"; 225). This existential uncertainty points to what Silvio Torres-Saillant terms an "ontological discomfort" faced by migrants. He writes, "Occupying the space of the diaspora has not come without a measure of ontological discomfort, stemming most likely from the sense that one has lost a homeland without necessarily gaining another" (*Intellectual History* 231). This chapter argues that the deviant positionality embodied by the male characters in *Ciudadano Cero* (Citizen Zero) by Rey Emmanuel Andújar, *P.A.R.G.O.: Los Pecados Permitidos* (P.A.R.G.O: Permitted Sins) by Waddys Jáquez, and *La cosa nostra dominicana* (Dominican Cosa Nostra) by Dió-genes Abréu perform the exclusion of subaltern subjectivities from orthodox national imaginaries and display the "ontological discomfort" of their transnationality. In their examination of "misfit" characters, it is no accident that the authors (and in two cases also the performers) of the pieces opt for the vehicle of solo performance to explore transnational states of being. Theatrical performance serves as a laboratory for producing identities because it explores identity as a performative construction and interrogates how it is represented. In *Straight White Male: Performance Art Monologues*,

Michael Peterson contends that performance art monologues represent "a highly concentrated, rarefied cultural production that depends on and participates in the construction of contemporary white male identity" (6). He examines the peculiar fact that despite a postmodern context of "rapidly shifting hierarchies, dizzying intertextualities, and crises in representation," solo performances of heterosexual white men continue to command large audiences (6).[1] By contrast, this chapter looks at monologue plays that revolve around nonnormative masculine types—for example, the artist-intellectual, the urban black, the drag queen, the homeless, and the Latino drug dealer. The characters in the works analyzed in this chapter lack the social power of white males, but in the context of the solo performance event they move into the spotlight, where it is their very alterity that captivates the attention of spectators with stories that upend the traditional patriarchal foundations of Dominican nationalism and model alternative collective solidarities.

Perhaps it is not surprising that over half the stories of migrants included in this book are one-person shows. As noted in the introduction, Dominican group theater projects in New York City have only recently developed, and in the main Dominicans have made their mark in the theater world as individual practitioners. Without institutional and collaborative support, artists turn to solo theatrical performance because it constitutes an exercise to refine their dramaturgical skills and represents a modest economic venture with better chances of finding a venue for production. However, this does not suggest that the monologue is a "lesser" dramatic genre cultivated only by necessity rather than choice. From the ancient Greek Thespis and the African griot, the European roving minstrels and troubadours and the one-man show of nineteenth-century American vaudeville, oral narratives performed by solo speakers have been performed across cultures throughout history (Bonney xiii). The focus on the individual and self-actualization that developed during the twentieth century explains in part the ubiquity of solo work at the end of the century and into this one. At the same time postmodernity questioned the notion of a stable identity and a complete and unified self, and many solo artists explored subjectivities influenced by the discourses and practices of popular culture, mass communications, and technology, monologue performances also became a space for previously marginalized voices and the assertion of identity politics. The solo pieces by Andújar, Jáquez, and Abréu—along with performances by Latino artists such as Guillermo Gómez-Peña, Coco Fusco, John Leguizamo, Carmelita Tropicana, and Rick Najera—straddle both positions, for they show a postmodern understanding of identity as constructed within multiple discourses at the same time as they serve as a vehicle for Latinos "'speaking' about the attempt to enter subjectivity" (Geis 3).

The different modalities of theatrical monologue can be broadly divided into the categories of solo performance and monologue drama. Both subgenres "involve a speaker who delivers speeches before an audience, sometimes directly addressing that audience, sometimes addressing a silent or invisible character-auditor" (Wallace 4). In addition, both solo performance and monologue drama share the artistic element of creating the illusion of privileging "reality" over "fiction." Peterson writes that the inconspicuous set typical of the monologue play creates the impression of an intimate connection between the actor and his/her character and the actor and the spectator, while instances of directly addressing spectators involve them in the fiction of the performance (16–17, 24). This is particularly so in what Peterson identifies as "performance art monologues" that unfold in their actual spaces—a stage, the street, a gallery, etc. Dramatic monologues, by contrast, tend to create a fictive space within which to situate both the speaker and the audience. The pieces discussed in this chapter demonstrate these different approaches to solo performance. *Ciudadano Cero*, a multimedia performance art monologue, is performed onstage, and, via video, on the streets. In *P.A.R.G.O.*, the fictional story takes place on a stage, in the context of a support group meeting where all the attendees take to the microphone to tell their stories, while the action of *La cosa nostra dominicana* unfolds in the audience of a play performance the solo performer has come to see. Even though none of these pieces frame the action in a traditional illusionist stage set, the latter two plays fall more closely within the category of dramatic theater, which "seeks to escape reality by overlaying the actual space with a fictive one" (Peterson 12). Similarly, the relationship between the performing body in *P.A.R.G.O.* and *La cosa nostra dominicana* and the text is dramatic. In these plays, an actor interprets roles written by a playwright, whereas in the performance art-oriented piece *Ciudadano Cero*, the body of the performer and author are one and the same. Peterson writes that with regard to spectatorship, "this overlay of authorial ghost and performative body usually means that the performance is read as a single artistic utterance, rather than as an interpretive, contingent version of an original. In performance art, it is the performing body of the author-figure that assumes the status of art object" (12). *P.A.R.G.O.* also positions the performing body as art object since Jáquez is both author and performer, but the piece exhibits some dramatic qualities that place it on a continuum between solo theater and solo performance art. Both *La cosa nostra dominicana* and *P.A.R.G.O.* are what Peterson terms "monopolylogues," in which a single actor plays multiple roles (14, 193). This draws attention to the break between the actor and character and suggests an "author-god" who created the different dramatic characters. *P.A.R.G.O.* and *La cosa nostra* are also more easily traced to a dramatic text, which opens the possibility of other actors interpreting the solo roles in the plays. By contrast, the performance text of *Ciudadano Cero* cannot be linked to a dramatic script. The piece evolved from Andújar's narrative writings and his participation in performance workshops, which makes it difficult to imagine how anyone other than himself could perform the title character.

Whether it is the author/performer or an actor who delivers the solo performance in monologue theater, both demand a virtuosic performance. In the preface to a collection of solo performance texts by black women, D. Soyini Madison writes: "The skilled, solo performer has made us experience and believe that the story cannot be performed in any other way. It is virtuosic because it is solo and it is solo because it is virtuosic" (xiii). In the absence of the stage set, dialogue, and plot conventions of dramatic realism, the audience's attention is concentrated on the physical presence and verbal delivery of the performer. Solo performance texts can capture the linguistic talent of the author, but it is only in performance that "the artists' physical presence, body language, rhythms of speech, command of dialects and sheer charisma can deliver" (Bonney xv). Even though in solo shows spectators are captivated by the brilliance of the solo performer's skill, they perform an integral role as well. Bonney writes, "the solo show expects and demands the active involvement of the people in the audience. They are watched as they watch, they are directly addressed, their energy resonates with that of the lone artist, and their presence in the room can trigger not only new levels of performance, but, more interestingly, new material" (xiii). Many solo performances are not published as dramatic texts. Those that do find their way into print are likely the product of many performances of the piece, each iteration always slightly different due to the variability of the audience response. All dramatic texts acquire a life of their own in the hands of new directors, actors, and audiences. For example, everyone knows famous productions remembered more for their directors than for the original author of the play. However, it seems somewhat different for solo performance texts. While they appear to be the product of a single person, they are not only the result of the author/performer, but, as suggested by Bonney, also the audience, and, I would add, other stage personnel. This collaborative effort is invisible on page, and by the time the solo performance is captured in print, it is so closely connected with virtuosity of a particular performer that it is hard to fathom how the text will serve as a blueprint for any other artist.

The apparent privileging of reality over fiction and the charismatic pull of the dazzling performer makes the examination of the self the predominant theme in solo performance. "The use of persona as a means of social critique, the undermining of gender stereotypes through role-play, blurring the outlines of the autobiographical, 'authentic' subject are recurrent features" of the plays examined in this chapter, which reflect a trend seen in monologue performances since the 1980s (Wallace 13). As Catharine McLean-Hopkins points out, performance "*sites* the self with the theatrical frameworks of space, time, and presence" (194). On a basic level, simply center staging the Dominican male characters and allowing them to tell their stories in their own voices in these solo performances enables an engagement with a diasporic culture that seeks to represent itself. At the same time, though, the solo performances "*cites* the self as remembered iterations" (194) and explores the performativity of identities. From Judith Butler's perspective, performativity is the act of repeating the norms that constitute and regulate us as subjects. In her theory of gender and sexual identity, Butler contends that heterosexual norms are "for the most part compulsory performances, ones which none of us choose, but which each of us is forced to negotiate" (26).[2] In reference to the performativity of black female identities, D. Soyini Madison asserts that inside theatrical performance, they "are not necessarily stylized repetitions that shape identity, because their alterity is illuminated and their stylized acts are constantly teasing identity" (xiii). The theatrical frame allows for "stylized acts," like play with persona and metatheatrical role-play, which undermine the notion of an authentic subject and highlight the discourses that shape subjectivities. The pieces examined here accomplish what Jon Rossini has called an act of "wrighting" he identifies in Latino plays that simultaneously correct (right) and create (write) ways of conceiving ethnic identities (10). By displaying nonnormative masculine Dominican identities—ethnoracial, gender, sexual, national, and otherwise—I maintain that the solo performances discussed in this chapter examine the complexities of the new subjectivities produced in relation to transnational migration networks.

Dominicanidad to the Beat of Hip-Hop: Rey Emmanuel Andújar's *Ciudadano Cero*

Through his award-winning short stories and novels, Rey Emmanuel Andújar has become one of the most acclaimed young Dominican writers in recent years.[3] His work displays an intellectual and aesthetic openness toward cultural experiences and forms of belonging that diverge from the patriarchal, heterosexual, and racialist values that framed Dominican developing nationalism in the nineteenth century and were later institutionalized during the twentieth-century Trujillo and Balaguer regimes. In addition to questioning the gendered, sexed, and raced underpinnings of Dominican nationalism, Andújar's multimedia performance art monologue *Ciudadano Cero* also unsettles geographically bounded conceptions of national identity. The prefix *trans* is useful for thinking about both the border spanning paradigm in which Andújar operates and the aesthetic strategies of his works. He is a transmigrant artist whose artistic, intellectual, and personal projects locate him variously in Santo Domingo, New York City, Chicago, Paris, and San Juan. As I discuss throughout this book, the simultaneous engagement with multiple discourses of citizenship and identity has been an important experience in leading Dominican transnationals to break away from the limited and hierarchical ways of understanding identity promoted by the nation-state. Like a growing number of Dominican writers who project a transnational diasporic consciousness in their works, in *Ciudadano Cero* Andújar envisions *dominicanidad* as a point of intersection in a web of African, Caribbean, and Dominican diasporas. More specifically, *Ciudadano Cero* marks a significant departure from the former Eurocentric and elitist constructions of Dominican identity because it showcases the cultures of urban black communities. Far from the soundtrack of whitewashed folkloric merengues favored by Dominican cultural nationalists, Andújar sets *Ciudadano Cero* to the beat of contemporary hip-hop, an aesthetic created in the transnational spaces of Afro-diasporic music.[4] By infusing the elements of hip-hop in his tale of an ill-fated *ciudadano cero* (citizen nobody) marginalized in an urban ghetto, yet at the same time entangled in a web of transnational relationships and desires, Andújar imagines *dominicanidad* as deterritorialized and in sync with globalized black popular culture.

Hip-hop is commonly noted as an example of how today's economic and technological interconnectedness enables shared cultural spaces across the globe. As the cultural studies scholar Juan Flores asserts, "it is becoming ever clearer that hip hop is the stylistic current most closely identifiable with contemporary globalization. It is perhaps the aesthetic remittance par excellence because it emerged just when financial remittances became the most visible, tangled manifestation of transnational social relations in our times" (*Diaspora* 10). Not only have the financial remittances from Dominicans in the United States become a major factor in the Dominican Republic's economy, the transnational migration patterns also have produced cultural remittances to the homeland that include, according to Flores, "customs and practices, ideological orientations, forms of artistic expression, and ideas of group identity acquired in diaspora settings" (*Diaspora* 4). The flows of Dominicans through Puerto Rico and New York City brought hip-hop culture back to the Dominican Republic, and though young people have embraced the hip-hop arts, cultural nationalists characterize the new styles and attitudes as dangerous and un-Dominican. The following observation about American hip-hop also holds true for the Dominican Republic: "Young members of the hip hop generation find themselves essentially in an antagonistic relationship with the institutions that attempts to structure and control their lives. Law enforcement, school systems, and popular media all identify them as internally dangerous elements of urban America, and this identification led to the social construction of rap as also fundamentally unsafe" (Crossley 504). Nevertheless, Dominican urban youths have been receptive to hip-hop precisely because, as Deborah Pacini Hernandez suggests, "Its clearly audible cosmopolitan and defiant attitude resonated with their own experiences of and resistance to racial and economic marginality" (72–73). World music scholars are quick to acknowledge that hip-hop is a commodity marketed by monopolies from metropolitan centers, and they point out that in the United States in particular, hip-hop culture has lost many of its subversive qualities. However, in the context of the Caribbean and other areas of the Global South, hip-hop continues to serve as what George Lipsitz calls "a conduit of ideas and images articulating subaltern sensitivities" (36). Hip-hop has thus served as an important means for articulating life in marginalized urban neighborhoods, a theme in the Dominican Republic mainly untouched in other forms of artistic expression.

It is, therefore, noteworthy that Andújar brings the rhythms, styles, and themes of hip-hop from the mass media and the streets to the "high culture" spaces of literary publication and theatrical performance.[5] Moreover, the very artistic methods employed by Andújar support the hybrid sensibilities of his work, for *Ciudadano Cero* is a multidisciplinary project that crosses artistic borders and combines narrative texts and spoken word poetry, rap music, body movement, video, and visual art. *Ciudadano Cero* was published in Andújar's 2005 collection of hybrid narrative and poetic stories, *El factor carne*, but it was developed earlier in a Dominican performance laboratory led by the poet, dancer, and performance artist Loraine Ferrand.[6] Andújar's training with Ferrand in the methods of Eugenio Barba's International School of Theater Anthropology has been central to his development of embodied writing techniques. Theater Anthropology practices include physical exercises that seek to "alphabetize" the performer's body, creating a language that transmits meaning and a performer's singular scenic presence. Andújar performs these exercises daily, bringing the body to his creative writing process. He explains:

> El único compromiso del escritor debe ser escribir mejor y esta posición toma dimensiones distintas cuando se involucra el cuerpo completo y lo escrito no es sólo un reflejo de la mente. Se escribe desde el centro, la columna vertebral, las costillas. Todo esto da paso a una múltiple apertura de ventanas, la creación de fábulas y las lecturas sensoriales de estas para de ahí llegar hasta un texto final para ser representado. ("Antropología" 43)
>
> *The only commitment of the writer should be to write better, and this position takes on different dimensions when it engages the whole body and writing is not only a reflection of the mind. One writes from the heart, spine, ribs. All this enables the opening of multiple windows, the creation of fables and sensory readings like these, that then become a complete text that is to be represented.*

Andújar's experimentation with what he calls *la dramaturgia del cuerpo del escritor* (the dramaturgy of the writer's body) resulted in *Ciudadano Cero*, an undertaking that first originated in his performance training, then evolved into a series of short texts, and was later staged as a performance piece in important theater venues in the Dominican Republic and Puerto Rico.[7]

The *Ciudadano Cero* project on the whole might be called an example of hip-hop theater. Recognizing hip-hop theater as a genre took flight in 2000, with the inauguration of the Hip-Hop Theater Festival in New York City. In 2003 it received further institutional recognition by the Ford Foundation, which conducted a two-day workshop in San Francisco called "Future Aesthetics: Hip-Hop in Contemporary Performance Project." The New York City festival founder and performer Danny Hoch defines the genre as "theatre that is by, for and about the hip-hop generation, which spans roughly ages 12 through 36" (qtd. in Euell 36). These generational parameters correspond to Bakari Kitwana's characterization of members of the hip-hop generation as born after 1965 and before 1984 (12). Another leading figure in hip-hop theater, Will Power, defines the genre as theater "that uses one or more of the four cornerstones of hip-hop culture—emceeing (rhyming or rapping), deejaying, break dancing and graffiti—to tell a story" (Euell 36). Andújar employs rap, break dancing, and graffiti art to express Ciudadano Cero's story; however, since the theatrical text does not include any stage directions that might indicate the cadence of the vocal delivery, body movement, costuming, or a soundtrack, it is only in performance that the elements of hip-hop become discernible.

Andújar's hip-hop performance reflects the emergence of new technologies and a historical shift from a text-based culture to a new media age of image and sound. *Ciudadano Cero*, along with several other pieces discussed in this book, might be described as postdramatic since it eschews the dramatic elements of plot and character development through action and dialogue and employs a hybrid performance language that combines the live vocal and gestural expressions of the actor with a music soundtrack and mediated images projected on a video screen.[8] The "postdramatic" performance does not translate a dramatic text to a performance text. Rather than interpreting a narrative story, the spectator is challenged to actively become in making meaning of the sights and sounds presented onstage. Thus, my analysis of *Ciudadano Cero* is based in large part on the music video version featuring the hip-hop group Lo Correcto, and I will reference a video of the live performance at the Sala Ravelo del Teatro Nacional as well.[9]

The video versions of *Ciudadano Cero* are essential for deciphering the cryptic and fragmented texts. For example, a brief reference to graffiti in the fragmented theatrical text might be overlooked: "Las frases de la pared se derriten con las agujas que caen, las pinturas de labios, carbón, crayolas de Goico" ("The wall's phrases melt like needles downward, lipstick, charcoal, Goico's crayons"; *Pieza* 75). Most spectators will not catch the reference to Carlos Goico, the self-proclaimed *pintor maldito* (cursed painter) of urban Santo Domingo.[10] However, in the theater performance, one of the backdrops clearly displays graffiti-style art, and in the music video version we see an urban industrial landscape with graffitied walls. In this version the camera cuts between Andújar's stage performance of the character Ciudadano Cero, and a video of street scenes that alternate between showing Dominican authorities engaged in street fire with rebel youth, rows of uniformed children in a classroom, a young man's wake, and a group of young men dressed in the newest hip-hop fashions roaming the streets like choral flaneurs, observing the chaos of urban poverty and looking for a space to break-dance. These visual scenes have as soundtrack a Ciudadano Cero rap performed by the well-known Dominican hip-hop collective Lo Correcto.[11]

In her pioneering study, Tricia Rose describes hip-hop as "a cultural form that attempts to negotiate the experiences of marginalization, brutally truncated opportunity, and oppression within the cultural imperatives of African-American and Caribbean history, identity, and community" (21). These experiences are explicit in the audiovisual components of the *Ciudadano Cero* project, and they are woven into the dozen segments of letters, monologues, and poetry that comprise the theatrical text in a more implic-

2.1. Ciudadano Cero reads a letter. Photo credit: Paul Grisanti.

it, metaphorical fashion. The global cultural economy and the imperatives of poverty place Dominicans in a transnational network in which they seek to improve their life opportunities. In *Ciudadano Cero,* the use of letters structurally communicates this web of transnational relationships and the character Ciudadano's desire to escape his environment. He writes and receives letters from his mother, who, we learn, is involved in the international sex trade in Amsterdam, and from friends in Norway and Switzerland he most likely met on the globalized spaces of Dominican beaches. Most telling is Ciudadano's letter to NASA in which he details his physical and mental readiness to become the first Caribbean astronaut. But Ciudadano cannot escape planet Earth, let alone his island, or, more precisely, his half island, his city, his barrio, or even his home. How Ciudadano situates himself in the world is a small but significant detail. When Ciudadano mentions he lives on an island, he recognizes that Hispaniola is shared by two nations by correcting himself, "media isla . . . este egoísmo" ("half island . . . this egoism";

Pieza 77). In line with other pieces studied in this book, this exemplifies a special sensitivity shown by Dominicans in the diaspora to the border issues between the Dominican Republic and Haiti.

According to Scott Crossley, in hip-hop music "the overwhelming majority of metaphors used to describe African American neighborhoods conceptualize them as restrictive rather than protective objects" (8). These metaphors of entrapment transfer to Ciudadano Cero's Santo Domingo context, which shares the social realities of socioeconomic inequality and racial discrimination experienced throughout the diasporic history of black people around the world. Marked as "different," for his style, his intellect, and perhaps his sexual orientation, the voices of neighbors in crowded housing projects reduce him to a "citizen nobody" who doesn't belong.[12] Ciudadano says, "En medio Barrio me tienen *desacreditao*" ("Half the neighborhood has *discredited* me"), and he repeats the voices of his community invoking his difference:

> Que el Tipo ese oye música *rara*
> Que el Tipo ese sí se viste raro
> Que el tipo del *cuarto* del frente sí habla *raro*
> Siempre filosofando
> Que el inoportuno de la pensión me mira *raro*
> El día que se meta conmigo lo parto en dos. (*Pieza* 76)
>
> *The guy listens to weird music*
> *The guy really dresses weird*
> *The guy across the hallway talks really weird*
> *Always philosophizing*
> *The poor weirdo from the boarding house looks at me weird*
> *The day he sticks his head into my business, I'll chop him in two.*[13]

The threat of physical violence demonstrates how Ciudadano's intelligence and personal style threaten the accepted norms of masculinity in the barrio.[14] He cannot find tranquility either on the streets, where macho *tígueres* roam and police perform indiscriminate round-ups, or in his home, where the sounds of nightly sexual encounters in other rooms give him insomnia.[15] At the same time, echoing the voices that impose the norms that rule "decent" society also reveals his sense of asphyxiation: "Me tienen harto. Harto. Estás mal . . . No andes con . . . No te fumes esa . . . si bebes . . ." ("I'm fed up. I'm sick and tired. You're bad . . . Don't walk with . . . Don't smoke that . . . if you drink . . ."; *Pieza* 79). But the very institutions that are to form upstanding citizens only serve to snuff out the aspirations of Dominican youth. For example, as students complete their secondary school education they are vetted for further educational opportunities. Recalling his aptitude test, Ciudadano's perspective mixes in with the questions of his examiners:

> ¿Qué puede usted estudiar?
> ¿Qué va hacer si logra salir?
> Le *joden* la vida a uno los psicólogos
> Yo quiero ser astronauta señorita psicóloga rodeada de monjas.
> (*Pieza* 76)
>
> *What can you study?*
> *What are you going to do if you get out?*
> *Psychologists* fuck up *one's life*
> *I want to be an astronaut Miss Psychologist surrounded by nuns.*

In short, the spaces and people that make up Ciudadano's immediate world are forces of immobilization. As Ciudadano ironically characterizes his neighborhood, "Esto no es un Ensanche, esto es un Callejón" ("This isn't a development, it's a dead-end street"; *Pieza* 76). The government-planned development where he lives, called an *ensanche*, from *ensanchar*, to widen or improve a street, is, in reality, for many young people, a dead-end street.

Artistic creativity might have provided an outlet from Ciudadano's oppressive socioeconomic circumstances, but it seems that his marginality carries over into his art, and as a self-proclaimed outcast *poeta soldado de la muerte* (soldier poet of death), he subscribes to a certain fatalism. Via mail correspondence from Europe, Ciudadano's friends encourage him to act, to carry on with his art and his life plans. Iván, for example, sends an anecdote about a crazy violinist playing on the rooftops in spite of the showers of rocks thrown at him, and he encourages Ciudadano to reconnect with his lost love, Jessica. In his letter to Jessica, however, Ciudadano asks: "¿Cómo transmitirte esta asfixia si ni siquiera me animo hablarte?" ("How can I even communicate to you this sense of asphyxiation if I don't even dare to talk to you?"; *Pieza* 80). In her reply, Jessica likens his passivity as walking "hacia su propia fosa" ("toward his own grave"; *Pieza* 81). As the title that frames all the Ciudadano Cero texts published in *El factor carne* foretells—"Ciudadano Cero: La antropología de un seppuku caribeño" ("Citizen Zero: the anthropology of a Caribbean seppuku")—the eponymous protagonist commits suicide. There is little evidence in the text, however, indicating how he dies, only brief allusions to what is probably his wake: his mother's tears and Ciudadano dressed in a nice suit (*Pieza* 80–81). The performance, nonetheless, fleshes out this part of the story: we witness Ciudadano, dressed in Asian garb, ingesting a large quantity of pills. Costumed throughout the

2.2. Ciudadano Cero as a boxer. Photo credit: Nelson Rivera.

performance as a boxer, this wardrobe change draws attention and might be best explained by the allusion to seppuku, the Japanese samurai ritual of suicide by sword, considered an act of great honor. Faced with truncated life chances and the realization that he could not combat his own limitations, the street fighter commits violence toward himself, a departure from the chronic outward acts of violence so often observed in urban ghettos.

Nevertheless, if we take Ciudadano Cero to be an alter ego of Rey Andújar, we may be able to substitute some amount of the story's fatalism with hope. As mentioned previously, in performance art it is typical for the author to be onstage as the performer, which is the case in Andújar's piece. While I would not label it an autobiographic solo performance in which the performing subject, Andújar, is the subject of the performance, the text includes details that play with and blur the lines between fiction and reality, as well as self-reflexive commentaries about making art. For example, in the following quote, it is Andújar's voice calling for Dominicans to find artistic inspiration in the social reality that surrounds them:

> Quizás la respuesta está parte atrás en los ritos de los callejones, y cañadas de bolsillos relegados que crecen sin planificación urbana; en familias que dejan el campo para ir a la ciudad para ocupar los lugares que dejan los que emigran para sustentar el imperio de remesas y salones de belleza. Quizás la respuesta está en empezar a considerar el arte sub-urbano como una realidad y no como un experimento de clases visto desde la periferia. ("Antropología" 42)
>
> *Perhaps the answer can be found in the rituals of the alleys, and pockets of abandoned gullies that grow without urban planning; in families that leave the countryside to go to the city to fill the places of migrants who have gone to sustain the empire of remittances and beauty salons. Perhaps the answer is to begin to consider sub-urban art as a reality and not a class experiment viewed from the periphery.*

This passage recalls how the urban space of Santo Domingo has been shaped by a double migration—first the movement from the countryside to the city, then abroad. For many, rural poverty translated to urban poverty and the growth of ghettos. As anonymous as Ciudadano Cero is among the masses of the urban poor, he, and the space he inhabits, is strongly embedded in an outward looking transnational web. The urban poor are keenly aware of the opportunities that migration to the United States or Europe may bring them. As the quote suggests, many, like Ciudadano, go nowhere, but they are economically sustained by the "empire" of economic remittances and Dominican beauty salon businesses abroad. The transnational flows of culture and capital have transformed even the most forgotten about spaces in Dominican society, and Andújar's art encourages us to see these realities as central to understanding contemporary *dominicanidad*.

Andújar further characterizes the space from which *Ciudadano Cero* was imagined as "la miseria del circo caribeño donde el proceso creativo envuelve crudeza, conflicto y sensualidad hasta llegar al ser" ("the misery of the Caribbean circus where the creative process invades one's being with rawness, conflict, and sensuality"; "Antropología" 42). On the one hand, a circus evokes the camaraderie of a marginal artistic community, a mobile tribe that transgresses, on a local level, the borders between institutional spaces of artistic creation and social spaces such as parks, cafés, and the street. On the other hand, the circus is also labeled *caribeño*, and the descriptors *miseria*, *crudeza*, and *conflicto*, suggest the challenges of creating art in this environment. *Circo caribeño*, moreover, evokes mobility and migration, and might be understood as a metaphor for the Caribbean diaspora. Unlike his character Ciudadano's isolation in the urban ghetto, Andújar's alternative artistic circles have presumably provided enough privilege and support to persevere in his artistic endeavors. By acting as a transmigrant, Andújar has been able to transcend obstacles faced by island-based Dominican writers such as the lack of channels for publishing outside government-sponsored publishers and the lack of career opportunities for intellectuals marginalized by the dominant political parties shaping public discourse.[16] Writing from a diasporic space in which Afro-American, Afro-Hispanic and Afro-Caribbean cultures overlap and intermix, Andújar draws from the sounds, sights, and sensibilities of hip-hop and creates a hybrid narrative and performance piece that recognizes the black, popular, and diasporic components of Dominican culture long disavowed in traditional constructions of national identity. The transnational diasporic consciousness embodied in *Ciudadano Cero* encourages us to imagine different forms of citizenship, social solidarity, and political action that might combat the increasingly inequitable allocation of resources and opportunities in a globalized world economy. Perhaps some hope may be found in the solidarity of Afro-diasporic youth cultures that counter resignation and despair by circulating dissentient sounds, images, and attitudes across the globe. As the rappers in Lo Correcto exhort in their *Ciudadano Cero* rap, "Quizás para muchos avanzar es un problema, pero más problema es si tú no avanzas / Anda Ciudadano, písalo y arranca" ("Perhaps moving forward is a problem for a lot of people, but it's more of a problem if you don't move / Get going, Citizen, step on it and go").

The Politics of Abjection in *P.A.R.G.O.: Los pecados permitidos*

The male characters in the solo performances discussed in this chapter explore an expansive understanding of *dominicanidad* by embodying identities that fail to align with the territorial and essentialist nationalisms produced by a legacy of political authoritarianism, US military interventionism, and the Haitian-Dominican border conflict. Waddys Jáquez's darkly comic play *P.A.R.G.O.: Los pecados permitidos* (2001) performs the exclusion of hybrid subjects marked by their race, class, gender, sexuality, and immigrant status from traditional national imaginaries.[17] In the play, four supposedly rehabilitated Latinos in New York City resist the normalizing action of a support group session—read here as assimilation—and display a politics of abjection that exposes the unremitting "ontological discomfort" of their transnationality.

The repugnance and attraction that the abject immigrant characters in *P.A.R.G.O.* presumably generate in their audience signals the anxiety of the sending and receiving societies in claiming them as subjects as well as their personal struggle in claiming a space in their resident country.[18] In his reading of Julia Kristeva's "The Powers of Horror," the Puerto Rican critic and creative writer Alberto Sandoval-Sánchez posits his sick, gay Latino body as "the ultimate embodiment of abjection" (313). If abjection is described by Kristeva as "what disturbs identity, system, order. What does not respect borders, positions, rules" (4), then Sandoval-Sánchez's body represents a contaminating threat to symbolic systems of order. "Expelled from the national body politic," he writes, "the unclean and improper other is translated as an alien, as a monster, an excess or lack that provokes anxiety, horror, and disgust" (317). The politics of abjection Sandoval-Sánchez proposes, however, exploits the boundary space of exclusion and integration, and he suggests that "The abject Latino gay subject in this liminal zone of abjection is capable of transgressing borders and hence of making possible a certain subversion and emancipation" (317). In *P.A.R.G.O.* Jáquez uses his queer, Afro-Latino body to transform into four immigrant characters, three Dominicans and one Puerto Rican, in what might be seen as an exemplary space hovering on the boundaries of social exclusion and integration: a fictitious support group meeting run by the charitable organization, P.A.R.G.O., which stands for *Patronato de Recuperación Global Organizado* (Global Organized Recovery Board). Abjection and migration are linked in that the ontology of the abject is concerned with place. In Kristevan terms, the abject is an exiled "deject" that asks "where" rather than "who" (15). She writes: "The one by whom the abject exists is thus a deject who places (himself), separates (himself), situates (himself), and therefore strays instead of getting his bearings, desiring, belonging, or refusing. Situationist in a sense, and not without laughter—since laughing is a way of placing or displacing abjection" (15). As we will see, laughter is central in creating the possibility for subversion in the space of social rehabilitation.

P.A.R.G.O. consists of four monologues linked by interventions by a leader of ceremonies and a male ballet dancer. One by one, María Cuchívida, a homeless and mentally unstable crack addict; Papichío Domínguez, a handsome but lonely ex-alcoholic *matatán* (macho big shot); Zaza, an ex-prostitute turned P.A.R.G.O. beauty queen; and Pasión Contreras, a drug-using transsexual, take to the stage to tell their stories. Some have been associated with the institution for over a decade and none have been truly *renovada* (rehabilitated) in the words of Marimba Cepeda, also known as *La señora del Busto Prominente* (The Large-Busted Woman) and who serves the meeting's host. In fact, each painfully funny monologue played by Jáquez underscores the many ways in which these characters continue to operate in an unassimilated space of abjection. As María puts it, "Años van y años vienen en esta

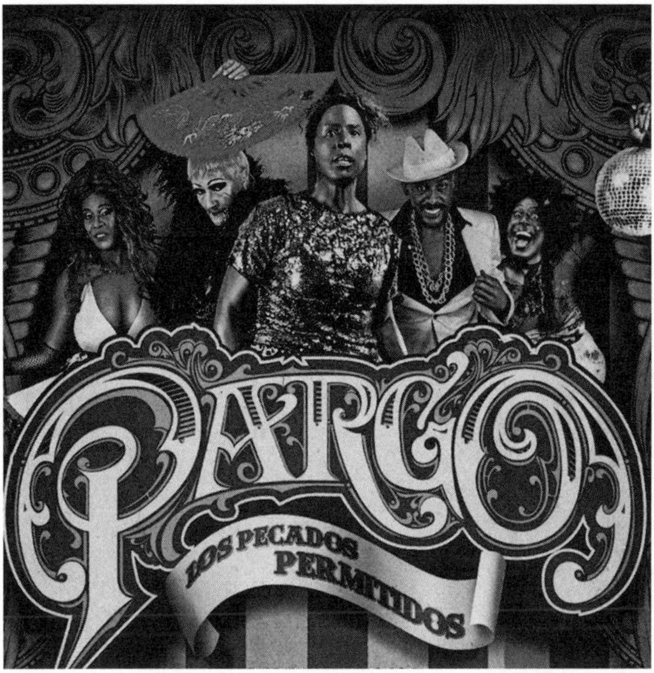

2.3. Waddys Jáquez and Verónica López in *P.A.R.G.O.: Los pecados permitidos*. Photo credit: Maglio Perez. Poster design: Evaristo Angurria.

recuperación de la que nadie se recupera" ("The years come and go in this recovery from which nobody recovers"; 9). María refers not so much to their various addictions, as to their status as immigrants, or, in my view, transmigrants, since it is evident that their loyalties and social networks go beyond their residence in one nation-state. To recover would be to assimilate, and their outrageous postures, idiosyncratic modes of expression, and tragicomic tales of survival are all signs of their marginalized position on the edges of mainstream society.

Perhaps the most therapeutic outcome of participating in P.A.R.G.O., then, is to inhabit a space where they can perform a narrative of the self, a persistently abject subjectivity productive in maintaining difference. Except for María, they have been invited to "testify" at a support group meeting that resembles a variety show. Each character has a special relationship with El Licenciado Betances (Betances, Esq.) the director and founder of P.A.R.G.O., and each is connected through the diva Zaza—she introduced María to prostitution in the Netherlands, she was once Papichío's lover, and she is a friend and neighbor of Pasión. Paradoxically, however, it is the disin-

2.4. Papichío in *P.A.R.G.O.: Los pecados permitidos*. Photo credit: Maglio Perez.

tegrative quality of their lack of bearings and sense of dislocation that joins them as an abject community more than their evident personal links and shared addictions.

María and Papichío's translocality is evident in their obsession with the past. Both are haunted by how they arrived in New York City and by familial stories of origins. After being excluded from the chain of migration formed by her nine brothers—a trauma from which she has never recuperated—María makes her journey to the United States via the Netherlands, where she worked as a prostitute, or, as she tells the folks back home, as a *niñera* (nanny), tending to "boys" from ages twenty to fifty, until she robs a passport from an unsuspecting Mormon and finally reaches the United States. Even though Papichío has been in "Nueva Yol" for fifteen years, he continues to relive his departure from home: "Miro pa'atrá y el tiempo no pasa, todavía veo a la vieja depidiéndose de mí" ("I look back and time doesn't pass, I still see my mom saying good-bye"; 11–12).[19] Papichío's body language and repeat amendments to his migration story add levity to the tale of his nightmarish illegal nine-week journey to the United States in a merchant ship: "Todo comenzó hace 15 años cuando este chamaco salió de Quisqueya la bella en un balco mercante . . . Digo en un furgón que estaba dentro de un balco mercante . . ." ("It all began fifteen years ago when this boy left his beautiful homeland in a merchant ship . . . I mean, in a shipping container that was inside the merchant ship"; 13).[20] On the surface, Papichío exudes style, sexuality—in his words, "carisma tropical" ("tropical charisma"; 12).

Papichío arrived to the United States poised for stardom, but the reality of depressing factory work and hard luck in love and with the law add up to nostalgia, loneliness, and alcoholism, leading him to admit: "Maldigo ese día en que yo me monté en el barco mercante (en el furgón que taba dentro del barco)" ("I curse the day that I boarded the merchant ship [the container that was inside the ship]"; 15). Just another marginalized hustler on the streets, at P.A.R.G.O. Papichío's abjection allows him to become, momentarily, the star of the show. By contrast, the compelling "pornografía verbal" that was María's life story once made her popular at P.A.R.G.O., but now on the brink of madness and death, she has reached a level of abjection beyond P.A.R.G.O.'s charitable interests and is no longer invited to testify as a model of recovery. Instead, she has crashed the meeting by pushing her shopping cart onto the stage and has captivated the audience through her rancid odor of homelessness, terrifying appearance, and stinging comments about her fellow P.A.R.G.O. participants.

Zaza and Pasión also radiate a repellant magnetism, and, through their bodies, they display part of their "diasporic discomfort." Zaza is described in the stage directions making her stage entrance as "Putona, putísima, pelucona, peluquísima, coronada y todo, como una pantera en celo" ("Slutty, super slutty, wiggy, super wiggy, crowned and everything, like a panther in heat"; 16) and by her own grandmother as "una bomba de sensualidad tropical, un aborto de la naturaleza" ("a bomb of tropical sensuality, an abortion of nature"; 16). Pasión Contreras also draws stares, for her contrary male/female passions prompted a surgical sexual crossover that has left her looking like a "truco mal hecho" ("bad trick"; 20). With the help of the artist Hochi Asiático, the foam-padded costumes worn by Jáquez display the grotesquely exaggerated physical merits of a Caribbean beauty queen and the failed quest for beauty that has left Pasión with an ugly exterior that only she knows harbors the beautiful soul of a beauty queen: "Ríanse si quieren, pero aquí parada donde estoy, yo tengo el alma de una Miss Universo de Venezuela" ("Laugh if you want, but here, as I am, I have the soul of a Venezuelan Miss Universe"; 22). These monstrous, alternately excessive, and ambiguous immigrant bodies perform a certain abject power that threatens the boundaries of homogeneous identities, systems, and order, in this case, both the Dominican and United States national body politics.

It is worth noting that, as in other important narratives of Caribbean identity, Jáquez imagines the queer identity categories of a transsexual Puerto Rican as embodiment par excellence of the contradictory cultural, economic, and political realities of the transnational Caribbean subject. Like Pasión's category-blurring sex/gender migration, Puerto Rican history and culture constantly problematizes such dichotomies as island/mainland, nation/colony, black/white, Spanish/English, and thus has been theorized as queer by numerous scholars. As Lawrence La Fountain-Stokes eloquently explains: "Puerto Ricans are a queer bunch: simultaneously Afro-Diasporic, Caribbean, Latin American, Hispanic, Latino/a, and American, at least since 1898; insular, migratory and translocal, with United States citizenship and passports since 1917; speaking Spanish or English or sometimes, perhaps rather often, some variation of both; living here and there and sometimes in several places at once"[21] ("Cultures" 275). In his more recent work on Puerto Rican drag/trans performance, La Fountain-Stokes has honed in on a more specific term, *translocas*, to identify the condition of inhabiting different locations, genders, and sexualities. The combination of *loca* as a sign of masculine effeminacy and *translocal* as a signifier of multiple spaces "bring together transgressive sexuality to a migratory spatial analysis" (La Fountain-Stokes, "Translocas"). By these terms, Jáquez's play with drag performance in his story of abject immigrants underscores how the transnational Dominican diaspora at the end of the twentieth century has similarly produced an increasingly translocal and queer collective identity.

In addition to their transgressive bodies, Zaza and Pasión's enthusiastic use of scatological (*caca*, *vómito*, *diarrea*) (shit, vomit, diarrhea) and vulgar language (*cocaína*, *coño*, *puñeta*) (cocaine, fuck, shit) are at constant odds with the institution's goal of presenting an inspirational discourse of rehabilitation. Similarly, Zaza's voice-over farewell speech ending her reign as P.A.R.G.O. queen parodies the charitable projects organized by pageant winners by proposing a manual for performing "happy suicides" and a plan for the elderly to build their own caskets (19). Even Marimba, *La Señora del Busto Prominente*, who as emcee should represent the official discourse of P.A.R.G.O., frequently betrays propriety and, in reference to herself, drunkenly shouts, "Desampará, borracha y emigrante. ¡Un éxito!, 'recuperarse es caminar el resto de la vida en una cuerda floja,' me cago en la teoría y le regalo a la doctora González la práctica" ("Helpless, drunk, and emigrant. A success! 'To recover is to walk the rest of your life on a tightrope,' Fuck theory and I'll gift Dr. González practice"; 19). Ironically, this institutional maxim evoking the unsteady balancing act of walking the tightrope of recuperation is suggestive of the irrepressible bodies of the performing characters. One of Jáquez's great accomplishments with this piece is expressing through his body what Vivian Martínez Tabares calls the "gestural essence" of each character—María's teetering between madness and lucidity, Papichío's rhythmic strut, Zaza's self-consciously unhurried beauty queen gait, and Pasión's edgy energy ("Caribbean" 28).[22] Each exudes an uncontrollable vitality that exceeds the normalizing efforts of the support group session.

Indeed, the authority figures and their attendant medical, psychoanalytic, and self-help discourses one would expect to frame and control the event do not appear to have much hold on the presenters. Betances and his medical staff never appear onstage, and they are characterized solely by the character's allusions to them, which generally ridicule and undermine their moral authority. The P.A.R.G.O. organizers, for example, hope to censor the content of the life stories shared by their model clients, and when they are not in the wings encouraging the performers to highlight the good episodes in their lives and to check their obscene language, they are frantically trying to remove María from the stage. At one point, Betances shuts off all the lights in an attempt to curb the torrent of "malas palabras y leyendas urbanas" ("curse words and urban legends"; 6) spewing from María. Later, he tries to drown out her voice by playing on the sound system, of all songs, the upbeat urban anthem "New York, New York" (9). In the end, Papichío takes over the situation and calmly counsels: "¡Betances! coja el bastón pa que no se caiga, déjeme esto a mí que soy experto en improvisación, quédese en la puerta de que esta gente me encargo yo porque lo mío es el carisma" ("Betances! Grab your cane so you don't fall down, let me handle this, I'm an expert in improvisation, stay by the door, I'll take charge of these people because I'm the charismatic one"; 11). Throughout, all the supposedly rehabilitated characters retain their nonnormative qualities, which might be perceived as a failure from the point of view of the organizers of P.A.R.G.O., but as a source of empowerment from the perspective of those who were able to use the forum to become a speaking subject and to assert their distinct subjectivity.

Moreover, the organization's performers interact with the audience in such a way that positions them as abject actors rather than simply objects of the evening's spectacle or the institution in general. Spectators are incorporated into the fiction of Jáquez's play and stand in for attendees of the support group session.[23] The play casts a critical eye on the work of social service agencies by hinting at Betances's suspect relationships with his female clients and by emphasizing the pleasure the audience takes in listening to the misfortunes of others. For example, Papichío cheerfully says, "Testificaré, pues quién soy yo para evitar que utede se divieltan con la degracia ajena" ("I'll testify, because who am I to keep you from having fun with other people's misfortunes"; 12), and Pasión has been asked to return ten times over the past year due to the demand for her "horribles narraciones" ("horrible stories"; 20). Apparently, the speakers, their audience, and the institution gain something from this arrangement, whether it is therapy, pleasure, or economic profit. This problematic relationship among clients, support group members, and the management is not lost on the performers, however, and Pasión speaks bluntly to the audience: "Ustedes con esa carita de: 'Mira nena, te perdono y te acepto' . . . ¡Hipócritas! No vinieron aquí por solidaridad vinieron porque le gusta el can, la chercha sincronizada o porque en el fondo quieren sentir que son buenos" ("You people with that little expression: 'Look, girl, I pardon and accept you' . . . Hypocrites! You didn't come here out of solidarity, you came because you like gossip . . . or because deep down you want to feel that you're good"; 24). However, the institution deflates any feelings of superiority on the part of the spectators by videotaping everyone who attends the event, therefore destroying their reputation and creating more business. As Marimba points out: "Si usted está sentado ahí es porque oculta algo y Viciosos Incorporados lo quiere ayudar. Querido compañero, que no te de vergüenza tu debilidad, mas bien afróntala, afróntala, afróntala . . . ¡Afróntala coño!" ("If you're sitting here it's because you hide something, and Vices Incorporated can help you. Dear colleague, don't let your weakness embarrass you, rather, confront it, confront it, confront it, dammit!" 2).

In the final analysis, semantics might provide a clue to the social work performed by the *Patronato de Recuperación Global Organizado*. P.A.R.G.O. is not only an acronym. "Para los que no dominan el término real" (For those who don't understand the term), Pasión explains, "pargo es el nombre que se le da a un encuentro casual, sexual premeditado con fines de lucro" ("pargo is the name given to a planned sexual encounter for financial gain"; 23).[24] The solidarity meetings, therefore, might be seen as a profitable "pargo": the organization's administrators prostitute their star clients who lure in clients who may turn out to be future luminaries of the show. In one way or another, the administrators, performers, and audience members exploit each other. If social agencies are to "cure" societal ills, within the conceit established by the play, P.A.R.G.O. should operate to purge or to assimilate what is perceived to be alien to the national body politic. On the contrary, for better or for worse, the fictitious support group cures nothing, and instead maintains a self-sustaining space of marginality in which its abject clients can bask in a spot light of difference rather than slip away into the anonymity of sameness. *P.A.R.G.O.* disrupts models of Dominican identity that demand allegiance to one nation-state and provides a space for "translocal, transgender, and transgressive" explorations of individual and collective identity (La Fountain-Stokes, "Translocas"). Likewise, as noted in the introduction, Jáquez's artistic method is transnational and represents a new direction for Dominican theater. The artist's popularity among audiences in both New York City and the Dominican Republic (and beyond) attests to his unassimilable transnationality and a more receptive climate for examining the "baggage" that comes with negotiating identity under conditions of transmigrancy.

Interrogating the Stereotype of the *Jodedor* in *La cosa nostra dominicana*

In *La cosa nostra dominicana* (2009), Dió-genes Abréu surprises audiences by center staging a *jodedor*, or drug dealer, in order to dissect a model of masculinity that has come to be identified with Dominican migrants and to reflect on the intersection of drug trafficking and transnationalism. Based in New York City since 1983, through literature, art, and community activism, Abréu has long confronted the challenges faced by Dominican migrants and the barriers to an inclusive understanding of Dominican identity.[25] His essay collections, *Perejil: el ocaso de la "hispanidad" dominicana* (Parsley: The Decline of the Dominican "Spanishness") (2004) and *Sin haitianidad no hay dominicanidad* (Without Haitianess There Is No Dominicaness) (2013) represent important, but relatively little-known contributions to the debates that have insisted on placing migration and multiculturalism at the center of the Dominican national imaginary.[26] Like the scholarship produced by professors such as Silvio Torres-Saillant and Ramona Hernández, Abréu's essay collections examine Dominican culture and identity from the perspective of the Dominican immigration experience. However, Abréu is not an academic, and his writings—in particular his 2007 essay collection, *Engañifas, Discurso y Práctica Social* (Tricks, Discourse, and Social Practice)—pointedly reminds readers and scholars like myself of the contradictions of producing a progressive academic discourse that is likely to exclude the marginalized sectors that it has as an object of its study. Perhaps this is why Abréu opts to cast in the limelight the figure of the drug dealer in *La cosa nostra dominicana.* In countering the negative representation of Dominican migrants, academic discourse tends to condemn the skewed media representations of Dominicans, particularly during the 1980s and 1990s, the difficult years in the drug wars in Washington Heights. While Dominican dealers or any other groups in the drug trade certainly do not represent their communities on the whole, they form a sector of society and a topic that merits analysis rather than being swept aside in accounts—academic or otherwise—of Dominican migration to the United States.

Since the 1980s, when the Cali cartel began using Caribbean islands as transshipment points between South America and the United States, drugs, geography, power, and politics converged to build a framework of geonarcotics in the region (Griffith 3). Weak law enforcement, inadequate technological resources, and remote geographical spaces made the Dominican Republic a prime location for the drug trade. At the same time, poor social and economic conditions pushed Dominicans to migrate, and many settled in Washington Heights, which had always been a center for distributing drugs on the East Coast due to its proximity to the George Washington Bridge and Interstate 95 (Kleinknecht 258). Before long, entrepreneurial Dominicans established themselves in the underworld economy, specializing in using legitimate businesses like bodegas and travel agencies to launder the proceeds of drug sales. The journalist William Kleinknecht notes the circular transnational quality of the Dominican drug trade, first, in the innumerable New York City money-wiring businesses that funnel laundered cash back to the Dominican Republic, and, second, in the fact that the drug kingpins "spend their lives as immigrants with one foot in the Dominican Republic, sustained by the dream that they will return to enjoy the good life in their native country when they have made enough money in New York" (295). As a result, it is doubtful that Dominicans will develop in the United States a well-structured crime organization with an extensive criminal portfolio like the Italian American Mafia, otherwise known as La Cosa Nostra, although the impact of drug trafficking on their community is significant enough for Abréu, in his play title, to acknowledge the criminal activity of dealers as *La cosa nostra dominicana*.

The stereotype of the Dominican migrant as a drug dealer looms large in the popular Dominican and American imaginations. Kleinknecht writes that "the drug trade has led many in law enforcement and society at large to saddle Dominicans with the same kind of criminal stereotype that has been foisted upon immigrants for more than a century. They are often dismissed as bands of criminals. . . . But Dominicans are not inherently immoral, lazy or criminal. They just come from a country that is frighteningly impoverished and whose emigrants, through accidents of timing and geography, have found themselves being tempted more than other ethnic groups by the siren call of the drug trade" (255–56). The stereotypic descriptor for Dominican migrants, Dominicanyork, links crime with migration. In the *Dictionary of Latin American Racial and Ethnic Terms*, the first definition listed for the term is "Dominican drug dealer," while the second is "Dominican-American" (Stephens 186). Like its predecessor Nuyorican, Dominicanyork distinguishes between Dominicans from the island and those in the diaspora, and it can be invoked as a pejorative, racialized label, though some have appropriated the term to celebrate a new, bicultural identity. Most striking, though, is how the first definition conflates migration with criminality, revealing the extent to which Dominicans in the United States have been categorized as drug traffickers. In public discourse, the Dominicanyork label for compatriots who have lived abroad carries the stigma of exclusion and is linked to class pretensions and criminal activities. Dominicans who have lived abroad have been referred to variously as Dominicanyorks, Dominican Yorks, Dominícans, and *cadenú*. Based on interviews with residents of Santo Domingo's lower-class neighborhoods, the historian Jesse Hoffung-Garskof teases out the different meanings of the terms: "*Dominicanyork* referred to a suspect place, and in its shortened version *dominícan*, to the English language pronunciation of the national marker, dominicano. But *cadenú* referred specifically to cultural artifacts, to symbols of consumer power. Gold chains stood in for the accusation of drug dealing, and more broadly for the foreign-inspired class pretensions of Dominicans with no real cultura [*sic*]" (230). In brief, for many Dominicans *aquí* and *allá*, Dominicanyork instantly conjures a look and a lifestyle associated with compatriots who have profited by the drug trade.[27]

Abréu's play with the stereotype of the Dominicanyork drug dealer in the context of performance counters discourses of prejudice and stereotype faced by immigrant communities. As psychologists explain, stereotypic thinking reflects a variety of cognitive and motivational processes, serving different functions in different contexts. Often, though, stereotypes are invoked "to make information processing easier by allowing the perceiver to rely on previously stored knowledge in place of incoming information" (Hilton and von Hippel 238). Scholars have noted how Latino theater complicates this perceptual process by highlighting alternative modes of representation that contest images of Latinos as hot-blooded machos or sex symbols, gang members, or illegal immigrants, among other stereotyped characterizations.[28] Jon Rossini's study, *Contemporary Latina/o Theater: Wrighting Ethnicity* (2008), usefully posits the notion of "wrighting," in Latino plays in which playwrights create new conceptual frameworks by simultaneously correcting (righting) and creating (writing) (10). Through the act of "wrighting," Rossini suggests that these playwrights open up "possibilities of what can be conceived by exposing and transforming the structures of what is perceived" (10). The frame of theatrical performance encourages audiences to see anew what they have seen represented before in popular and political discourses and images. In what follows, I argue that distancing techniques employed by Abréu in *La cosa nostra dominicana* trouble the spectator's stock perception of the *jodedor.*

Abréu employs several dramatic devices to complicate the drug dealer stereotype: he creates three dealer characters played by one actor, breaks the fourth wall, punctuates the plot with music and multimedia, and uses humor. Like *P.A.R.G.O.*, *La cosa nostra dominicana* is a "monopolylogue," but it has a different quality of virtuoso performance since it calls for the actor to transform into different characters seamlessly, with no change of scene or costuming.[29] The play's setting is the theater itself, specifically the auditorium, and the action consists of the dealer fielding continual cell phone calls while seated among the audience. The site-specific location of the action of the play deliberately disrupts the illusion of the fourth wall, as does the direct audience address when the character occasionally interacts with fellow audience members. Most of the play, though, consists of the dealer's animated telephone conversations with multiple, unseen interlocutors. Unlike the conventional realist play in which spectators passively follow the intrascenic dialogue, here, they must be prepared to respond to the actor, and, different from voyeuristic eavesdropping, they must listen intently and fill in the blanks of the one-sided conversations, to some extent becoming cocreators of the story. In *La cosa nostra dominicana*, the spectators are enfolded in the fiction of the play, while the actor inserts himself in the space of reality of the audience. The spectators know the play is a fiction, but they also know that outside the performance event, there are drug dealers on the streets of their community. Blurring the lines between art and life places spectators in active interpretative roles and allows them to engage with a social problem rather than being the passive recipients of media representations or political discourse.

La cosa nostra dominicana also foregrounds the artificiality of acting conventions since the presence of one actor who plays three characters constantly makes the spectator aware of the distinction between actor and character. In this monologue piece, the performing subject and subject of performance are not the same, as in an autobiographical solo performance. The multiple roles played by the actor never allow the audience to conflate the actor with the character, therefore drawing attention to the role of the Dominican drug dealer as a social construct. Each dealer uses a different variety of Dominican Spanish that identifies him variously from New York City, Santo Domingo, or from the Dominican countryside. The Dominicanyork character is further identified by a soundtrack of rap and house music, the *capitaleño* is associated with merengue and salsa, while the campesino is introduced by bachata and *perico ripiao* (traditional merengue associated with the Cibao region). As noted previously, stereotypes often simplify the cognitive demands on the perceiver, but Abréu's play asks audiences to process incoming information from the three characters rather than relying on a simpler, singular, and previously constructed understanding of the *jodedor.* Furthermore, the cell-phone conversations of the three characters invoke a web of characters including mothers, girlfriends, wives, friends, and business partners and refer to social, political, and personal matters in both in the United States and the Dominican Republic. The play's different drug dealer characters and their telephone conversations underscore the transnational quality of the everyday lives of Dominicans, adding layers to the one-dimensional stereotype and multiple angles through which to scrutinize it.

While Abréu's drug dealer characters are representative of a deterritorialized *dominicanidad* that moves between two nation-states, the trio and their activities cannot be said to represent the Dominican community on the whole. In his essay "What up, Nigga? El Dominicanyork como terrorista cultural" (What up, Nigga? The Dominicanyork as a Cultural Terrorist) Abréu confirms that a discourse *de desprecio y estereotipo* (of disdain and stereotypes) has been forged to categorize Dominicans living in New York. However, he concedes that "algunas de esas actitudes son justificadas, dadas las vergonzosas maneras de comportamiento mostrados por una minoría nuestra que, mordida por la ansiedad de mostrar opulencia, logros y realización personal, pisotea y vuelve caricatura bufónica la realidad y condiciones de vida de la mayoría de nuestras comunidades" ("some of these attitudes are justified, given the embarrassing behaviors of a minority of us, who, bitten by the desire to show opulence, achievements, and personal success, trample and transform into a ridiculous caricature the reality and life conditions of the majority of our communities"; 168). In *La cosa nostra dominicana*, as the stage directions indicate, slide projections and video serve as a counterpoint to the negative image the *jodedor* has cast over the entire community (18).[30] In line with Erwin Piscator and Bertolt Brecht's legacy of stage techniques highlighting reason, didacticism, and documentary reality, the slide projections provide socioeconomic context, such as scenes from the impoverished Dominican countryside and testimonials by immigrants of various backgrounds in the United States, to foreground the factors that compel people to migrate and some to engage in illegal activities to survive. This distancing effect creates intellectual empathy, perhaps diffusing some of the prejudices produced by emotion. However, in the use of video projections, Abréu's piece will also emotionally draw in the spectator if the director follows the stage directions and screens clips from Dominican cable television shows such as *Nueva York de Noche* and *Lluvia Musical*.[31] These cult favorite shows will trigger personal memories and group solidarity, most likely distracting spectators, at least momentarily, from the social problem examined in the play.

Nevertheless, Brecht always insisted that didactic theater should be pleasurable, and I suggest that laughter also serves as an effective distancing technique in *La cosa nostra dominicana* (72–73). Simply shifting the *jodedor* from his territory on the street to a theater auditorium has a humorous distancing effect because it heightens the representation of the character to the point of caricature. The dealer personas break all the conventions of the hushed, polite anticipation that generally precedes a performance by asking to smoke, ordering *tostones* and *carne frita* for delivery, playing music on their cell phones, and sustaining loud, nonstop conversations that reveal their involvement in the drug trade. As the audience members begin to realize that this unruly spectator is the performance they have come to see, their initial responses—curiosity, surprise, and annoyance—will be refocused as they become observers and interpreters.

Tuning in to the conversations, spectators are likely to be placed in an uncomfortable position of both recognizing and rejecting the overblown masculine attitude and behaviors associated with *jodedor*. For example, in the following dialogue, Jodedor 1 is characterized as both stupid and sexist:

> ¿El título? ¿De la obra? Qué sé yo, una vaina ahí que tiene que ver con "ostras" dominicanas. *Otras* no, te dije "Ostras." Got that? I said Ostras. ¿Que yo si'toy fino? Coño, pero tú ere una mujercita bruta . . . (leyendo el programa de la obra) Óyeme bien, pay attention to this: La obra se llama *La cosa nostra dominicana*. Nostra quiere decir ostras en italiano. You know what I'm saying, ah? (19)
>
> *The title? Of the play? Who knows, something that has to do with Dominican "oysters." Others, no, I said, "Oysters." Got that? I said, "Oysters." Do I think I'm high class? Damn, aren't you a dumb woman . . . (reading the playbill) Listen carefully, pay attention to this: the play is called The Dominican Cosa Nostra. Nostra means oysters in Italian. You know what I'm saying, ah?*

In all three monologues, the fact that none of their cell-phone interlocutors can believe that drug dealers are attending a play performance pokes fun at their lack of culture. This produces an anxiety that exacerbates their macho bravado—*coño, pero tú ere una mujercita bruta*—that establishes a gender hierarchy that denigrates women and mistakenly attributes the stupidity to her. The telephone banter does nothing but confirm the *jodedor* as an untrustworthy player who hustles the streets and the women in his home life. In the third and final monologue, the *jodedor* switches between conversations with a work associate and several women. He speaks warmly of Nana, the woman who has stood by him throughout all his criminal adventures. "Ya no encuentra una mujel así: fiel así" ("You just don't find a loyal woman like this anymore"; 27), he gushes. In the same breath, Jodedor speaks to someone he refers to as Mami. Unlike the sheltered Nana, whom he doesn't allow to work, Mami earns a salary as a factory worker, but she needs money to spring a friend from jail. Jodedor will provide the funds, but it's clear that he expects the favor to be returned, sexually. Finally, as he's talking about a Boricua (a Puerto Rican) he's currently romancing in hopes of marrying to obtain a green card, a hysterical Nana calls to tell him the police are searching for him. The piece ends with the authorities handcuffing Jodedor and tearing the phone away as he calmly signs off, "Te llamo más talde polque parece que va a empezal la obra. Chilao bro!!" ("I'll call you later because it looks like the play is beginning. Chill out, bro!!" 29).

By the end of *La cosa nostra dominicana*, not only are the police on to Jodedor, so are the spectators. By spotlighting a stigmatized characterization of Latinos, *La cosa nostra dominicana* runs the risk of perpetuating a stereotype. Certainly, the dialects, attitudes, and styles presented in the play are instantly recognizable to the Dominican community. The play invites identification and laughing along with the types represented onstage, but even more strongly, the piece creates an intellectual distancing that results in laughing at, or rejecting, the culture and behaviors of a Dominican minority that has often colored how most Dominican migrants are perceived both in the United States and the Dominican Republic. Abréu acknowledges the criminal activity of drug trafficking in transnational migration, as "our thing," a Dominican problem, but like the express mission of the community center where the play premiered—"to enrich and empower our youth and adults"—his play takes up a social problem in art, in order to interrogate how we perceive a criminalized model of Dominican masculinity.[32]

The subaltern masculinities performed by the solo artists in the three plays discussed in this chapter make visible marginalized subjectivities at the same time they foil their stigmatized representations. In Andújar's *Ciudadano Cero*, black global culture represents a space from which to cultivate a form of belonging that resists the cultural homogeneity of traditional nationalist imaginaries, as do the politics of abjection displayed by the immigrant members of the P.A.R.G.O. support group so vividly brought to life by Jáquez. Implicit in taking on the figure of the *jodedor* in *La cosa nostra do-*

minicana is an awareness of how Dominican identity has been transformed geographically and culturally and a challenge to Dominicans both *aquí* and *allá* to think about the qualities of *dominicanidad* they may wish to embody, or, alternately, reject. Like Peterson and many other theater scholars have suggested, solo performance offers a unique space to observe the structures and discourses involved in the production of identities. In contemporary Dominican culture, migration has been the foremost catalyst in changing how Dominicans grapple with personal and collective modes of belonging, and the activity of theater represents a laboratory where artists work through and experiment with the new subjectivities that have been generated by mass migration. As Rossini notes, playwrights "foster recognition of the complex cultural forces that help shape the literal and metaphorical staging of identity and community. Symbiotically creating and correcting, revising and reorienting, they highlight the edges of existing conceptual frameworks to point to a space beyond" (22–23). The theatrical texts and performances by Andújar, Jáquez, and Abréu acknowledge the new borders of *dominicanidad* and challenge received notions of national identity by locating their male characters on the margins and drawing attention to their relationship to transnational social fields. In the following chapter, the creative and corrective impulse of the theatrical frame similarly focuses on gender and sexuality in plays by Marco Antonio Rodríguez in order to "wright" identities that have been silenced through the heteronormativity of Dominican nationalism.

Chapter 3

Breaking the Silence of Heteronormativity in the Theater of Marco Antonio Rodríguez

Like the experimental solo pieces examined in the previous chapter, the theater of Marco Antonio Rodríguez interrogates the intersections of migrant identities and nonnormative masculinities, but it does so from a radically different context. Whereas the characters in the solo plays grapple in public street and stage spaces with transnational identities that position them "queerly" with respect to traditional, territorially bounded understandings of national belonging, Rodríguez presents a Dominican American world of immigrants and their children long settled in the United States within the frame of dramatic realism. With the plays *La luz de un cigarillo* (*Ashes of Light*) (2011) and *Barceló con hielo* (*Barceló on the Rocks*) (2014) Rodríguez has become the most visible and consistently staged Dominican playwright in the United States.[1] Perhaps the descriptor *Dominican American* best suits Rodríguez, for if we were to place the playwrights in this book on a continuum spanning the United States and the Dominican Republic, as a second-generation immigrant, he would be the most rooted in the United States. Rodríguez was born and raised in New York City, although he spent extended periods of time in the Dominican Republic during his childhood.[2] Fluent in Spanish and English, Rodríguez writes versions of his plays in both languages and promotes his work on a bilingual website.[3] Nevertheless, his plays show that being a second-generation immigrant born in the United States is not mutually exclusive with transnationalism; in fact, part of Rodríguez's success is creating stories that speak to Dominicans at home and abroad (however they define where *aquí* and *allá* are).

An entangled family tree and the depiction of Dominican spaces encourage us to consider *La luz de un cigarillo* and *Barceló con hielo* as founding narratives for Dominican American drama. In the tradition of the Puerto Rican and Cuban family dramas from the 1950s and 1960s such as *La carreta* by René Marqués and *El súper* by Iván Acosta, Rodríguez populates the stage with Dominican immigrants and their children in New York City. Indeed, the realist domestic set designs of Rodríguez's contemporary plays closely approximate the scenography of previous generations of Latino dra-

3.1. Luz, Divina, and Julio César in *La luz de un cigarillo*. Photo credit: Anthony Ruiz.

ma, suggesting that some aspects of the Latino immigrant experience in the US Northeast have not changed much over time.[4] Through the visual cues of apartment set designs, *La luz de un cigarillo* and *Barceló con hielo* offer, to my knowledge, the first fully Dominican American onstage universe for US audiences. In one, an Upper West Side efficiency with barred windows and pink painted walls, we see a giant portrait of Pope John Paul II dominating one wall, an oven/cupboard stuffed with clean dishes, stacks of LP records, and various nonfunctional electronics. This space creates a sense of ordered disorder, which for the mother character, is comforting, whereas for her son, is asphyxiating. In the second play, a father shares a Washington Heights apartment with his two sons. From the streets, the sounds of youth hanging out and hip-hop music permeate the conservative home decorated with Caribbean artwork, a dried palm in the form of a cross, and a plastic encased portrait of the sacred heart of Jesus Christ. In addition to these visual signs, Rodríguez encourages identification with Dominican culture in both pieces by crafting dialogue that reflects the voices of Dominicans both in the United States and the Dominican Republic. An author's note on dialect preceding the texts and a glossary following them underscores the playwright's intent to bring the specificity of the Dominican Spanish to the stage. To achieve authentic renderings of both characters from the island and Dominicans born in the United States, Rodríguez employs at least four linguistic registers in the plays: standard Dominican Spanish, a regional *cibaeño* dialect from the Dominican countryside, a *cibaeño*-inflected Spanish of someone who has lived in New York City for many years, and a Dominicanyork Spanglish vernacular. Finally, Rodríguez further encourages sensorial identification with the onstage cultural milieu by frequently incorporating music and the preparation of culinary dishes into the stories as they unfold.

While earlier plays about migration focus more on the journey and the difficult experiences of adaptation, the characters in *La luz de un cigarillo* and *Barceló con hielo* are established in New York City and have already established a transcultural identity. As I have noted throughout this book, social scientists consider the Dominican Republic's sizeable migration within a compact time frame a model case of contemporary transnationalism (Itzigsohn 318). The anthropologist Jorge Duany characterizes the Dominican Republic's transnational relationship to the United States as "neocolonial" to highlight how military intervention and economic dependence has created enduring social, economic, and political links between the two nations (*Blurred Borders* 6). As Rodríguez's dramas illustrate, many Dominicans are attached to both places in their daily lives even though they may never actually cross the national boundaries between the island and their place of residence. In both plays, the characters definitively live *aquí*, in New York City and Dallas, but I argue that *allá*, the Dominican Republic, still weighs heavily on their lives through Dominican technologies of gender that have sustained a national culture of authoritarianism to this day.[5]

Aside from the meticulously constructed Dominican American spaces, both dramatic comedies explore fragile parent/offspring relationships that are threatened by family secrets, and an intriguing twist that facilitates a spectator following is the creation of a family genealogy that encompasses both stories. *La luz de un cigarillo* and *Barceló con hielo* are companion pieces that depict a transnational Dominican world not unlike Junot Díaz's literary project that spans urban New Jersey and the Dominican Republic and includes characters like Yunior de las Casas who appear in multiple texts. In terms of dramatic action, chronologically *Barceló con hielo* precedes *La luz de un cigarillo*, even though Rodríguez wrote the latter play first. The plays' protagonists include the patriarch Nino Antonio Ortiz and the matriarch Luz Hortensia Cruz, both in their late forties or early fifties. They migrated to the United States in the 1970s, where they split up because of Nino's infidelities. Nino has three sons by two women who left him, Sergio and Dennis, whose mother is Norma, and Julio César, whose mother is Luz. Both Luz and Nino have siblings who enter the action through dialogue and flashbacks in the Dominican Republic and in the plays' present, through visits to the New York City homes. Rodríguez creates rich and memorable characters in the sons and siblings, leading one to suspect that a third installment of the series may focus on one or more of these characters. In both plays, the impending death of the patriarch sets the dramatic action in motion. A serious illness precipitates Nino's disclosure of some long-held secrets in *Barceló con hielo* and in *La luz de un cigarillo* we learn that Nino has died, because Julio César returns to New York City to attend his funeral. During his brief visit, another family secret is revealed.

Memory and Masculinity in *Barceló con hielo*

Barceló con hielo centers on Nino Antonio Cruz's relationship with his sons. Sick with stomach cancer and facing major surgery, Nino's home is in disarray, as his elder son, Sergio, is packing to leave for college in the Bronx. From the perspective of Washington Heights residents, notes Dennis, his younger sibling, leaving Manhattan for another borough is like moving to "otro continente" (232) ("another continent"; 97). Dennis, a *tíguere* slacker who sports a Pablo Escobar T-shirt, seems ill prepared to take on the role of dutiful, caretaker son. Sensing his solitude and mortality and aided by the free flow of Dominican Barceló rum, ghosts of the past visit Nino, leading him to confront President Joaquín Balaguer's legacy and its impact on his family. While Rafael Leónidas Trujillo is the prototypical Latin American dictator remembered in literature and history books, Balaguer is the political figure whose socioeconomic policies and political persecutions are connected to the massive outflow of Dominican migrants to the United States.[6] Rodríguez thus fills an important gap in Dominican theater by dramatizing this historical figure. In performance, I sensed the impact of bringing Balaguer back from the dead when the audience audibly gasped when the actor playing the political leader stepped into the domestic story onstage. Later, a different, but related sense of unease became palpable when spectators laughed during a sincere and heartfelt scene in which two boyhood friends share an intimate embrace. In what follows, I suggest that these scenes produce discomfort because they explore the authoritarianism that silences interrogation of the sociopolitical status quo and the marginalization of nonnormative sexualities in Dominican culture.

Balaguer's three-decade dominance in island politics represents a sequel to the thirty-year Trujillo dictatorship, another authoritarian regime, but with "a more convincing democratic façade" (Horn 52).[7] To this day, Dominican families, including Rodríguez's own, are politically divided over opposing views of Balaguer.[8] Even after the end of the Balaguerato in the mid-1990s, the deeply engrained culture of authoritarianism has silenced serious interrogation of the social order and the political status quo, as Silvio Torres-Saillant explains: "The conservative sector . . . has had the power to name reality and render the opposition mute, which has put serious limits on what the new generation of Dominican scholars has been able to do for their people. . . . There is no question as to who really has the last word" ("Tribulations" 1106). Nevertheless, since the turn of the twenty-first century, the sociologist Ana Liberato has identified a surge in memory work around the figure of Balaguer, and she argues that "the images, representations, and narrative frames used by social actors to make sense of, and mobilize, meanings of the Balaguer Era" contribute to a collective reckoning with the authoritarian past (13). For Liberato and the literary studies scholar Lucía Suárez, opening a dialogue on the past is crucial in the Dominican Republic because, following both the fall of the Trujillo dictatorship and the most oppressive period of Balaguer's regime, the state effectively repressed the memories of traumatic political violence. Liberato and Suárez observe that unlike countries such as Argentina, Chile, and Haiti, state-sponsored acts of memory, truth commissions, and criminal trials never developed in post-dictatorship Dominican Republic.[9] Suárez asserts: "The politics of silence—or rather denial—have been dominant in Dominican memory" and that "the Dominican Republic has continuously rejected any investigation into human rights infringements during the Balaguer years" (7). Furthermore, Suárez suggests that "women, Haitian Dominicans, and homosexuality" are still silenced in official accounts of Dominican lives (7). It is perhaps not surprising, then, that it is from the diaspora Rodríguez might more comfortably not only stage Balaguer, a historical figure that has been all but absent in Dominican theater, but also critique the regime by exploring the scripts of normative masculinity that have supported a persistent culture of authoritarianism.[10]

Liberato affirms that "from the time of independence in 1844 to the time of Balaguer's rise to power in 1966, there has been no shortage of authoritarian Dominican leaders," and she characterizes their authoritarianism as a monopolization of power, including the pursuit of reelection beyond the legal term, controlling the military, paternalism, and clientelism (44). This form of totalitarianism is clearly linked to Latin American patriarchal culture with its roots in the Iberian colonial past. In his study on political authoritarianism in the Dominican Republic, however, the political scientist Christian Krohn-Hansen argues that "specific ideas and categories which structure discussions of masculinity among Dominicans correspond to a dominant political discourse—or to a legitimate problematic which helps structure and give form to particular power relations in Dominican society" ("Masculinity" 120). To be masculine is to embody an authoritarian position predicated on oppressive power relations. Maja Horn sums up this authoritarian power structure as dyadic, competitive, and gendered in her literary and cultural study *Masculinity after Trujillo*: "Having power and being powerless, domination and subordination, and being a leader or a follower are often phrased in gendered terms and through notions of virility. These sexualized forms of differentiation masculinize the political and public sphere, inscribe men and women in particular sexualized gender dynamics, and tend to divide women among themselves" (12–13).[11] In *Barceló con hielo*, shifting between time periods and spaces, Washington Heights today and the rural Cibao region in the Dominican Republic in the late 1960s, highlights the continuities of Dominican culture—in particular, the discourses of masculinity—in the development of a transnational society.

Although he has lived in New York City almost his entire adult life, Nino reinforces the elitist, racist, and authoritarian qualities of Dominican nationalism cultivated by the island's long string of dictatorial heads of state. Balaguer's appearance in his Washington Heights apartment underscores the persistence of the past in Dominican collective memory and the haunting of the private sphere by state violence. The visual presence of Balaguer helps audiences recognize Nino's domineering desire for order in his household as conduct that mimics the state's control over its people. Nino's repressive methods for controlling Sergio and Dennis include demanding that they make the sign of the cross upon entering and leaving the apartment, insisting that they speak Spanish, critiquing their sloppy dress and posture, insulting their friends, barking out orders, and slapping them. In the tradition of phallocentric dominance, he also models *machista* and heterosex-

3.2. Balaguer visits Nino in *Barceló con hielo*. Photo credit: Michael Palma Mir.

ist behavior for his sons. For example, even though a Caribbean landscape painting hangs on the wall of the living room, Nino rejects Sergio's artistic talent as effeminate and unproductive. When Nino finds a sketched portrait drawn by Sergio, he responds:

> NINO: ¿Tú 'tá dibujando muchachos que se parecen a Jesú Crito? Yo no quiero hijo' maricóne,' ¿tú me oye?
>
> SERGIO: Oh my God.
>
> NINO: Yo te he dicho a ti que eto' garabato' no te van a dai un poivenir. (170)

NINO: You drawing boys that look like Jesus Christ? I don't want no faggot kids, ya hear me?

SERGIO: Oh my God.

NINO: I told you there's no future in this doodling crap. (36)

In addition to insulting homosexuals, Nino manages to belittle everyone in the community that surrounds him—African Americans, recently arrived illegal immigrants, uneducated pregnant Dominican women, and the mother of his children, to give a few examples. His constant invectives afford him a sense of power that, as a racially mixed, working-class, immigrant single parent, he lacks outside his domestic domain. However, Nino does not recognize the physical and verbal control he exercises in his home as a microcosm of the authoritarian Dominican state, as evidenced in this exchange with Balaguer:

NINO: La veida' que eso' lente' que uted lleva pueto no son pa' mirai mejoi. Son binoculare.' Enfocan y desenfocan a su conveniencia.

BALAGUER: ¿Ve su reflejo en ellos?

NINO: No soy como uted.

BALAGUER: Mírelos bien. (259)

NINO: Those glasses you have on don't really help your vision. They're binoculars. Focusing in and out of whatever is most convenient.

BALAGUER: Don't you see your reflection in them?

NINO: I am nothing like you.

BALAGUER: Look closer. (123)

Indeed, the events of *Barceló con hielo*—namely, facing his past—force Nino to confront why he has adopted a Balaguer-style authoritarian persona to manage his personal relationships.

Rodríguez presents this portrait of an angry and repressive father with humanity and a good dose of humor through the juxtaposition of Nino's ultra-traditional attitudes with the thoroughly contemporary Dominican-york perspectives of his sons that reflect different attitudes toward race, class, and religion. When Nino insults Sergio's friends, calling the young women pregnant high school dropouts and the young men "black monkeys," Sergio counters by pointing out that Nino can barely read and mocks his claim of white, Spanish blood (38–39). Sergio also challenges his father by questioning his supposed religiosity:

NINO: ¿Quién ha dicho? Yo leo mi Biblia.

SERGIO: La Atalaya no e' Biblia.

> *Nino le da un golpe detrás de la cabeza.*
> NINO: ¡Muchacho 'e mieida! ¡Cierra el josico y anda y presínate! (159–60)

> *NINO: Says who? I read my Bible.*
> *SERGIO: The Watchtower isn't the Bible.*
> Nino smacks him across the back of the head.
> *NINO: Shut your damn mouth and cross yourself.* (26)

Nino's oppressive response does not stop Sergio and Dennis from smoking marijuana and humorously recalling the time they attempted to set their grandmother's Bible on fire (it was apparently fire-resistant) and were consequently disciplined by being struck by a Dominican sausage link and sprinkled with *agua florida*. The façade of the household's traditional religious upbringing is again apparent when Dennis misinterprets *agua florida* as water from Florida and is corrected by Sergio: "¡Eso no e' agua de Miami, inútil! E' como agua bendita" (234) ("It's not water from Miami, dumbass. It's like holy water or something"; 99). In the same scene, they also jovially remember classic 1980s merengue music and the folkloric Dominican bottle dance. Sergio and Dennis identify as Dominican, despite never having been to their parents' country of origin and their distancing from the nationalism reflected in their father's racism and arrogant identification with Spanish Catholic heritage. Their neighborhood is part of the Dominican transnation, what Dennis calls "Dominicanlandia punto com" (239) ("Dominicanlandia dot com"; 104), filled with bodegas, young people hanging out, bootlegged media sold on the streets, and electronics stores fronting for a shadow lottery that pays off the winning numbers in the homeland lottery. While they may not participate in institutionalized transnational practices of the first generation, Sergio and Dennis show how the everyday lives and identities of the second generation continue to operate in a transnational symbolic framework that is marked by enduring authoritarianism.[12]

It turns out that adhering to traditional Dominican scripts of masculine behavior is largely responsible for Nino's bitterness and oppressive behavior. Nino has secrets from his past that, on one level, are political, but they are also bound up in questions of male identity. Nino has lived in the United States his entire adult life filled with rage and regret. Flashbacks to the rural Cibao region in the late 1960s, triggered by the appearance of Balaguer onstage, reveal that he was forced to migrate to the United States to escape the fate of his father, who was killed under the Trujillo regime, and of his brother, Aurelio (Fello), who meets a similar fate during the action of the play during the time of Balaguer. Nino's closest childhood friend, Jaston, is a pro-Balaguer military man of Haitian descent. Tragically, Nino passes along information about Fello's involvement in student protest groups to Jaston, which inadvertently leads to his brother's death and Nino's subsequent migration to the United States. The culpability Nino feels for his brother's death is intensified by the fact that the political conflict between Nino, Fello, and Jaston is also a personal one. The personal becomes political when the horizontal bonds of fraternal love for his brother and friend are broken by hierarchical state violence. Immediately following a monologue in which Nino details his brother's cruel death, Balaguer comments: "Las dictaduras del corazón son . . . distracciones para el hombre. Han confundido y destruido desde los más grandes poetas, viriles generales y, más que nada, los más simples de provincianos" (252) ("Dictatorships of the heart are . . . distractions. They have confused and destroyed from the greatest of poets to the most virile of generals and, more than anything, the most provincial of peoples"; 117). Nino's perceptive response, "¿Y la política? ¿No ha hecho lo mimo?" (252) ("What about politics? Hasn't it done the same?"; 117), rejects the notion that bonds based on sentiment and solidarity destroy men and highlights instead the devastating effects of politics on those affiliations.

These flashback scenes depict how family and friendship relationships are destroyed under the pressures of authoritarian regimes, and they display models of masculinity that add depth to play's examination of a Dominican father's relationship with his New York City-raised sons. Fello plays the contradictory role of the budding revolutionary who is elitist, sexist, and xenophobic. Dialogue between brothers reveals university-educated Fello to be critical of the Balaguer regime, while Nino, who is open to his brother's ideas, also represents the point of view of the pragmatic campesino impressed by Balaguer's national modernization projects. Fello's university education in the capital has introduced him to classical music, philosophy, and French poetry, while tending the family store with his mother has kept Nino at home. On the one hand, Nino making fun of his brother's newfound love of Bach amusingly highlights their increasingly different cultural tastes:

NINO: Ay, tú. Suena como si 'tuvieron toitruando violine.'

AURELIO: La compuso Bach.

NINO: ¿Behk?

AURELIO: Baach.

NINO: ¿La compuso un chivo? (180)

NINO: Sounds like somebody torturing violins.

AURELIO: It was composed by Bach.

NINO: Bech?

AURELIO: Baaach.

NINO: It was composed by a goat? (46)

On the other hand, when Nino offers him a meal of homemade *lambí* (stewed conch), Fello condescendingly responds: "Tú sabes que no soporto esa porquería de provincianos" (181) ("You know I don't eat provincial garbage"; 47). More seriously, when Fello grows frustrated with Nino's naïve support of Balaguer and the nation's apparent embrace of yet another strongman ruler, he exclaims: "Que van a saber ustedes. Balsa de analfabetos" (250) ("You'll never get it! Bunch of illiterates"; 115). He also insults Nino and women in general when he praises him for dating Norma, whom he deems attractive and educated, and for having broken off with Luz, a campesina who migrated to New York City "a freí tusa con lo' jodio' yanqui' del diablo eso" (185) ("to be with those piece of shit Yankee gringos"; 50). Fello's repeat references to Norma's ample breasts and his lack of nuance in understanding of migration as a national betrayal make his political position as a vanguard intellectual suspect. Finally, Fello's remarks about Jaston make visible the reactionary attitudes of many Dominican nationalists regarding Haitian immigrants in their country. Fello does not simply discredit their family friend for his support of Balaguer, he denies his right as a citizen to serve his country: "¿Y a mí qué carajo me importa lo que diga ese Haitiano asqueroso? Queriendo mandar en un país ajeno" (249) ("What the hell do I care what that Haitian trash has to say?! Barking orders in a country that's not even his"; 114). With Fello, Rodríguez avoids aligning moral righteousness with the play's strongest anti-Balaguer character. Rather, *Barceló con hielo* presents the prototype of the progressive revolutionary with ambiguity, inviting the audience to meditate on the complexity of identifying as pro or contra *balaguerista*, whether it is in the fiction of the play, the historical past, or the present.

Characters like Fello and Jaston serve to lead spectators to consider ideological positions that transcend whether a character is for or against the political status quo during the time of Balaguer. If we link Jaston with the context of the play's premiere, in which there has been a recent upsurge in xenophobia and new legislation that has made hundreds of thousands of Haitians stateless, we might conclude that Rodríguez joins a chorus of criticism of anti-Haitianism that has emanated from the Dominican diaspora.[13] Jaston and Nino's childhood friendship and love for each other metaphorically unites the border that divides Hispaniola, and Jaston's position as a lieutenant in the army suggests that Haitians can be Dominican patriots. From a reactionary and homophobic point of view, however, Jaston betrays his nation and his gender in numerous ways. His Haitian heritage clouds his commitment to the Dominican army because he is never truly considered Dominican. He must continually assert his nationality, which is casually doubted even by Nino. For example, questioning why his friend left school, Jaston replies:

> JASTON: Pa' seivir a mi país.
> NINO: Tu país.
> JASTON: ESTE e' mi país. (211)
>
> *JASTON: To serve my country.*
> *NINO: Your country.*
> *JASTON: THIS is my country.* (76)

When Nino points out the irony of serving a country that rejects him by suggesting Balaguer is probably no different than Trujillo in his distrust of Haitians, Jaston exclaims: "No soy de ese paisito jediondo y atrazao, ¿tú me oye'? Hace tiempo que tengo mi ciudadanía dominicana (222) ("I am not from that backwards, piece of shit country, you got me?! I've had my Dominican citizenship a long time now"; 86). In a sense, Jaston betrays his Haitian origins since he disavows them to the point of internalizing Dominican prejudices, yet his allegiance to his adopted country is always suspect in the eyes of Dominicans. In addition, by loving another man, he betrays the heterosexual machismo that sustains the nation's political and military institutions. Consequently, Jaston is compelled to love his adopted nation over Nino to prove his *dominicanidad.* That is, since he does not embody the expected model of male sexuality, Jaston must reassert his commitment to the nation by squashing Fello's revolutionary movement and killing him. Jaston thus destroys his loving relationship with Nino in favor of displaying his devotion to the totalitarian state.

As I have noted, Rodríguez breaks new ground in Dominican theater by pairing the themes of authoritarianism with gender and sexual identity, and the intimate relationship between Nino and Jaston startled some spectators.[14] Jaston affectionately calls Nino *Bèl nonm* (beautiful man), and gives him a hand-drawn sketch, he removes his shirt, and they sit together in an embrace drinking rum and listening to a rainstorm. Although they are alone in this scene, we might assume that others know of the nature of the relationship. For instance, when discussing Nino's girlfriends, Fello asserts: "Por lo menos rompiste el compinche que tenías con el dichoso Haitiano" (185) ("At least the weirdness with the Haitian is over and done with"; 50). Antonio de Moya and Rafael García's study of Dominican male bisexuality suggests that intimate friendships among young men are not necessarily rejected among their friends and families, "provided that neither of the friends is suspected of being 'effeminate' and both show a proper erotic interest in girls or women in their daily talk. In many cases, 'passing' strategies are developed in order to maintain the secrecy of these bonds, in situations where male partners may not even know that what they do with each other is understood as homosexual behavior, and both may sequentially or simultaneously have non-suspecting girlfriends" (129). Nino's girlfriends and Jaston's role as lieutenant in the military display heteronormative behaviors and provide cover for their relationship. Fello's voiced approval of his brother's relationships with women signals his awareness and discomfort with his brother's bisexuality, but there is no explicit denunciation on his part. One of the passing strategies de Moya and García observe in Dominican culture is identifying close male relationships as familial (brother, cousin), or as inseparable companions (129). We see something similar in the scene in which Jaston and Nino reminisce and reenact their youthful play activities:

> JASTON: Parece que fué ayei que 'tabamos volando chichiagua' junto': "Oooh. Pero miren donde van . . . el blanquito bonito con el prieto feo."
>
> NINO: Yo nunca lo vi así.
>
> JASTON: Y a ti te fascinaba jugai a lo' indio y a lo' vaquero.' ¿Te acueida? (216–17)
>
> *JASTON: Seems like yesterday we were flying kites: "There they go! The pretty white boy with the hideous Haitian."*
>
> *NINO: I never saw it that way.*
>
> *JASTON: And you just loved playing cowboys and Indians, remember*? (81)

The white/black and cowboy/Indian pairings invoke linkage, and the innocent notion of the boys' inseparability might be expressed in any number of idioms, such as "peas in a pod" or "thick as thieves." In a dialectical Hegelian sense, though, the couplings are unavoidably hierarchical: the construction of one role depends on the "other"; the white boy's "beauty" comes into existence through the black boy's "ugliness," while the same racism undergirds the character traits of the white cowboy and the "savage" Native American.[15] This underscores again one of the play's arguments, that Haiti and the question of race cannot be extricated from constructions of individual and collective identity in the Dominican Republic.

Jaston's involvement in the military dissolves the close bonds he had with Nino. We do not know how their semi-clandestine homoerotic relationship might have developed as adults; we can only see the impact of Jaston's affiliation with an authoritarian institution on their personal relationship. When

Jaston admits his bullets hit Fello at the student uprising, a brutal physical scene ensues because Nino threatens Jaston with the only power he has over him, knowledge of his sexual orientation: "¡NEGRO MARICÓN!" (255) ("You faggot!" 119).[16] According to de Moya, "the emphatic social stigma attached to the homosexual identity in predominantly patriarchal societies imposes public silence upon sexual relations between men. The stigma against male homosexuality partially results in the perception of this role is feminine, weak, and lacking power" (90). Jaston's explosive response to Nino's threat to break the silence surrounding their relationship is telling about Dominican attitudes toward homosexuality:

> ¿QUÉ E LO QUE TU TE CREE'? ¡CAMPESINO IGNORANTE! ¡E' CON UN MACHO QUE TÚ 'TA' HABLANDO AQUÍ, CARAJO! UN TENIENTE 'E PRIMERA! ¡NO LE AGUANTO YO ESA MIEIDA A ESO' HIJO' 'E PUTA AHÍ AFUERA CONTIMÁ A TI! (255)
>
> *WHO THE HELL DO YOU THINK YOU ARE?! IGNORANT PIECE OF SHIT! THIS IS A MAN YOU TALKING TO RIGHT HERE! A TOP-CLASS LIEUTENANT! I WON'T TAKE THAT BULLSHIT FROM THOSE BASTARDS OUT THERE MUCH LESS FROM YOU! (120)*

Jaston insists that he is a "man" and a "top-class lieutenant," suggesting a "faggot" cannot be either. His homosexual bond with Nino must remain hidden if he is to enjoy what de Moya calls "the patriarchal dividend" (88), the power afforded those who embody a hegemonic heterosexual masculinity. Jaston's rejection of being identified as gay by Nino—"much less from you"—might be interpreted as an expression of Jaston's hurt by the man who best understands his precarious footing as a gay Haitian in Dominican society. Or, it might be read as a denial of his sexual orientation and the outing of Nino as the "faggot." That is, being the active partner in a stigmatized personal and sexual relationship allows Jaston to consider himself as heterosexual, while Nino holds the submissive position in the relationship and is labeled homosexual for playing a passive role. In this raw moment of confrontation, the powerful word *faggot* is used to wound, underscoring the deep extent to which Nino and Jaston have internalized the very homophobia that stigmatizes them.

As much as Nino may try to approximate the role of dictator in his home, seeing the ghosts of Balaguer and Jaston leads him to understand that continuing to perform the authoritarian masculinity that supports Dominican culture will destroy his rapidly deteriorating relationship with his children. Furthermore, as we have seen, Nino cannot embody a hegemonic male identity because he has not been exclusively heterosexual. In the diaspora, Nino fully invested in heterosexuality and suppressed his love for his Haitian-Dominican friend because it led to his brother's death and the fragmentation of his family. His expression of *machista*, homophobic, and racist prejudices thus stems in part from his anxious need to enact a normative masculinity to maintain his reputation and influence over his household, which is made vulnerable by his status as a working-class immigrant. For example, Nino's harsh rejection of Sergio's artistic inclination manifests the repression of his love for Jaston, who was also an artist and had given him the landscape canvas hanging on the living room wall long ago. In the scene during which Sergio and Dennis get high and reminisce, they discuss how their mother never liked the painting, and Dennis impulsively tosses it out the window (241; 105).[17] When Nino returns and asks about the missing landscape, the family tension reaches a climax in a physical and verbal altercation. Nino reveals why he insists on displaying the painting, calling it "his cross," to refer to the guilt he has shouldered for the death of his brother (248; 113). The painting hung, too, as a reminder of the shame associated with homosexuality. To repress his sexual orientation and to rule over his sons, who were adopting cultural practices and attitudes that departed from traditional *dominicanidad*, Nino over emphasized the discourses of respectability and exaggerated the role of the heterosexual male in his household.

Now, having alienated Sergio and Dennis and facing his mortality, the play's protagonist defeats his antagonist, his own self in a hypermasculine and homophobic role. The following admission by Nino references both the political—the traumas of the Balaguer era—and the personal—the repression of his sexual identity: "Eso e' lo que se hace allá, ¿tu ve? To'lo que no se entiende . . . Se esconde. No se dice. Se entierra. En un hoyo hondo. Hata que no aguante ei dolor" (257) ("That's what you do over there. Whatever you don't understand . . . You hide. You bury it. Way deep. 'Til you can't stand the pain"; 122). *Barceló con hielo* digs up and reveals the secrets of the Balaguer regime to address its devastating effects on Dominican families. At the same time, it supports Horn's conclusion that "discourses of gender and sexuality, rather than being merely 'personal' expressions, have important broader political ramifications and effects in the Dominican Republic" (139).

Barceló con hielo does gesture to an opening in gender norms from one generation to another, a signal perhaps of how repressive modes of conduct in Dominican culture might change. Sergio expresses a sense of relief knowing that a lifetime of shouting, surveillance, and physical abuse was not brought on by something he or Dennis had done. He also feels relieved discovering his father had emotions of which he was never aware. He states:

"Yo pensaba tú te había muerto hace tiempo. Que no había na' ahí. Y mírame eto . . . Ahí dentro hay de to.' Bien vivo que tú 'tá. To' esa' otra' cosa' . . . Me la tragaré, no me la tragaré . . .¿Qué se yo? Pero papi, que tú te sonreíte como te 'taba sonriendo ahí. Que tú quisiste a alguien tan bonito así . . . Con tanto amor. Que tú tiene la CAPACIDÁ.' Eso me da' alivio" (261) ("I thought you died a long time ago, pop. But look at this . . . You are most definitely alive. All that other stuff . . . I'll accept it, I won't accept it . . . I don't even know. But, dad, the smile I just saw . . . that you loved somebody so much . . . That you have the CAPACITY. That's . . . a relief"; 125). At the end of *Barceló con hielo*, the ghost of Balaguer has been banished, and the three men admire the sunset from their fire escape. Sergio sketches a portrait of Dennis without the usual attack from his father, and Nino belts out, "Sin remedio," his song with Jaston, without Dennis mocking the old-time bolero.

Closing the story on a note of artistic creation and camaraderie contrasts with the play's opening line, uttered by Nino: "Caramba . . . cuanto silencio," (157) ("So quiet"; 24). I link the notion of silence to one of Rodríguez's epigraphs to the play, a quote by Orlando Martínez Howley, a Balaguer critic and left-wing journalist murdered in the 1970s. Martínez Howley warned, "Si el silencio, sobre todo el auto impuesto, vuelve a expandirse entre nosotros, estamos perdidos. Irremisiblemente perdidos" (147) ("If silence, especially self-imposed silence, grows among us again, we're lost. Irretrievably lost"; 14). In this past decade, pieces like *Barceló con hielo* and other forms of memory work have begun to probe the social and political consequences of silencing.[18] The act of remembering Balaguer in Rodríguez's play acknowledges his haunting presence in the Dominican collective memory. Nino's silence—his sexual orientation and the political motivation of his migration—is broken in a cathartic fashion. By contrast, near the end of *Barceló con hielo*, after Nino recalls and narrates Balaguer's funeral, the statesman repeats the very same line: "Caramba . . . Cuanto silencio (266) ("So quiet"; 130). Here, I read "quiet" not as a silencing or a forgetting, but as the abandonment of Balaguer, a tuning out of his ideologies in favor of listening to points of view that have been long marginalized in Dominican culture. This may account for the audience unease I noted during the play in performance. As Liberato's study suggests, memories of Balaguer are quite divided. On the one hand, some Dominicans employ a narrative of exceptionalism in which they recall Balaguer as a superior and honest leader who helped solidify democracy and stimulated economic progress, while others may challenge this narrative by remembering the corruption, repression, and terror associated with his efforts to monopolize power (Liberato 2–4). *Barceló con hielo* represents the latter position and allows the audience to confront not only the

3.3. The cast of *Barceló con hielo*. Photo credit: Michael Palma Mir.

country's violent political past but also notions of masculinity that have naturalized patterns of political and social relation based on authoritarianism.

Family Secrets in *La luz de un cigarillo*

By contrast to the male-centered *Barceló con hielo*, *La luz de un cigarillo* features a trio of memorable female characters in its exploration of a transnational family tree that undermines the patriarchal model of heterosexist nationalism. In the play, the death of a father (Nino) reunites a mother (Luz) and son (Julio César) for a tense visit that explores unconditional love. Two secrets—first, that the mother hid from her son the fact that his father never legally acknowledged him, and, second, that the son is gay—create the dramatic tension of the piece. Luz and Julio César are first- and second-generation immigrants firmly planted in the United States, and although neither is involved in the concrete practices that sustain a Dominican transnational social field, their framework of identity is Dominican. As a young, single parent, Luz's focus during Julio César's childhood was to establish a place in American society for herself and her son. Yet the play shows a transnational orientation through the family's strong affective ties with the homeland and the enactment of the Dominican practice of silencing of nonnormative sexualities. Just as Nino's bitterness and oppressive behavior was fueled by the social mores that sustain Dominican authoritarianism, Luz's loneliness and estrangement from her son can be attributed to her homophobia.

Luz is a complex portrait of a Latina mother. She beams with pride over Julio César, her handsome, grown son, endlessly prepares food for him, and chastises him for distancing himself from her. However, she never depended on her son to negotiate the complexities of immigrant life in New York City. Luz came to the United States with little education, learned English, worked in factories to provide for her son, and earned her US citizenship while raising him on her own.[19] Luz smokes cigarettes, speaks Dominicanyork Spanish, frequently curses, and in one humorous and raunchy scene, discusses middle-aged sexuality with her sister. She also makes deeply homophobic statements and nags her son to get married, have a family, and find a "real" job. She cannot understand his passion for the theater or truly appreciate his ability to perform Shakespeare. Thus, from her son's perspective, Luz is closeminded, ignorant, and provincial. They are ultimately estranged; Julio César lives in Dallas and this is his first return in five years. When Julio César offers to help Luz during his next visit, she retorts: "De aquí a que tú regrese 'toy yo siete metro bajo tierra. Y yo mima arreglo mi cosa. To' la vaina que necesito 'tan aquí mismo, en éta cuatro parede" (37) ("By the time you come back I'll be six feet under. It's okay. I can take care of my own things. Got everything I need right here within these four walls"; 35).

The stage directions and the character's voiced perceptions of the domestic space in *La luz de un cigarillo* create character subjectivity and help develop the dramatic conflicts. Within the walls that comprise her small and stifling hot efficiency apartment, Luz's crammed belongings are perfectly organized in a system likened by the stage directions to a jigsaw puzzle that can only be solved by her (34; 33). For Julio, who grew up with his mother in this one-room apartment, the space simultaneously elicits warm childhood memories and a desire to flee. While listening to boleros and eating the Dominican national stew, *sancocho*, the characters recall the music, movies, and telenovelas of Julio César's childhood. The recollections invoke artists and cuisine from all over the Hispanic Caribbean and Mexico, reminding us that the largest waves of Dominican migrants entered the United States when major urban centers were already global Latino spaces. In this way,

Luz's domestic space does not represent a retreat into nationalist nostalgia. But now that Julio César has grown up and left and her Latino neighbors are being pushed out by gentrification, Luz is increasingly isolated and vulnerable. The enclosed space of the home is suggestive of both mother and son locked in different comfort zones, unwilling to venture out.

Luz, for example, uses working seven days a week as an elder caretaker as an excuse for never visiting her son in Texas. In addition, unlike many Dominicans on a transnational loop, she has not returned to the Dominican Republic in fifteen years. Whereas her free-spirited sister, Divina, makes periodic visits home and cherishes her connection with the Dominican countryside, Luz rejects any attachment to the homeland. For Luz, the island represents a dirty *campo* (countryside) with burdensome relatives who expect her financial help. Furthermore, the sisters have competing memories of their home country: Luz remembers humidity, blackouts, polluted water, and reckless drivers, while Divina remembers family reunification scenes in the airport, relaxing at the beach, and local cuisine (70–71; 59–60). Julio César has happy memories of living with Divina in the Dominican Republic during a time when Luz struggled to get her financial affairs in order in New York City. Thus, part of Luz's rejection of her birthplace stems from her envy of the close relationship that developed between her sister and her son. Julio César calls Divina weekly and his mother only rarely. Just as Luz feels cut off from Julio César, Divina points out that the family back home feels disconnected from Luz. It takes Divina's insights and her son's return visit for Luz to face the reality that her stifling apartment and the daily grind of her work routine have become part of a system of self-defense that has protected her from facing certain truths, such as the sexual orientation and illegitimacy of her son.

These secrets have driven Luz and Julio César apart, but so has their different experiences as immigrants. Luz's lack of nostalgia for the Dominican Republic and her pride in gaining US citizenship does not set up the kind of first- and second-generation conflict seen in earlier Latino plays about migration. Both mother and son are Dominicanyorks firmly planted in an American life that continues to remain connected with the home country. Luz's comment, "Uno na' ma' viene aquí, coño, a pasa' trabajo. Fajao trabajando to' lo día y lo chele se le van a uno como si na.' Te digo a ti . . . La promesa de ete país son poco lo que la difrutan" (21) ("You come here, work like a dog and barely have anything to show for it. I'm telling you . . . only a select few enjoy the promises of this supposed land of the free"; 23), however, underscores the limitations confronted by first generation immigrants. Her hard work and sacrifice enabled Julio César to attain a post-secondary education that has made further upward movement on the socioeconomic ladder possible for him, but not necessarily for her. Like Fello and Nino in *Barceló con hielo*, Julio César's educational attainment puts him at odds with his mother. For instance, in her attempt to learn more about his life, Luz asks him about his work and to perform for her. Julio César explains what it means to perform plays by Shakespeare in repertory, to which Luz replies, "Repe-who?" (42) and humorously repeats the famous dramatist's name as "Chupacabras" (43) and "Chancleta" (43).[20] These moments, and several others, signal the social differences between mother and son and provoke gentle laughter in the audience. By contrast, audiences are likely to cringe when Julio César, wounded by Luz's inability to accept his sexual orientation, lashes out: "¡La vida na' má no e' la televisión, la maldita funda plástica y fotos del Papa! Edúcate, mujer. ¡No sea tan bruta! (103) ("Life is not just television, plastic bags, and pictures of the Pope! Get an education, woman. Stop being so fucking stupid"; 83). The stupidity Julio César alludes to is the stubborn adherence to heterosexism in Dominican culture that has supported authoritarian models of political and social relation. Ultimately, Luz cannot simply enjoy the sample performance she requested, since she is uncomfortable with her son working in what is stereotyped as a gay-friendly profession. She questions his role as Oberon, "king of the fairies," and wonders out loud why he didn't become a teacher (47; 43).

The question of Luz's knowledge of her son's sexual orientation is the most intriguing and novel aspect of the play. In his book *Tacit Subjects: Belonging and Same-Sex Desire among Dominican Immigrant Men* Carlos Decena describes the dynamic of broaching the topic of male homosexuality in Dominican culture as tacit. He uses the grammatical metaphor of the *sujeto tácito*, which is the subject that "is not spoken but that can be ascertained through the conjugation of the verb in a sentence" to describe how homosexual Dominican men perform their sexual identity (19). Julio César's homosexuality is knowable in a tacit way to the people close to him, which is very much in line with Decena's ethnographic research in which men "described their sexuality as something present yet not remarked upon, something understood yet not stated, something intuited yet uncertain, something known yet not approached by either person in a given exchange" (18). Decena's analysis of Dominican male sexual identity suggests that the narrative of disclosure should not be held as the standard for all cultures. In that vein, *Ashes* dramatizes the complexities of the open secret of Julio César's sexuality and can only be viewed as a "coming out" play in a uniquely unspoken way. At turns provocative and protective, Luz comes to understand the truth of Julio César's sexuality without an admission on his part.

Scenes of female camaraderie between Luz and her Mexican neighbor, Lydia, and Luz and her sister, Divina, provide comic moments in the play, but they also bring into focus how women bond over homophobia. On the one hand, the play affords Luz, a middle-aged mother, a sex life, which is often repressed in patriarchal cultures that promote women as nonsexual maternal Virgin Mary figures (Melhuus 249). Not only does Luz have a sexual partner, she has no interest in giving up her independence by marrying him. Divina has an extended, hilarious response to the news that her sister is sexually active that includes trying to find out the degree of sexual satisfaction Luz has achieved:

> DIVINA: ¡AJÁ! ¡Dímelo tigresa!
>
> LUZ: ¡Qué no!
>
> DIVINA: ¿Ya tú lo 'tá llamando "papi"?
>
> LUZ: ¿Qué?
>
> DIVINA: Porque si ya tú lo llama papi, eso quiere decir que—
>
> LUZ: Pero qué lo que tú 'ta—
>
> DIVINA: ¡Ay papi, ay papi, ay papi! (75).
>
> *DIVINA: AHA! I want details! Locations, number of times, reviews . . .*
>
> *LUZ: No!*
>
> *DIVINA: Are you calling him "papi" yet?*
>
> *LUZ: What?*
>
> *DIVINA: 'Cause if you're calling him papi, you know what that means . . .*
>
> *LUZ: What are you—*
>
> *DIVINA: Ay papi, ay papi, ay papi!* (63).

This unusually frank treatment of female sexual pleasure contrasts with the silencing of Julio César's sexual orientation. As de Moya observes, women are key players in enforcing gender conformity: "From ancient times in the Dominican Republic, women have been seen as playing a pivotal role in the cultural transmission of gender anxiety and homophobia to younger generations" (72). Luz and her neighbor Lydia are bound together by their gay sons (Lydia's has died of AIDs) and their homophobia. Lydia's sole interest, "Oye, ¿ya tienes novia?" (27) ("Where's the girlfriend?" 28), is to ascertain if Julio César has a girlfriend. Speculating "Un muchacho tan guapo como tú me imagino que tiene filas de admiradoras" (28) ("I bet you have lines of women fighting for you"; 28) reinforces the expected promiscuity of males and promotes heterosexual procreation: "Ya mero mero te da nietos"; (28) ("Ya mero, he's gonna give you grandbabies, qué no?" 28). To a similar effect of pressuring Julio César to perform his expected gender role, Luz counsels

Julio César to tell nosy family members he has been too busy to get married. Even an offhand comment such as when Luz tells her son not to cross his legs is representative of a "stereotyped and paranoid (totalitarian) etiquette of gendering both the verbal and non-verbal behavior of young boys away from 'femininity'" (de Moya 72).[21] The ostensibly loving and supportive motherly behaviors displayed by Lydia and Luz are a constant sign of their rejection of nonnormative sexualities.

In addition to the everyday gender work performed by mothers to stifle the threat of their sons' possible nonhegemonic masculinity, Luz makes hurtful, derogatory comments about gays in hopes that Julio César will react and force them to acknowledge what they both already know. She mentions that Lydia's son got what he deserved (his death): "Eso le pasa a la gente por 'tar andando en vagabundería" (18) ("That's what you get for having no shame"; 20). In addition, on two occasions she draws Julio César's attention to what is airing on television to blatantly condemn homosexuality: "Ay, dio,' mira. Dique un show de pájaro. Te digo a ti. Este mundo está perdido" (41) ("Look at that! Some crazy thing about queers. I tell you, this world is going to shit"; 38). She later comments on a news program report on gay marriage: "Mira mira. Dique una balsa e' pato que se quieren casar. Te digo a ti. En este mundo se ve cada horror, verda Julio César" (60) ("Can you believe this? A bunch of faggots that wanna get married. I swear . . . This world is full of all kinds of horrors right, Julio César?" 52). Luz is stymied by the frustration of wanting to know more about Julio César's life and her reluctance to know the truth, thus during his short visit she tries to force the issue by goading him into responding to her insults. His measured responses reveal little about his personal life. Tensions do rise at the end of the first act, suggesting that Luz's jabs are having their intended effect, but his outburst does not challenge her homophobia.

As I have observed, the space of the apartment helps characterize mother and son as closed off to one another and to certain truths. Thus, in the play's climactic confrontation, Julio César has reached his limits with feeling stifled, and his cry to renovate the house constitutes a plea to repair his relationship with this mother:

Julio César sube la ventana y rompe la reja.

JULIO CÉSAR: ¡ARREGLA ETA MALDITA CASA! ¡ESTA FUCKEEN REJA! ETA MALDITA PAREDE!

LUZ: ¡DÉJAME LA CASA TRANQUILA!

DIVINA: ¿PERO MUCHACHO, TÚ 'TÁ LOCO E'?

JULIO CÉSAR: ¡YO NO 'TOY MUERTO! ¡A MÍ TÚ NO ME VA A ENTERRAR! ¡LA QUE 'TA ENTERRÁ EN UNA TUMBA ERE TÚ! (106)

> Julio César runs to the front window. He raises it and breaks the guardrail.
> *JULIO CÉSAR: FIX THIS HOUSE! THESE RAILS! THESE GODDAMN WALLS!*
> *LUZ: LEAVE MY HOUSE ALONE!*
> *DIVINA: MUCHACHO, ARE YOU CRAZY?*
> *JULIO CÉSAR: YOU'RE NOT GONNA BURY ME! YOU'RE THE ONE THAT'S BURIED! WAY FUCKING DEEP!* (85)

The domestic space has served to shelter their secrets, and, more powerfully, the Dominican ideologies of gender and sexuality embodied and reproduced by his mother have "buried" or suppressed his identity. In this exchange, Julio César turns the table and suggests that his mother is "buried" and that she risks ending up isolated and emotionally "dead." Mother and son can only reconnect if they break through the barriers that separate them to confirm what they already know and move forward to repair their home/relationship with that understanding.

While Luz's implicit knowledge of Julio César's sexual orientation creates much of the tension of the drama, it represents only one facet of the mother-and-son relationship examined in *La luz de un cigarillo*. Being raised by a single mother and knowing the sacrifices she made during his childhood have weighed heavily on Julio César, but any guilt he feels is not transformed into expressed gratitude because his mother's rejection of his sexual identity drives them apart. Nevertheless, Julio César's dutiful return for his father's funeral dispels a family myth and ironically underscores his closeness with his mother. When Luz lets slip that it was the father who refused to sign the legal documents that would give his son his surname, Julio César's vision of his mother changes: "Yo pensando que fuiste tú la que no lo había dejado firma [y] te lo repeté. Coño ata te lo admiré. Pero eso na' ma' e' puro cuento" (57–58) ("This whole time I thought it was you who didn't let him sign. I respected that. Christ, even admired it. But it was just lies"; 50). Luz lied by omission to protect her pride and to shield her son from the hurt of knowing that his father never legally acknowledged him. Now, as a young adult, Julio César fully understands the rejection that bound him so tightly to his mother. Consequently, at the end of the play, when Julio César finds a photograph of his parents as a happy couple, he weeps, comforted by knowing that love did bring him into the world.

This cathartic moment, in turn, enables a second one in which mother and son tacitly acknowledge Julio César's sexual identity. In response to Luz's earlier accusation that he may as well be dead to her given how much she knows about his life, Julio César insists, "Yo no estoy muerto mami" ("I'm not dead, Mami"; 90). She replies, "Yo sé. Yo sé. Yo lo sé todo, mijo" (113) ("I know. I know everything, mijo"; 90), tacitly recognizing his secret.

3.4. Mother and son in *La luz de un cigarillo*. Photo credit: Anthony Ruiz.

Further, Luz tells Julio César that she would like to invite his friend over for some Dominican *sancocho*, and he responds by kissing his mother on her forehead (93). The only other words exchanged are Julio César's request for Luz's blessing, which she gives, and we are left with the image of Julio César drifting off to sleep with his head in his mother's lap, watching the fading light of the final cigarette she smokes before bedtime. No verbal admission was needed to confirm what Luz had already intuited.

By acknowledging the resistance to nonnormative sexualities in Dominican culture, confronting family and national conflicts, and highlighting contrasting views of the homeland, Marco Antonio Rodríguez's plays leave open multiple possibilities of the changing ways the characters might define their identities and their relationship with their place of origin and their place of migration. *La luz de un cigarillo* and *Barceló con hielo* are notable for featuring single-parent households and homosexual characters that contest conventional family and kinship constructs, but the plays stop short of imagining the transnational Dominican community as a queer, affiliative set of social practices or political commitments; rather, they remain within the frameworks of common ancestry and filiation that structure traditional diaspora narratives. In this way, Rodríguez's work is linked to the legacies of realist domestic Latino drama that carved a space on the US stages for

Latinos explore their migration and adaptation experiences. Thus, it is no surprise that Rodríguez's adept combination of familiar tropes and milieus with the particularity of the Dominican experience of transnationalism has been met with a positive reception by audiences eager to engage with the stories of today's waves of global migration. The story of return constitutes another, increasingly common narrative in contemporary patterns of circular migration. In the next chapter, women populate the stage and serve as protagonists in plays and performances about the experience of return migration. In these stories, some characters adopt a bifocal lens through which to critically view changing conceptions of gender, family, and home in the homeland and the host land, while others reveal a resistant stance on such cultural transformations.

Chapter 4

"Home Is Where Theatre Is"

Dominican Women's Stories of Return Migration

As suggested in the introductory chapter, despite representing one of the fastest growing populations of Latinos in the United States, a survey of recent literature on Latino playwrights and performers might suggest that Dominicans have yet to make a home in the Latino theater community. However, rather than dwelling on the apparent absence of a playwright or director who might serve as catalyst for a Dominican enclave theater in the United States, this book contends that a transnational approach to Dominican performance brings to light an abundance of plays and performances that take up the theme of Dominican-US migration. This chapter looks at the experience of return migration depicted in plays by four women playwrights and performers. The pieces analyzed—*Por hora y a* Piece-Work (Hourly and Piece Work) (1993) by Elizabeth Ovalle, *Ay Fefa, Where is the Wind?* by Zaida Corniel (1994), *Nuyor/Islas* (New York/Islands) by Chiqui Vicioso (2006), and *Dominicanish* by Josefina Báez (2000)—show that for transnational migrants, "home" can be conceived of as pluri-local and mobile. Likewise, as I have maintained throughout this book, we might consider Dominican theater and performance as a multi-sited transnational practice in which authors, actors, and audiences make temporary homes for displaying bodies and discourses not always recognized by the majoritarian culture of the nation-state.

Along with peoples and cultures on the move, the theater has always crossed local, regional, and national borders. From the more modest reach of itinerant players, community-based theater projects, and experimental intercultural performances, to national theater productions and blockbuster musicals exported internationally, play performances circulate in new social and cultural milieus. What distinguishes contemporary diasporas in the age of rapid movement of bodies, cultures, and, above all, capital, "is the intensity and reciprocity of the ties between emigrant or exiled populations and their countries of origin" (Flores, *Diaspora* 22). To speak of the creation of transnational networks or communities is to map the transmigrant's provisional positioning in their homeland or their homeplace, as a shared, yet multi-sited social field. The cultural work of Dominican theater and performance artists who move between the Dominican Republic and the United States addresses both locations and helps imagine a transnational Dominican community. Juan Flores's study of Hispanic Caribbean return migration, *The Diaspora Strikes Back*, shifts the focus of much transnational analysis from economic remittances, and their social and political consequences on the sending societies, to what he calls "cultural remittances" (44). As Flores notes, a good deal of contemporary migration is characterized by circular "counterstreams" of return migration—physical or socioeconomic, temporary or permanent, forced or optional—to the homelands (39). Flores writes that "by means of return and circulatory migration and multiple conduits of mediated and direct communications, cultural customs and practices, ideological orientations, forms of artistic expression, and ideas of group identity acquired in diaspora settings are remitted to homeland societies" (44). While Flores looks to music and youth culture for examples of cultural remittances, I turn to the specific performance activity of theater, which has yet to appear on the radar screens of most Dominican cultural analyses. As I have noted, theaters and performers travel, and though its cultural remittance may not be as pervasive as the mass market of music and fashion, the performance event offers a unique setting where new styles and ideologies are rehearsed in front of a collective body of people who may, or may not, identify with them.

Staging scenarios of migration amounts to a cultural remittance that exerts pressure to expand notions of national identity. Transnational diaspora life, Flores observes, "necessarily stretches the meaning of national belonging by disengaging it from its presumed territorial and linguistic imperative, and de-centering it in relation to any putative 'core' values or markers of greater or lesser 'authenticity'" (*Diaspora* 45). Studies on migration spanning the humanities and the social sciences have extended the geographic and linguistic boundaries of Dominican national culture and have illuminated the many ways in which the diaspora has contested elitist, Hispanocentric, and paternalistic official constructions of *dominicanidad*. In the field of literary and cultural studies Silvio Torres-Saillant has been an insistent voice in placing migration at the center of the Dominican national imaginary. He argues in *El retorno de las yolas: Ensayos sobre diáspora, democracia y dominicanidad* (The Return of the Yolas: Essays about Diaspora, Democracy and Dominicanness) (1999) that whether or not they voyaged to the United States on rickety boats known as yolas, all Dominican residents abroad are survivors of a perilous journey, a forced migration provoked by the state's failure to provide social and economic security for the clear majority of its population ("Epílogo" 424). Yet the discourse on migration that has emanated from the Dominican Republic has rarely acknowledged state responsibility for the exodus; in fact, this discourse has reacted defensively by portraying migrants, at best, as traitors and, at worst, as stereotyped Dominicanyorks.[1] The "retorno" referred to by Torres-Saillant is not the nostalgic return to the homeland; rather, it is a cultural remittance and a transnational lens through which to view the Dominican Republic and the Dominican community abroad.[2] It is a critical gaze directed at reconceptualizing Dominican identity from the perspective of the lessons learned from the diaspora ("Retorno" 38). I submit that the performance texts *Por hora y a* Piece-Work, *Ay Fefa, Where is the Wind?, Nuyor/Islas,* and *Dominicanish* embody Torres-Saillant's "diasporic perspective" to varying degrees.[3] In what follows, by considering what Alberto Sandoval-Sánchez and Nancy Saporta-Sternbach call the "politics of representation" in the performance of return migration, I will highlight the work's resistance (or acquiescence) to dichotomist nativist/diasporic positions on *dominicanidad.*

The performance pieces, all written and performed by women, constitute examples of Dominican transnational performance not only because they explicitly treat the theme of migration but also because each author's creative process and vision is generated in a social network that spans two nation-states. The transnational character of their work helps explain why these and other playwrights and performers are neither considered central to Dominican national culture nor are included in studies of US Latino theater. Nevertheless, *Stages of Life: Transcultural Performance and Identity in U.S. Latina Theater* by Alberto Sandoval-Sánchez and Nancy Saporta Sternbach provides a useful framework for posing questions about what I call transnational theater. Similar to Jon Rossini's theory of how the art of writing and staging theater can serve to innovate and amend ways of conceiving ethnic identities discussed in chapter 2, the authors of *Stages of Life* call a "politics of representation" the process by which "playwrights dismantle and undo dominant stereotypical representations at the same time that they revise and rearticulate new ways of seeing" (4). In the same way Torres-Saillant's diasporic perspective creates a space for countering negative representations of Dominican migrant identity, the plays reveal a complex portrait of the Dominican migrant community by showing how the migrant community is comprised of men and women from various regions and social backgrounds who have migrated for different reasons at discrete historical junctures, and who have lived the diaspora in diverse ways: as ethnic enclaves in the Northeast, as returnees to the Dominican Republic, and as Dominican migrants who continue to circulate.

The context of transnationalism and globalization problematizes the understanding of migration as a one-way process of emigration (leaving) and immigration (arriving) and invites analysis of patterns of circular migration. The migration studies scholar Anders H. Stefansson writes that in the context of return migration, "The stress on symbolic homelands as sources of diasporic identity has given way to a focus on the many concrete global ties that immigrants often maintain with their countries of origin" (7), and he suggests that earlier conceptualizations of one-way migration neglect the practice of homecoming (5). In the following analyses, I look at the cultural encounters experienced when the protagonist either returns to her homeland permanently or at least for a short-stay visit. The common denominators of Chicano, Puerto Rican, and Cuban theaters identified by Sandoval-Sánchez and Saporta Sternbach—"migration, nostalgia, ethnic memory, transcultural identity and home" (48)—are salient in Dominican theater as well, though in response to its own migration experience. The return event depicted in the plays analyzed here can be understood as one of the "stages of life" outlined in the authors' theory of transcultural subjectivity. They argue that "at specific moments of cultural crisis, identities are reevaluated, revised, reformed, and transformed," and that the ongoing process of negotiating identity represents the core dramatic action in Latina theater and solo performance (9). Nonetheless, in the framework of transnationalism, the concepts of home and return must be employed differently. Sandoval-Sánchez and Saporta Sternbach's study speaks to earlier migration narratives of assimilation and multiculturalism/diaspora. For example, in *Stages of Life* the authors discuss the theme of home: "The search for 'home' is crucial in the process of establishing a bilingual, bicultural Latina/o identity, both for new immigrants as well as for those generations born on the mainland of the U.S. Since the 1980s, in the theater, as in other literary genres, the mythical return to the homeland becomes a rude awakening from those expected utopian or imaginary spaces. This painful but necessary process of returning to one's ethnic and cultural roots as well as geographical origin helps to consolidate and establish a Latina transcultural identity" (48). To establish a bicultural and bilingual home in the United States, however much this transcultural identity is continually negotiated, represents a sort of stop point or denouement to the drama of identity. Return migration, by contrast, extends this drama and multiplies homes and identities. Upon return, the identity and home forged in the United States is scrutinized from the perspective of Dominican national culture; conversely, the returnee evaluates what once was home, and what it means to remake a home there.

Gender informs migration as well, and as Ramona Hernández and Anthony Stevens-Acevedo observe in their overview of the field of Dominican studies, "Women are the backbone of the Dominican community in the U.S.," because they are the first to migrate, a significant portion serve as head of their families, and many become grassroots leaders in their communities (13). The female protagonism of the plays and performances studied here heightens awareness of the Dominicanyork label as a masculinist construction. Unlike the images of young Dominican men returning to the Dominican Republic in caskets, victims of drug violence disseminated by the press and popular films such as *Nueba Yol*, in the theatrical portrayals of return migration the outcomes for the female protagonists are open-ended. As the scholarship in *Migrations and Mobilities: Citizenship, Borders, and Gender* indicates, women's movement across borders are rarely a question of single individual; rather, her mobility constitutes "a nodal point in a network of relationships" that involves dependents and partners (Benhabib and Resnik 13). The motives for migrating and returning are conditioned by both this network of relationships and US-Dominican Republic economic interdependencies. Similarly, women's conceptions of their social and economic roles are informed by family relationships and by different notions of gender roles in both societies. Homecomings, notes Stefansson, "often contains elements for rupture, surprise, and perhaps, disillusionment" (4). The affective power of this social scenario inevitably evokes theatrical metaphors such as the "drama of return." Undoubtedly, shifting understandings of gender roles at home and in the diaspora add to these tensions.

Por hora y a Piece-Work: An Exilic Perspective

Elizabeth Ovalle's social realist drama *Por hora y a* Piece-Work plays out the anxieties regarding the unprecedented growth in Dominican migration during the 1990s.[4] In many ways, the play's account of the struggles of Dominican laborers in New York City exemplifies the negative islander view of the diaspora described by Torres-Saillant in his essay "El retorno de las yolas": "La mirilla a través de la cual se nos ve, privilegia una narrativa marcada por la delincuencia, la precariedad, y los demás males implícitos en la marginalidad social. Rara vez dicha mirilla se fija en la lucha denodada de la diáspora por enaltecer su dignidad humana" ("We are seen through a vantage point that privileges a narrative marked by the delinquency, precariousness, and other evils implicit in social marginality. This view is rarely focused on the diaspora's determined struggle to extol its human dignity"; 43).[5] *Por hora y a* Piece-Work premiered in Santo Domingo in 1994, a year after Ovalle had returned from a four-year stay in New York City, where, like many other compatriots, she held working-class jobs in supermarkets and factories, and, in effect, serves for Santo Domingo audiences as a cautionary tale that details the dangers of abandoning the homeland. The jury awarding the prestigious Casa de Teatro prize seems to have been receptive to this message, for it awarded the play first place in its annual competition.[6]

The dramatic action takes place in a work space and, at first glance, seems to be about arrival and adaptation rather than return, because it tells the story of a recently arrived Dominican campesina named Juana who takes a job at a garment factory in New York City.[7] The workers are Dominican, but there is little sense of solidarity; rather, Juana discovers a hierarchy based on their regional origins and mode of arrival, length of time in the United States, and legal status. In this regard, *Por hora y a* Piece-Work does highlight the complexity of Dominican migrants as social group. Through the workers' daily conversations, we intuit that the burden of survival erodes most efforts at building camaraderie. They speak of New York City as a hostile and dangerous urban space, of the ways to acquire legal status and to maneuver the welfare system, and of the pressures to perform at work, where the boss makes sexual advances and constantly threatens to impose sweatshop conditions by paying by the piece rather than by the hour. The workers also emphasize the struggle to subsist in New York City, let alone the imperative to provide material goods for family back in the Dominican Republic and save enough money to be reunited, whether in the United States or by returning to the island.

Through the factory environment created by stage objects and the idiosyncratic speech of over ten working-class Dominican employees, Ovalle creates a recognizable reality for audiences. The stage directions note that there should be no built set, only the machines and objects used in the manufacture of garments (246). Dominican music plays at varying volumes throughout, and time regulating the daily routine of the workers is marked by the sound of sirens and the act of punching into the time clock, as well as, in two instances, lowered stage lighting to signify the passage of more than a day of time. The one-act play is faithful to realism in drawing attention to the working conditions in manufacturing plants, but it loses some credibility in the overwhelming number of "realistic" details that cast migration in a strongly negative light and its relative silence on the social structures and economic processes that create the conditions for migration.[8]

For example, Ovalle includes a myriad of details to characterize the space of the factory as violent. The factory, a metonym for New York City, helps to naturalize the notion that Dominicanyorks are inherently dangerous. The factory is filled with the verbal aggression and jealous behaviors committed by males against other males, males against females, and females against females, making for a workplace filled with psychological and physical violence. A verbal dispute between Capitaleña, Freddy, and Manuel escalates when Freddy pulls a knife, grabs Capitaleña by the throat, pushes her up against the wall *como un animal* (like an animal), and says: "Mira mujercita de cabaret, la próxima vez te cuida tu lengua" ("Look little cabaret dancer, next time you'll watch your tongue"; 251). Seconds after this denigrating assault, the characters' attention is averted to shots ringing out below in the street:

> MANUEL: Ay, mataron a Marcelo, está tirado en la acera. ¡Cuánta sangre!, corra Sr. Recio.
> AÍDA: (*De pie, junto a otras personas mirando. Mientras el señor Recio corre al auxilio de su hermano.*) ¡Ese no se salvaba, demasiados líos con drogas, no se parecen en nada eso dos hermanos, qué diferentes!, el que se mete en drogas eso es lo que le espera. (252)

> *MANUEL: Ay, they killed Marcelo, he's down on the sidewalk. So much blood! Run, Mr. Recio.*
> *AÍDA:* (Standing next to the others, watching. Meanwhile, Mr. Recio runs to help his brother.) *He won't live, too many troubles with drugs! Those brothers don't seem at all alike, how different they are! This is what happens when you get mixed up in drugs.*

The individualistic quest for economic security dehumanizes the Dominican characters, and they live and die like animals. In the theater, the audience does not see the lifeless body on the sidewalk, but Manuel's exclamation about the quantity of blood underlines an image that audience members have already seen repeatedly on the front page of any number of island newspapers. The play thus reiterates the narrative of Dominicans in New York City falling prey to delinquency and violence.

In its damning portrayal of the experience of migration, *Por hora y a* Piece-Work generates little empathy and identification with the characters. The male figures are underdeveloped and simply reify stereotypical Dominican masculine types. These characters include Sr. Recio, the abusive social-climber boss, the requisite drug dealer shot in front of the factory; the intellectually empty and style-conscious *cadenú*/Dominicanyork, Manuel; and the effeminate lottery seller, Fifo, whose gay identity is signaled by his difference. Manuel adds some levity to *Por hora y a* Piece-Work by intervening mainly by singing his lines to an American-style rock music beat: "Quisiera ir a la escuela a aprender, pero quiero dinero, dinero, dinero: camisa ancha, pantalones jean, tenis altos y un corte a lo moderno, con eso soy feliz" ("I'd like to go to school to learn, but I want money, money, money: a wide-neck shirt, jeans, high tops and a hip haircut, and with this I'm happy"; 256).

With his *cadena de gofille* (gold-fill chain) Manuel personifies the *cadenú*, the ostentatious Dominicanyork stereotype. Through Manuel, Ovalle suggests that the access to education many cite as a motivating factor in leaving the homeland becomes a dream perverted by the materialistic values acquired in the host land. The play's male characters are precisely the types stigmatized in island discourses that question their conformity with traditional Dominican values, and, who, in a Santo Domingo theater might be met with misgivings or even derisive laughter. By contrast, even though the female characters appear equally one-dimensional, the problems they discuss might be received with a measure of sympathy.

Much of the women's dialogue about their hardships rings true, but *Por hora y a* Piece-Work does not allow for a portrayal of an honest, hardworking immigrant character. The characters initially inspire pity because they work long hours for wages that are insufficient to support their families. As Aída's lament suggests, they sacrifice their lives and happiness so that their children can grow up in the United States: "No, no, no soporto trabajar, trabajar 20 años de mi vida, trabajando sin parar, quiero irme, quiero irme, no puedo, no tengo nada ni aquí ni allá" ("No, no, no I can't bear working, working 20 years of my life, working nonstop, I want to leave, I want to leave, I can't, I don't have anything here nor there"; 255–56). The repeat references to their illegal status and strategies for scamming the welfare system, however, characterizes them as dishonest. The women mention friends getting by in households supported by welfare subsidies combined with income gained in the drug trade (249). Aída could become a naturalized citizen, but she prefers to remain illegal so she does not have to report her earnings. Moreover, Aída depends on her salary and the taxpayer-funded welfare programs that support her US-born "anchor" babies: "Voy a tratar de coger toda la ayuda que me dé el gobierno" ("I'm going to try to get all the help government will give me"; 255), and she plans to have another baby with *cualquiera* (whoever) to continue receiving benefits. These strategies are real, and so is the socioeconomic vulnerability of the characters, but the play lacks realism in leaving out any suggestion of undocumented female workers using honorable tactics to survive.[9]

Within the logic of *Por hora y a* Piece-Work, Aída and the cadre of female factory workers represent what Juana will become, thus her deportation is cast as a favorable outcome. The theme of return enters at the play's climax, when migration officers seize the factory and deport the undocumented workers. This is a melodramatic deus ex machina moment, since Juana's young daughters, who had just arrived from the Dominican Republic to be reunited with their mother, instantly reject New York City and wish to return home: "Allá está mi abuelita, mi gato Tito, la gallina jabá y hasta una hortaliza que hice con mamá, me gusta más allá, quiero estar allá, allá" ("My grandmother, my cat, Tito, and our hen, and even a garden I made with my mom is over there; I like it better there, I want to be over there, there"; 261). At this crisis moment, *allá* (the Dominican Republic) signifies family, land, and a whole host of values that contrast with what the play has presented as the world of *aquí* (New York City). Like her daughters, Juana identifies with the land: "Mire yo soy muy pobre aquí y en mi campo, pero por lo menos que si sembraba 10 matas de batata, iba a conseguir 50 batatas y son mías" ("Look, I'm very poor here and in my country, but at least if I planted 10 bunches of sweet potatoes, I would get 50 sweet potatoes, and they were mine"; 262). For Juana, deportation is a happy outcome, as it means free tickets home (and the knowledge that her abusive boss will be punished for employing undocumented workers). The return in *Por hora y a* Piece-Work marks a moment of cultural crisis in which the protagonist disidentifies with adopting a diasporic identity and reaffirms traditional constructions of *dominicanidad* by linking territory and authenticity. The untold story is how Juana and her daughters experience reterritorialization. On the one hand, one might assume that the family's short-lived experience in New York City spared them from the stigma of returning to the Dominican Republic with *costumbres* (customs) acquired abroad. On the other hand, one could consider the possible gains in Juana's short sojourn in New York City. In his review of Francesco Cerase's typologies of return migration, Flores writes that a "return of innovation" would signify a returnee who would carry social change—values, lessons, skills—back home to help resolve problems in the sending country (*Diaspora* 35). I question whether Juana would have this kind of "successful" return. The city/country binary constructed by *Por hora y a* Piece-Work highlights the utopian return to the land and omits any suggestion of how a single mother's return migration to a poor, rural, and patriarchal world might signify a loss in whatever small social gains Juana achieved in New York City. Rather than reading *Por hora y a* Piece-Work as having a happy conclusion, we might ask: Will the accumulation of cultural or economic capital during her brief stay equip Juana to constructively confront the conditions that forced her original migration? That is, will Juana's return migration be simply a stopping point on a migration circuit fueled by economic inequities? Home, for Juana and today's global migrants, may never be an enduring haven.

Lorgia García-Peña argues that the desire to return differentiates the exilic and diasporic perspectives of Dominican writers located outside of the island and that "the poetics of *dominicanidad ausente* breaks away from the nostalgic trope of migration narratives in order to propose a transnational critique of the relationship between power, the production of history, and the construction of (trans)national citizenship and identities" (174).[10] *Por hora y a* Piece-Work embodies an exilic perspective, while the remaining plays examined in this chapter display a diasporic poetics in their critical engagement with migrant identities. These plays also depart from the realism of Ovalle's ensemble drama by using solo performances, which for Sandoval-Sánchez and Saporta Sternbach "stage to the fullest Latinas' subjectivities-in-process in relation to given historical formations and discursive locations" (95). I argue that in these pieces, the already complex historical formations and discursive locations of transnational subjects are further complicated by the experience of return. In the contemporary context of transnationalism and globalization, whether or not there is a nostalgic desire of return, the possibility of return exists due to the unequal power relationships that continue to catalyze global migration. Thus, in the diasporic transnational performance pieces I analyze, the question of return remains and complicates the exilic-diasporic dichotomy.

Arrival in *Ay Fefa, Where is the Wind?*

While Ovalle's *Por hora y a* Piece-Work is directed to an island audience and includes only a few phrases of heavily Spanish-accented English, Zaida Corniel's bilingual poetic monologue, *Ay Fefa, Where is the Wind?*, was performed in New York City to a primarily English-speaking audience. *Ay Fefa* takes the theme of return a step further than *Por hora y a* Piece-Work and dramatizes the very moment of arrival home after a thirty-year absence.[11] The return scenario unfolds as the expected welcome home party for Fefa fails to materialize and she is left alone to deliver a poignant and increasingly inebriated monologue in which she grapples with the reality that even at "home," she finds herself in a state of cultural limbo. This liminal state is reinforced by the bare stage, which features a set of trunks, and, at one point, a doll house. "Home" has become as portable and transient as luggage, and both the trunks stuffed with material goods and the doll house signify the economic forces and material desires moving mass numbers of people around the world.[12] Throughout the monologue, Fefa's mother intermittently joins her onstage, repeatedly asking in Spanish if she has found the wind. The mother has died, and Fefa is tormented by not having returned to the Dominican Republic before her death. In *Ay Fefa*, there is to be no reunion with the mother, a figure for the *madre patria*.

Dominican transnational theater has served to counter reductionist portraits of the Dominican migration in political and media discourse because the fictional stories it stages juxtapose a myriad of experiences that contradict one-note stereotypes. For example, Fefa's reasons for migrating and her urban and middle-class origins contrast with Juana's poor rural background and desperate and illegal journey to the United States. The image of young Fefa running in pursuit of the wind with her arms making a windmill motion establishes her as a quixotic dreamer: "Cuando era niña acostumbraba a jugar con el viento. Mis brazos siempre buscaban otros espacios y ellos cortaban el aire como remolinos" ("When I was little I used to play with the wind. My arms were always looking for other spaces and they cut the air like windmills"; 8). However, Fefa's migration story is less of a pursuit of her personal dreams than it is a forced journey. We learn that Fefa was the daughter of a colonel under Trujillo and that she never knew him. He was "a good man in bad times" (3), and we can surmise that he was killed by the regime, since Fefa's mother was adamant about sending her away after 1965 civil war and US military intervention.[13] During the conflict, the constitutionalists who supported the democratically elected government of Juan Bosch were defeated by the US-backed conservative forces, allowing Trujillo's former right-hand man, Joaquín Balaguer, to rise to power. Migration, for the moment, became an outlet for ridding the country of dissidents. The play thus serves to remind spectators that the Dominican diaspora is very much linked to US imperialism.[14] The push of the political crisis was a trigger in Fefa's migration, but the pull of economic opportunity was strong as well. Along with her desire to protect her daughter, the mother and daughter were swayed by stories of the fast-paced modernity and material abundance of New York City. A family friend who migrated would visit and "she brought that smell of new clothes, new radios, new Barbie dolls. . . . We called it the smell of Nueva York. Then I knew why they call it New York and I wanted to go where everything was new" (5).

The different socioeconomic origins of Juana and Fefa, however, matters little in the eyes of the US labor market. Both women face the challenges of being single mothers and manual workers in factories. In the United States, Fefa's aspirations of becoming a singer quickly become sidetracked by the reality of supporting two sons on her own, but she does achieve financial security by working at a factory that makes pacifiers. The monotonous job of checking the quality of pacifiers invades her nocturnal dreams. In one, enormous pacifiers overtake her room and melt: "My breath was getting short. I screamed mamá, mamá. Then a pacifier shut me off" (9). The link between pacifiers and maternal sustenance is significant. Fefa is haunted by being sent away by her mother—"I lived your dream, I did it!" (3)—and she is devastated that her mother thought "her future, her Green Card" (3) was more important than reuniting with family. Fefa was forced to break with the mother/land, and the economic success she achieved could serve only as a pacifier, or a false mother that satiates the desire for money but does not nourish the soul.

By depicting a fraught personal and political relationship with the homeland and using poetic images, Corniel's play achieves a sense of emotional poignancy. Another detail that rings true in *Ay Fefa* is its engagement with the theme of race, a theme that is virtually absent in Ovalle's play, even though it is inseparable from discourses of *dominicanidad* and the experience of migration.[15] The play evokes race through music and references to Afro-Dominican religiosity. A percussionist plays a classic merengue during Fefa's arrival at the airport and again during a scene in which she becomes possessed by *misterio*, or a spirit from Dominican voodoo, known as *Las 21 Divisiones*. García-Peña argues that "Afro-religious practices such as spiritual possession contest hegemonic understandings of Dominicanidad at home and abroad by making visible the too-often silenced bodies of Dominican racialized subjects. Through Afro-religiosity, artists, particularly diasporic writers, are finding a diction that allows them to interpellate the Hispanophile version of Dominican history, reimagining an *other* truth that can finally confront the passivity and silencing of hegemonic texts" (83). In the same vein, Bony Raposo, the musician who played the percussionist in the performance, developed the musical group La 21 División in New York City with the express purpose of teaching young Dominicans in the diaspora about rural Afro-Dominican traditions (Austerlitz). The visual presence of the figure of the drummer and the sounds of Afro-Caribbean rhythms help develop the play's inclusive understanding of *dominicanidad*. As García-Peña notes, this component of national culture has long been silenced by a national archive that excludes and erases blackness. Scaling the socioeconomic ladder has long been a means of racial "whitening" in Latin America and the Caribbean. In the play, the erasure of blackness is seen in Fefa's newly perceived whiteness. Playing the part of her friends (who never appear onstage for the welcome party), the friend, voiced by Fefa, notes how much she's changed: "Pero hasta the color, you are so white that you look American. Yes, the color. I told you that in Nueva York people turned white" (8). Many would argue that it is quite the opposite. In this view, Dominicans discover their blackness in the diaspora, in a contradictory pull between the freedom from dominant homeland notions of national identity that deny blackness and a dichotomist conception of the race in the United States that perceives Dominicans as black. Indeed, Torres-Saillant asks whether "upholding a sense of racial identity that stems from the imposition of one's environment can in the end be considered liberating" (*Introduction* 54). Corniel's story of return migration makes spectators aware of the complexities of racial identifications for Dominicans back at home and abroad.

Although Fefa was not able to satisfy her personal dreams—"I think that my arms could not find the right wind" (9)—she is able to retire in the Dominican Republic comfortably. As she sits alone and contemplates the contents of a doll house, however, we wonder if achieving material success was worth the crisis of identity Fefa now faces. From the moment Fefa lands in Santo Domingo, it is evident that she is not perceived as Dominican: a customs officer tells her she does not look very Dominican, a money changer immediately identifies her as someone with dollars to change, and a taxi driver tries to overcharge her as though she were a foreigner. The airport money changer calls, "Change, change, change. Cambio de dólares, cambio dólares. Change, change, change. Cambio dólares, cambio dólares. I had arrived." (6) Literally, Fefa had arrived at the airport, but the fact that she is singled out as someone with dollars suggests she's perceived as someone who "has arrived," or has capital. Fefa's socioeconomic success, nevertheless, comes with the price of "change" in the sense that neither the migrant nor the world spaces she has occupied have remained static. The overwhelming disorientation and anonymity Fefa feels is like an immigrant arriving in a new land: "I was confused among the crowds that were waiting for families and friends. I was looking for a familiar face but there were too many faces and I didn't recognize any of them. Nobody seemed to know me" (6). While Fefa may insist that spiritually she never left the Dominican Republic and that she has not changed, the hurt of not being welcomed home launches her into adopting an outsider perspective: "Mierda, this is what you call a Banana Republic. I don't know why I have to come back. I must be crazy when I thought about this. Here people don't respect the line, the traffic is a mess, black outs all the time. I better go back where I came from" (10). Fefa is forced to reassess what was previously a given, that "home" is identified with land and birthplace.

Too often transnational identity is invoked to commend nomadic and hybrid identities without recognizing the vulnerability of this identity position with respect to the dominant cultures in the sending and receiving nation-states.[16] Fefa is perceived as a foreigner *aquí* and *allá*. She feels estranged from her American-born sons and feels she was not able to raise them "properly"—that is, within the norms of traditional Dominican masculinity: "My boys became little generals without an island, the only thing they did was hang out at the corner with their friends. I couldn't control them" (3). Fefa's sons fail to understand that she has worked her entire adult life—first, to provide for them, and, second, to realize her goal of returning home—and they refer to the furniture and household items she has collected to bring with her as "junk" (8). When her elder son asks about his origins, she assures him that he is American, but she asks herself, "Am I American?" (7) and feels distanced when she would hear them talking: "I would say to myself: this is my family. They are speaking another language, but this is my family. And I felt strange" (7).

Now, having returned with no welcome and feeling estranged from her homeland as well, Fefa sarcastically remembers the photo booth picture she took at the airport to remember "this glorious trip: the return to your motherland" (10). She nearly missed her plane waiting for the photo, which never came out of the machine. This telling detail speaks to Fefa's fragile sense of identity. Without the photo to confirm her existence, it is as though she has left no trace in either of her life spaces. The anonymity and loneliness Fefa felt in New York City—receiving a telephone message, she says, "is like an invitation not to kill yourself" (6)—turns out to be similar Santo Domingo. At the end of *Ay Fefa*, the phone, a lifeline of communication, rings, and Fefa answers, explaining that she's *la hija de la Toña* (Toña's daughter) back from New York City. It appears that the call is just a wrong number, but the stranger on the other end of the line stays on and inquires if Fefa has any US goods to sell, and Fefa, desperate to talk to someone, animatedly begins listing items: "Cosmetics, carteras, leather, leather shoes, colonia Jean Nate, pampers, t-shirts." (10). In this final moment, how Fefa will negotiate her transnational identity is left unanswered, while the economic interdependence of the island/diaspora relationship is made abundantly clear. Unlike *Por hora y a* Piece-Work, however, Fefa's comparatively stable financial situation is not likely to motivate a remigration. Instead, *Ay Fefa*'s drama of return displays what Stefansson identifies as the "mismatch between the imagined and experienced homecoming" (8), which "can be more difficult and emotionally destabilizing than leaving home and settling in a new part of the world" (8). The monologue leaves its audience doubting whether Fefa's return will be permanent. If Fefa cannot find a fit in her new/old home, one outcome could be rejoining her adult children in the United States—that is, returning to her old/new home.

Nuyor/Islas: The Insularity of Returnee Communities

In Chiqui Vicioso's play *Nuyor/Islas*, the protagonist, Doña Ramona, is in a slightly different stage of return, since she is an elderly woman settled in a returnee community. Vicioso's own mother's return to the Dominican Republic inspired the play, which is written in Spanish and has had numerous stagings in New York City and Santo Domingo. Vicioso's transnational perspective is different from most of the authors included in this study because her family moved to New York City in the late 1960s, before the nonmigrant perception of the diaspora took a negative turn.[17] Like many of her compatriots in New York City, Vicioso held jobs in factories, but she also acquired a university education, was active in student movements, and had work and volunteer experiences in Africa, and Central and South America, all of which contributed to radicalizing her thinking about gender, class, and race. Vicioso returned to the Dominican Republic after eighteen years abroad, where she writes journalism, literature, and literary criticism, and has held important posts as an advocate for women's rights.[18] It is valid to note that her middle-class background and education has afforded Vicioso with choices regarding employment and residence. Torres-Saillant, in reference to Vicioso, suggests that we do not equate "exilio con la condición diaspórica. El exiliado regresa y se acomoda; el deportado, no" ("exile with the diasporic condition. The exiled return and settle; the deported, no"; "Antelación" 401). As a middle-class intellectual, Vicioso evades the stigma of being associated with the new class of arriviste returnees by traditional island elites. However, her literary production, including *Nuyor/Islas*, clearly reflects a "diasporic" perspective that confronts the realities of exclusion that are unique to her transnational community.

Nuyor/Islas stands out because it grants visibility to an aging woman, Doña Ramona, who has the play's sole speaking role.[19] Asking audiences to tune in to her perspective is significant, because as Emilia María Durán Almarza notes: "El hecho de que Ramona sea una anciana sin estudios sitúa su discurso en la periferia del marco discursivo dominante" ("The fact that Ramona is an elderly, uneducated woman situates her discourse on the periphery of the dominant discursive frame"; 105). Rather than the damning, male-dominated portrayal of vulgar and even dangerous migrants often depicted in popular media and elitist discourses, Vicioso offers the story of a woman with a traditional middle-class upbringing who lived abroad for thirty-five years. By featuring an older character, the play shows that even the most deeply ingrained attitudes are subject to change, and it allows for an exploration of the migration experience of the second generation (through references to Ramona's daughter). Ramona's unfiltered and rambling monologue reveals a transnational subject positioning that encompasses practices and ideologies from both *aquí* and *allá*.

The title of the play, *Nuyor/Islas*, references different levels of insularity: the islands of Hispaniola and Manhattan, the spaces of isolation experienced by migrants and returnees in both locations, and the solitude of old age. The stage directions, setting, and monologue structure underline the loneliness experienced by the play's protagonist. In the play's introduction, Vicioso writes: "Atrapados por la nostalgia del país que conocieron y la añoranza por los hijos que dejaron fuera, o que optaron por quedarse en el país en el cual crecieron porque no están interesados en regresar a una isla donde ningún lazo les ata, es esta población víctima de la soledad" ("Trapped by the nostalgia of the country they knew and the longing for their children they left abroad or who chose to stay in the country they grew up in because they are not interested in returning to an island with which they have no ties, this is the population victimized by solitude"; 67). After three decades of modernization and urbanization, there is no going back to the island that Ramona knew when she left. Moreover, the returnee imperative is to ascend the social ladder, thus there is no return to one's once familiar neighborhood. Instead, Ramona settles in a development built for returnees in Santiago de los Caballeros, the Dominican Republic's second largest city. The stage directions note that when the bill collector rings, Ramona approaches the iron gate that surrounds her house, and the theater scholar Beatriz Rizk observes that in the New York City production of the play, the staging highlighted her entrapment "al ponerla dentro de una estructura que semeja una caja, con cuatro paredes que se cierran, al final de la pieza" ("by placing her in a structure that is like a box, with four walls that close at the end of the play"; 45).[20] In built environments, gates serve to mark social spaces and control movement. Writing about Puerto Rico, but equally relevant to the Dominican Republic, the sociologist Zaire Dinzey-Flores writes, "Locking in and out, gates reflect and effect social relations; they shape race and class inequality" (22). Ramona is both locked in and out. Ostensibly, Ramona's gated community keeps its privileged returnee residents safe by keeping intruders out, but the physical and symbolic boundaries of the community also locks its residents in, isolating them from the mainstream population. Whether it be due to her advanced age (she no longer drives), lack of social ties after a thirty-five-year absence, or a sense of ostracism for having migrated, Ramona never ventures outside of her home, even opting to attend church via a televised service. On the one hand, Ramona asserts a sense of social superiority and refuses to betray her vulnerability by insisting she cannot be bothered with dressing up for church and that she cannot abide by the overlong sermons and poor-quality chorus (74). On the other hand, she is anxious to interact with others and has established a routine of watching telenovelas with the vegetable peddler who still travels by burro (74).[21]

Similarly, Ramona desperately tries to engage the bill collector by repeatedly inviting him in with offers of food and drink. *Nuyor/Islas* is structured as a monologue, but the presence of a silent interlocutor creates an unspoken dialogue, which is significant because, similar to the voice on the other end of the telephone line at the end of *Ay Fefa*, it adds the implicit perspective of the islander.[22] In both instances, the one-sided conversations evoke a desire for more dialogue between the island and the diaspora. We can only assume that the bill collector tolerates the lengthy, rambling conversation because Ramona's mix of charm, good humor, and pathos makes him a captive audience. Ramona is a compellingly contradictory character. She brought traditional elitist Dominican notions of race, class, and gender to New York City, and she seems anxious to reassert them in front of a nonmigrant national who understands that she has economic power but is looked at with distrust for having migrated.[23] Ramona reiterates, for example, that in New York City she always maintained her status as a classy lady from a good family and lamented having to work at a pocketbook factory. As forelady of her shift, she distanced herself from her fellow Haitian factory workers and played music by Chopin as they worked: "Su música me tranquilizaba y además ponía bien claro que yo era una *lady*, bien comida, bien vestida y bien educada" ("His music calmed me, and besides, it made it very clear that I was a *lady*, well-fed, dressed, and educated"; 70). As Ramona's monologue progresses, however, she admits that she is the illegitimate daughter of a tobacco factory owner and that she ultimately enjoyed listening to popular Haitian merengue music (70–71). She also shows some degree of solidarity with her Haitian coworkers by commiserating over the racial profiling both Dominicans and Haitians suffer in the Unites States and offering advice on how to enter retail establishments like Macy's without feeling intimidated (71). In the diaspora, Ramona's ingrained anti-Haitian nationalism begins to show cracks.

As Vicioso's play and personal experience suggest, new understandings of race, class, and gender are some of the lessons that form part of the cultural remittances of the diaspora that "return" directly and indirectly to the Dominican Republic: "The New York experience, which was so crucial to my discovery of my Caribbean and racial identity, has made me a very, very critical person with respect to my own society. Things I had never noticed before, I now see. Like racism, for example. Class differences. Santo Domingo is a very societally structured city. The situation of women is atrocious" ("Oral History" 316). In *Nuyor/Islas* Ramona loses her battle to instill traditional Dominican racial and social values in her daughter, who she hoped to groom as a Grace Kelly, but who chose to emulate the looks and social and political activism of Tracy Chapman (72). On the topic of marriage and potential progeny, Ramona's sexism and racism rears its ugly head. For Ramona, implicit in *casarse bien* (marrying well) is whitening the family tree. She is not concerned about her blond son, for his blond hair makes him automatically attractive, while her "almost black" daughter must select a partner with potential to "improve" her looks. She is, therefore, dismayed when her daughter divorces her white, American husband and has relationships with a black man and a Chinese man. These statements recounted to the bill collector play out a generational conflict between migrants and their children. In the face of rearing children away from the homeland values, there is a reactionary tendency to assert these ideologies. Meanwhile, Ramona's monologue simultaneously reveals her changing attitudes, and the audience witnesses how she ultimately let go of some of her most traditional beliefs. She comes to understand what her socially conscious daughter pointed out all along: "Todos los dominicanos somos negros y que a los gringos les importa un carajo si eres Báez o Viccini" ("All us Dominicans are blacks and the gringos don't give a damn if you're a Báez or Viccini"; 70). The surnames Ramona refers to belong to the Dominican elite.[24] Now residing in the Dominican Republic, Ramona admits: "Ella siempre tuvo la razón. Tanto fastidiar con los haitianos y ellos son tan pobres como nosotros y nosotros somos los haitianos de Nueva York" ("She was right all along. So much conflict with the Haitians and they are as poor as we are and we are the Haitians of New York"; 76).[25] Through Ramona, we see how values attributed to here/there and now/then shift and combine over time, creating a transnational point of view. In New York City, Ramona asserts her most traditional Dominican attitudes, but when she relays them to the bill collector in her current context, these views ring hollow. In the following slip, Ramona locates her space of enunciation as New York City, suggesting that the homeland may no longer be her primary point of reference: "Cuando uno llega aquí, digo allá" ("When one arrives here, I mean there"; 69). Now with her "here" relocated to the Dominican Republic, Ramona displays new understandings of the workings of gender and race in her place of birth.

Nuyor/Islas includes more examples of cultural exchanges and forms of hybridity than the first two plays discussed in this chapter. It also avoids portraying the Dominican population as entirely traditionalist or trapping it in a nostalgic gaze. For example, even though the nonmigrant character in the play does not speak, we can surmise from Doña Ramona's conversation that he is not the typical male that she might remember from the 1960s: he is not overly macho, he does not practice a religion, and he does not eat meat. Food is a cultural signifier, and, ironically, it is Doña Ramona, the returned migrant, who delights nonmigrant locals with "authentic" *pan de agua* no longer made in the Dominican Republic (69). Conversely, in New York City, *Nuyor/Islas* shows that Dominicans and their cultural impact extends beyond the labor force. Doña Ramona's gringo boss would jokingly chide her for eating a sandwich, yogurt, and salad for lunch, while he longed for the delicious rice and beans that she would make with Dominican ingredients bought in New York City *marketas*. Doña Ramona's obvious loneliness and isolation in a returnee community, however, suggests the ambivalent and marginal space afforded to return migrants who embody hybrid subject positions.

The returns performed in Ovalle, Corniel, and Vicioso's plays embody varying degrees of cultural remittance, and, as I have suggested, varying probabilities of rediasporization. In these plays, hegemonic views of Dominican identity as homogenous and territorially bounded contrast with alternative diasporic perspectives, but the experience of return contains and complicates both positions. The politics of representation Ovalle's *Por hora y a* Piece-Work provide the least amount of space for a dialogue, for the play does little to question entrenched positions on *dominicanidad* and is characterized by an exilic, nostalgic relationship with the homeland. The monologues by Corniel and Vicioso, by contrast, place audiences in a more complex interpretative position, and, like the one-sided conversations in both plays, invite a two-way exchange on the problem of transnational identity. Josefina Báez's solo performance piece *Dominicanish* (2000) takes a more drastic step and forces such a conversation by bombarding the spectator with verbal and visual references to migratory experiences that cross at least three national borders as well as intra-ethnic boundaries.[26] By way of conclusion, I will briefly examine *Dominicanish*, a spoken-word poetry/dance performance text in which Báez poetically and gesturally recreates her immigration to New York City and her subsequent movements within the city, return trips to the Dominican Republic, and visits to India.

Dominicanish: Performing a Diasporic Perspective

Unlike the previous migration scenarios in this chapter, in which the protagonists leave the United States and return home to the Dominican Republic, in *Dominicanish* the home to which the author/performer returns is New York City. In the text's preface Báez defiantly states: "Yo soy una Dominican York. Y esta condición me otorga una infinidad de estímulos constantes y variados. Enriqueciendo mi cultura personal en formas inesperadas" ("I am a Dominicanyork. And this position grants me infinite, constant, and varied stimuli. It enriches my personal culture in unexpected ways"; 7). On the one hand, "una Dominican York" identifies a particular US Latina identity and suggests that her drama of identity has been making a bicultural home in New York City. Indeed, at the heart of the performance is the story of the artist as an adolescent exploring a new language and a new racial and gender identity. On the other hand, Báez's declaration suggests that her bicultural condition uniquely positions her to be open to the world of cultural influences surrounding her, implying that her identity can never truly be fixed and is always undergoing change. Although *Dominicanish* is clearly the most US-anchored text included in this chapter, Báez's story of migration does not end with the formation of a transcultural Latina identity; rather, it is one narrative thread included in the performance of the multidirectional movement of transmigrants and the ties they maintain across cultural, political, economic borders.

This dynamism is reflected in Báez's simultaneous recitation of her poems while in constant motion as she performs rhythmic steps and hand gestures from the South Indian dance tradition of Kuchipudi.[27] The Kuchipudi moves are accompanied by the sounds of melodic jazz played on the saxophone and flute by an onstage musician, Luis Disla. This unexpected pairing exemplifies the constant and varied stimuli that Báez embraces in the construction of her identity. The text itself, a flip book, also performs motion, for each page of *Dominicanish* features a small image of Báez in the lower right corner that varies incrementally. Quickly flipping the pages animates the image, imitating the dance movements one sees in the performed version of the text. The reader thus views the text and a dance performance as well as reads it; moreover, the graphic arrangement of the words, much like a list, defies the linear process of reading from left to right and encourages the reader to look from top to bottom as well.

The multiplicity of linguistic registers—ranging from public service announcements, the voices of teenagers and vendors, song lyrics, language lessons, acronyms, to snippets from tales from the *Panchatantra*—keeps the non-Aristotelian structure of the narrative flowing from one story to the next. Similarly, the bare stage enables the viewer to imagine Báez in any number of spaces, including a city street, a subway train, a kitchen, a business, or a school in New York City, the Dominican Republic, or India.

The experiences of Dominican transnationalism are interwoven throughout the performance poem. Like Corniel's *Ay Fefa*, Báez alludes to the political unrest that motivated Dominican migration in the mid-1960s:

> One way to Santo Domingo
> Exchange today 12.50

4.1. Josefina Báez in *Dominicanish*. Photo credit: Jorge Vismara.

4.2. Josefina Báez in *Dominicanish*. Photo credit: Jorge Vismara.

Trips to the airport rest in peace
Balaguer leave us the fuck alone leave us alone
man leave Me alone Dominican cake any
occasion march to take back our streets
March against police brutality celebrando
Abril translations (23)[28]

The reference to death, "rest in peace," suggests that perhaps the one-way tickets to Santo Domingo are for the dead to return to be buried in their homeland. By contrast, the daily exchange rate and multiple "trips" to the airport evoke the connectedness that has become normalized between the Dominican Republic and the United States. For example, Dominican cake can now be procured in either location. The bifocal transnational point of view comes into focus with the invective against Balaguer in English, followed by a concern that echoes 1970s US social justice movements in the reference to violence against women (the plea to be left alone and a march "to take back our streets") and to police brutality. The mention of "abril" shifts the focus to island politics and the civil war that ultimately brought Balaguer to power. Finally, "translations" evokes the speaker's expansive and oscillating investment in both island and diaspora politics.

Although repeat return trips help sustain transnational connections, they also foreground the impossibility of returning to one's origins and to the creation of a transcultural identity. Home, like many scholars of diaspora and exile have observed, "is a place of no return, even if it is possible to visit the geographical territory that is seen as the place of 'origin'" (Brah 192). The passage that follows depicts Báez as somewhat of a stranger in her original homeland. "Here," New York City, has become, through lived experience, the home with which she identifies:

I went back there on vacation
There is La Romana
Here is 107th street ok
Tú sabes inglés?
Ay habla un chin para nosotros ver si
tu sabes
I was changed they were changed he she it
Were changed too
. . .
Back home home is 107 ok
Full fridge full of morirsoñando con minute maid
To die dreaming of a maid in a minute (31)

The phrases in bold represent the voices of nonmigrant Dominicans and capture Báez's experience of being treated as a tourist or an outsider in her home country, while at the same the phrases sounding like a grammar lesson remind us that all the participants in the return visit scenario have changed. That the speakers are interested in finding out how much English Báez knows reflects more than curiosity on the part of the nonmigrants—it reveals how the cultural influences like language return to the Dominican Republic and make an impact on national culture. *Dominicanidad* has changed both here and there, and Báez's diasporic perspective is not focused on recuperating an "authentic" national culture or attempting to replicate such an identity in New York City. Rather, the links between "here" and "there" are sustained through creative reinvention. In New York City, a classic Dominican fruit drink, *morirsoñando*, is still made, but with commercially produced Minute Maid orange juice. The play with the words *minute* and *maid* reveal the asymmetrical power relationships governing transnationalism and remind us of the vulnerable socioeconomic and legal status of many Dominicans in the United States, but the linguistic creativity of the poetic voice and the improvised version of *morirsoñando* also suggest strategic adaptation and resistance as well.

Báez's dominance of English in the context of the United States performs transnationalism differently than it does during her return trips to the Dominican Republic. Learning English is depicted, at first, as awkward and painful, but, by the end, as liberating. The text is a celebration of "Dominicanish," which is Báez's Dominican Spanish-inflected English and her hybrid, "sort-of" Dominican identity. Caught between the bilingual students and the North Americans, young Báez had no "homeroom" at school where she could feel comfortable (32). She notes that "Hablo como Boricua/Y me peino como Morena" ("I talk like a Puerto Rican/And I style my hair like a black girl"; 43) and arrives at celebrating her Afro-Latina roots not through formal education but by means of the alternative school of popular music. Báez finds teachers and texts in the album covers and songs of groups like the Isley Brothers and soon she is "frequent flying to the dictionary grooving it" (30) and going on a "tour of idiomatic expression" (35). At the same time, Báez finds a language in the African American soul music of the 1970s; her body also moves to the Latin beats of the Dominican New York City-based musician Johnny Pacheco and the balladeer idol Fausto Rey.

Sports, too, along with language and music, forge racially inflected transnational sociocultural sensibilities. In the following segment, in which Báez affirms her black identity, I argue that she alludes to Chico Escuela, a role played by Garrett Morris, the first African American actor to perform on the television sketch comedy show *Saturday Night Live*:

> Discos del alma con afro. Con afro black is
> beautiful. Black is a color. Black is my color.
> **My cat is black.**
> But first of all baseball has been very very
> very good to me (26)

Between 1975 and 1980 Morris played Chico Escuela, a fictional Dominican baseball player for the New York Mets, who helped Jane Curtin with the nightly news broadcast. His English was limited, and the running joke was for him to insert the accented phrase "baseball has been berry, berry good to me" whenever he was unsure of how to respond to the newscaster's questions. The sketches aired on *Saturday Night Live* have always pushed the envelope of sexual, political, and racial humor. In the case of Chico Escuela, I think the dynamic with the female newscaster played by Jane Curtin served mainly to parody the stereotype of the dumb male athlete. For example, in response to Chico's bungled sportscast, Jane Curtin replies (with genuine enthusiasm): "Great job, Chico. I'm glad that we haven't hired just another stupid ex-jock sportscaster" (Weekend Update). Yet the skit seems to be on thin ice in its parody of the figure of the immigrant who lacks fluency in English. I would argue, though, that Chico's struggles with English pronunciation encourage a misreading of his intelligence. In fact, he cleverly wrests control of the script by tossing out the popular North American sports of football and hockey and focusing on baseball and his own self-promotion; however much viewers may laugh his expression, Chico is the star of the segment. The gesture of remembering Chico Escuela is complex. He may have been the only Dominican character on American television in the 1970s, and he may have been the butt of what might be perceived as a racist joke, but above all I think Báez's recuperation of this character serves as a playful reminder that the cross fertilization of US and Latin cultures is nothing new. The character Chico Escuela, as Lawrence La Fountain-Stokes points out, is likely based on the Afro-Cuban player Orestes "Minnie" Miñoso (1925–2015), the first black Cuban to play for Major League Baseball ("Speaking Black" 252–53). Baseball has long been a transnational sport with deep roots in Latin America and the Caribbean. Today, Major League Baseball is indisputably global—players from Asia, Latin America, and the Caribbean bring money, skills, and styles across borders and perform for fans all over the world. While baseball has been "good" to minority athletes by creating social and economic advancement, at the very end of her monologue Báez emphatically claims that "I have been good to baseball too" (49), suggesting that Latino talent has transformed Major League Baseball, "America's pastime," in positive ways.[29] By extension, one woman's story performed in *Dominicanish* illuminates how the cultural remittances of Dominicans and Dominicanyorks have enriched both US and Dominican economies and cultures.

The four performance pieces discussed in this chapter stage women on a transnational US- Dominican migratory circuit who return home, in each case, at least temporarily. Living across physical and cultural boundaries involves transmigrants in acts of imagining, moving, creating, and remembering homes—physical places that signify one's sense of national, cultural, and social belonging. In each text, the characters who return are engaged in claiming and being claimed by two nation-states, a paradoxically vulnerable and empowering position that informs how they articulate their gendered concepts of self and collective belonging. Likewise, the playwrights have lived a transnational life in different ways, ranging from Ovalle being the most permanently situated in the Dominican Republic, to Báez choosing New York City as her home base. A diasporic lens highlights the particularities of the Dominican migration experience and is useful in unpacking the politics of representation in constructions of *dominicanidad*. Not only do Dominican plays about migration counter stereotypical images of Dominican identity, they articulate new ways of understanding the meanings of national belonging. Furthermore, from the exilic perspective projected in Ovalle's traditional social realist drama to the most radically diasporic perspective embodied in Báez's experimental performance piece, we witness a shift in forms employed in approximating the experience of migration. Báez's self-reflective play with genre—dance, poetry, performance—and her constant, fluid movement between cultures enable her to express more a more radical and open conception of *dominicanidad*. The transnational circuit of Dominicans moving between the island and the United States has created for some the sense that they occupy what Báez calls "El Ni é" in her 2011 performance text *Levente no. Yolayorkdominicanyork*. "El Ni é" is short for the phrase *ni es una cosa, ni es la otra* (it's not one thing or the other). As we have seen in the works analyzed in this chapter, the experience of return migration sharpens the sense that the space of belonging for transnational migrants is permanently suspended between the homeland and the host land. García-Peña envisions this in-between space as mainly uncomfortable, owing to the "dual marginality" Dominican migrants face at home and abroad.[30] Nevertheless, this chapter's title references a line near the end of *Dominicanish* in which Báez declares, "Home is where theatre is" (37), reminding us that the artistic endeavor of theatrical performance is a hopeful and creative act of homemaking. As I will detail in the following chapter, the theater constitutes an interstitial space of conviviality where stage and auditorium bring together performers and spectators to forge a transnational public sphere that recognizes the rights of belonging of Dominicans inhabiting “El Ni é.”

Chapter 5

Borrowed Identities

Performing Undocumented Migration and Rights of Citizenship

The various stages of Dominican transnational migration dramatized in the plays in this study—travel, arrival and adaptation, settlement and assimilation, and return—demand different theatrical forms ranging from cutting-edge solo performance to conventional ensemble drama for engaging audiences with their stories of migration. In this chapter and the next, I focus on the aesthetic strategies employed in representing both the undocumented migrant's quest of citizenship and the transnational playwright's quest for recognition. I consider how the collective endeavor of theater affords opportunities to think through what the social scientists Stephen Castles and Alastair Davidson call "new rules for conviviality" that would cultivate equality, cross-cultural interaction, and the creation of new kinds of collective belonging (viii). Works such as Claudio Mir's *Mondongo Scam* (1994) and María Isabel Bosch's *Las viajeras* (The Women Travelers) (2003) give voice to undocumented Dominican immigrants and place audiences in the ethical position of having to assume a stance on the topic of human rights and citizenship. Through their engagement with hybridity as a theme and an aesthetic strategy, Bosch and Mir's performances not only explore new understandings of political, personal, and artistic belonging, they also join people in sites of conviviality that imagine a more accessible and expansive body politic. As I take up in chapter 6, by positioning Dominicans in a wider framework of global migration and experimenting with diverse aesthetic approaches, Frank Disla develops an artistic method that speaks to practices of transnational theater broadly.

The task of fostering conviviality is urgent in an age of burgeoning international migration in which more people than ever reside outside their country of birth and maintain strong links to more than one society.[1] Distinct from the one-way migration narrative of assimilation characteristic of the late nineteenth and early twentieth centuries, today's circular counter streams of transnational migration exert pressure on both the sending and receiving societies to extend frameworks of membership and to expand human rights. Citizenship has long been conceived of as a compendium of rights, responsibilities, and legal statuses grounded on membership in a territorial state. Underscoring the geographically bounded and political quality of citizenship rights in contrast to the universal character of human rights, Gershon Shafir and Alison Brysk write, "The idea of citizenship in the present, as in the past, anchors rights in membership in a politically sovereign entity, whereas human rights are rooted in the individual by virtue of his or her humanity and not due to his or her status in the body politic" (277). Over the last half-century, processes of globalization such as transnational migration have eroded the autonomy of the nation-state. Indeed, as the political theorist Seyla Benhabib notes, "From a philosophical point of view, transnational migrations bring to the fore the constitutive dilemma at the heart of liberal democracies: between sovereign self-determination claims on the one hand and adherence to universal human right principles on the other" (2). In this context, renewed debates about citizenship have focused on problems of human rights—that is, "the vindication of the right of every human being 'to have rights,' that is, to be a legal person, entitled to certain inalienable rights, regardless of the status of their political membership" (Benhabib 3). Nevertheless, there is no global legal framework with authority over sovereign nation-states to ensure these rights. The nation-state continues to be the institution that guarantees rights of citizenship and the political framework in which immigrants form different senses of belonging in a wide range of migratory contexts, such as rooted ethnic minority enclaves; transitory transnational circuits; economic, environmental, and war refugee displacements; and free-floating cosmopolitanisms. The stakes for developing new approaches to citizenship are high, for democracy cannot be maintained, let alone strengthened, in nations that have large populations of residents without citizenship. Any solution, suggest Castles and Davidson, "must lie in a mode of citizenship that reconciles the pressures of globalization with the reality that states will continue, for the foreseeable future, to exist as the most important political unit. One aim must be to dissolve the nation part of the nation-state and to replace it with a democratic state based on open and flexible belonging" (viii). Such a project would counter the contemporary anti-immigrant climate that seeks to block access to the rights associated with citizenship and, on the contrary, would expand citizenship with the objective of fostering healthy democratic states.[2] It is my contention that the grounded, collective activity of making and witnessing staged stories can contribute powerfully to this project of reimagining citizenship.

In his study on theater and human rights, Paul Rae frames his argument by noting that theater both treats the subject of human rights and is the object of those rights (6). When the theater addresses the subject of human rights, it becomes a place in which "lives are given voice and experiences form, and where representatives of one group can make their address to others" (22). As we will see in *Mondongo Scam* and *Las viajeras*, the voice and visibility granted to undocumented immigrants is central in confronting restrictive agendas of citizenship. Furthermore, as an object of human rights, the act of making theater is an exercise of assembly, free speech, and the sharing of cultural life (Rae 24–29).[3] While Bosch and Mir do not practice their art in places where these basic rights are threatened, as transnational artists their entry into the public sphere is complicated by the translocal US-Argentine-Dominican space from which their art is produced and received.[4] Just as political theorists posit models for global citizenship, so, too, should arts organizations develop a global vision for supporting cultural production. To be sure, fomenting border crossing cultural activity will encourage the intercultural and international communication necessary for imagining democratic global rights.

The theater constitutes a model for rehearsing (theorizing) and performing (putting into practice) new forms of conviviality because it is an inherently social activity. As the Argentine theater theorist Jorge Dubatti states, "Sin convivio—reunión de dos o más hombres, encuentro de presencias en una encrucijada espacio-temporal cotidiana—no hay teatro" ("Without conviviality—the gathering of two or more people, the encounter of presences in an everyday crossroads of time and space—there is no theater"; 43). Dubatti finds the essential qualities of theater in the symposium, convivium, and banquets of ancient Greek and Roman cultures, unrepeatable and finite communal encounters that implied orality, the distribution of roles, physical proximity, sensorial experience, and ritual transcendence (46–47). The theater, like the rite of sociability of the banquet table, joins people together and assigns them different roles. In similar terms, the political philosopher Hannah Arendt theorizes the public realm as individuals brought together at a dinner table: "To live together in the world means essentially that a world of things is between those who have it in common, as a table is located between those who sit around it" (52). For Arendt, the public realm is comprised of two related components—the space of appearance and the common world. Maurizio Passerin d'Entrèves writes that Arendt's public sphere "refers to that sphere of appearance where citizens interact through the medium of speech and persuasion, disclose their unique identities and decide through collective deliberation about matters of common concern" (146). This space is only possible "if we share a common world of humanely created artifacts, institutions and settings, which separates us from nature and provides a relatively permanent or durable context for our activities"

(146). In my view, the theater is an exemplary context for enabling spaces of appearance in which people engage in speech and action, take on the roles of actors and observers, and disclose, in Arendt's terms, "who" they are, that is, their unique identity (184–88).[5] The theater, for Arendt, is by definition a political art because "only there is the political sphere of human life transposed into art. By the same token, it is the only art whose sole subject is man in relationship to others" (148). I would add, however, that it is not only the subject of theater that is about human relationships, it is the collective and participatory nature of its making and reception that makes it a microcosm of the public sphere.

Thus, in the chain of relations set in motion by the theater event—from the playwright, to the production (producers, directors, actors, and theater personnel), and to the audience (metaphorical political community)—performance offers an apt site to rehearse new rules of conviviality in an age of intense intercultural contact. Though the theater is a part of the common world that facilitates the creation of the public realm, it often represents an alternative space where groups made invisible in the public sphere of politics can be seen and heard and imagined as a collectivity. The theater, like the public realm, summons people to a temporary arena in which the dynamics of reciprocity, solidarity, and difference are constantly at play. As Arendt notes, the collective identity of the polis is not a fixed location but rather an activity organized out of action and speech (in performative terms, polis is a "doing").[6] In the theatrical space of appearance created by Mir and Bosch's performances, a Dominican polis that embodies a transnational mode of collective belonging emerges. Their performances construct a public space where homeland notions of *dominicanidad* are revised and the host society is encouraged to acknowledge universal human rights rather than membership-based citizenship.

"Stand Up, Stand up for Your Rights": In Pursuit of Recognition and Citizenship

Despite their contrasting tones, intersecting thematic and formal components lend *Mondongo Scam* and *Las viajeras* to a tandem reading. Both solo performance pieces present the plight of undocumented Dominican immigrants through metatheatrical "monopolylogues" in which the actors play all the roles in dialogue with imaginary characters.[7] In Mir's comic play, the main character borrows the identities of dead people in order to access the citizenship that is denied to him by his undocumented status in the United States, but he is able to scam the legal system for only so long before he is caught and brought before a court of law. Achieving invisibility—that is, making his Dominican identity disappear into another—is a Caribbean trickster survival strategy that ultimately fails because the increasingly hybrid cultural identity he performs never completely sheds his *dominicanidad*. Rather, borrowing identities constitutes a translation strategy that does not result in assimilation—replacing one nationalist attachment with another—but in hybrid identities that embody multiple identifications. Bosch also plays various roles, but the characters she embodies are based on real Dominican women she encountered in Buenos Aires. By borrowing their identities and performing their stories through narrative monologue and visual dramaturgy, Bosch gives visibility to a growing global social problem of the illegal trafficking of women. As we will see, both pieces employ strategies that place spectators in active interpretive roles and exemplify what Nicholas Ridout considers the theater's ethical role in "managing the way people think about their relationships with one another and their potential for creating societies in which everyone can enjoy freedom as well as social solidarity" (7–8).

The unique interpretative positions in which *Mondongo Scam* and *Las viajeras* place their spectators are generated by some of the aesthetic qualities Hans-Thies Lehmann identifies as "postdramatic."[8] In postdramatic theater, the narrative representation of action and speech of drama is no longer the privileged starting point. Rather than reading *Mondongo Scam* and *Las viajeras* as pieces of dramatic literature, they are better understood as theater works that are only fully realized in performance, because although the artists work off of written scripts, the text is only one element in the scenic creation that might be seen as a crossroads of visual arts, dance, and music (31). Free from the teleological constraints of an Aristotelian-structured play, solo performance is a particularly effective theater form for exploring a single topic, in this case, the experience of being an undocumented migrant, from various intellectual and affective vantage points. Monologues, moreover, create the illusion of privileging "reality" over "fiction" in that there often appears to be a direct connection between the actor and his/her character and the actor and the spectator. This impression is created by a shift from intrascenic communication to stage-audience communication. Lehmann writes: "The actor's speaking is now accentuated above all as a 'speaking to' the audience; his/her speech is marked as the speech of a real speaking person, its expressiveness more as the 'emotive' dimension of the performer's language than as the emotional expression of the fictive character represented" (127). The monologue theatrical address in *Mondongo Scam* and *Las viajeras* is strongly extrascenic, which emphasizes "the communi-

5.1. Claudio Mir in *Mondongo Scam*. Photo credit: Alex Guerrero.

cation taking place in the here and now of theatre."[9] As I have argued, the theater event is, above all, the relations established in the "here and now" of the *convivio*. It is the convocation of a public to see and hear stories that encourage spectators to imagine communities of citizens irrespective of legal status and geographical location.

The solo performance in *Mondongo Scam* comprises a court defense in which the character Casiano Doroteo Antonio Tapia, who has been charged with impersonation and false identities, defends his case.[10] Throughout *Mondongo Scam*, Mir plays a dizzying array of characters in dialogue with unseen interlocutors and given that the audience implicitly serves as the jury (and in one scene, members of a Pentecostal church), Mir's address is equally extrascenic as it is intrascenic. During Casiano's defense, a typical migration narrative emerges in which transnational households and dreams of American material goods and an improved social status lure Dominicans to the United States at the same time as a stagnant economy pushes them to leave. Though not explicitly part of Casiano's defense, this story foregrounds the inevitability of border crossing in a globalized world organized by economic hierarchies and social transnational networks, thereby presenting to the judge and jury the factors that compel people to work and settle illegally in the United States.

Although Casiano went to New York City knowing that he would overstay his visa and face the risks of becoming an undocumented worker, his hybrid cultural identifications and transnational sense of belonging make it difficult for him to accept that he is perceived as an illegal alien. For example, when he was young, the subject of Casiano's aunts in New York City and Puerto Rico were so embedded in daily conversations that he thought they must be connected to the Dominican Republic by bridges. For Dominicans, New York City (a synecdoche for the entire United States) represents a better life—money, education, and an elevated social status—even though obviously this does not turn out to be the case for all. Disappointed that his mother did not migrate, Casiano had to settle for used American goods sent by family members abroad (such as prized athletic shoes he wore even though they were too small) and images of American culture transmitted on the television (the cop show *Kojak*) and in film (John Travolta and *Saturday Night Fever*). In a parodic moment of colonial mimicry Casiano exuberantly imitates Dominicans disco dancing and phonetically singing songs from *Saturday Night Fever.* While the hybridity of Casiano's cultural identifications is a comic moment that evokes the euphoria of the disco era, for Dominican nationalists, *Travoltismo*—the influence of the music, style, and rebellious attitude of Travolta's film characters on Dominican youth culture—signaled cultural imperialism and the erosion of native customs and culture.[11] With regard to culture and capital, national borders undoubtedly have become porous. The migration studies scholar Mae M. Ngai reminds us, however, that "nation-states remain committed to restrictive immigration policies, so that states' regulation of the transnational movement of bodies differs greatly from that of capital, goods, and information" (270). In a dialogue in which Casiano repeats lines from English lessons, Mir sharply articulates his similar critical point: that the interpenetration of American and Dominican popular culture does not mean that Dominicans will be welcome in the United States. In the lesson, Casiano repeats, "America is a democratic country, isn't it? That is called the tag question, like, you aren't American, are you?" (5). By the late 1970s and 1980s, the cultural imperialism and the economic remittances from the United States had made the Dominican Republic a fundamentally transnational society. Before Casiano even fulfilled his migratory destiny—"vamos a Nueva York, todos nacimos para venir a Nueva York" ("we go to New York, we're all born to come to New York"; 2)—his sense of collective belonging spanned the two nation-states. Despite the ever-increasing attempts of states to secure national borders, transnational migration has produced Dominicans like the fictitious Casiano, whose everyday life practices bridge sovereign communities and complicate traditional definitions of citizenship.

Casiano's defense involves a different kind of border crossing, what I describe more fully in chapter 6 as a sort of metatheatrical migrancy in which he moves from one role to another in his survival strategy of using the documents of dead people to secure employment and a driver's license. While it is clear that Casiano is a culturally dexterous pretender and that he has "scammed" the system, he presents part of his actions as out of his control and the result of supernatural forces. He explains to the judge and the jury that he is merely a caballo, or medium, in the *espiritista* tradition of Afro-Caribbean religions, possessed at will by spirits who live through him. Therefore, Casiano argues, "I wouldn't call what I did impersonation, I'll call it occupation or better yet possession" (5). Throughout the course of the monologue, when Casiano attains documents—intentionally, but also by chance—we witness his transformation from a mulatto Dominican male to his temporary embodiment of black and white, Latino American and North American, evangelical Christian and Jewish, and male and female identities.[12]

In addition to Casiano's possessions that temporarily transform his gender, race, and ethnicity, *Mondongo Scam* foregrounds how the experience of migration produces paradoxical racial transformations for all Dominicans. Their ascension to a higher social class "whitens" them at the same time they become racialized "others" in the United States. For example, Casiano repeats an offhand compliment often bestowed upon migrants during return visits to the Dominican Republic: "Tú te has puesto más buen mozo y hasta más blanco desde que te fuiste pa Nueva York" ("You have gotten better looking and even whiter since you went to New York"; 2).[13] The tendency in Dominican culture to disavow blackness is also seen when Casiano occupies the identity of Ramón Cortines, beauty product entrepreneur. In this vignette, Cortines sets up shop on the sidewalk and demonstrates a *desrizado*, a chemical hair-relaxing treatment using his proprietary blend of muriatic acid, margarine, eggs, Pine-Sol, Clorox bleach, Ajax dish soap, and some flour (10). The curious and dangerous ingredients are sure to provoke laughter, as the recipe for these products are closely guarded secrets in the competitive Latino (especially Brazilian and Dominican) beauty industry dedicated to hair straightening. However, many consumers are willing to use questionably safe products to produce their desired look. Moreover, Cortines notes, consumers will pay anything for a product "to make curly hair look like Chinese" (8). Chemical relaxers and other straightening techniques aim to tame what is known as *pelo malo* into *pelo bueno*, and, in the process, transform the client's racial identity. In her study of Dominican racial identity, the sociologist Ginetta Candelario explains: "Central to Dominican hair culture have been the twin notions of *pelo malo* (bad hair) and *pelo bueno* (good hair).... *Pelo bueno* is hair that is soft and silky, straight, wavy, or loosely curled. There are clearly racial connotations to each category: the notion of *pelo malo* implies an outright denigration of African-origin hair textures, while *pelo bueno* exalts European, Asian, and indigenous-origin hair textures. Moreover, those with *pelo bueno* by definition are 'not black,' skin color notwithstanding" (182). Candelario notes that the desire is to be "not black," but it is not necessarily to be white. The favored racial category is an intermediate one, not mixed race like mulatto, which carries the shame of blackness, but *indio* (Indian). *Indio* rejects blackness, but it recognizes color and native historical roots in opposition to external Spanish and African influences (17–19). While *indio* is the preferred category for self-identification and Indo-Hispanicity is still celebrated as the foundational Dominican national identity, through Cortines, Mir shows that term carries some stigma as well. Hawking his hair product, Cortines says: "Si usted es negro y no le gusta que lo identifiquen como tal, si es indio y no le gusta que le llamen indio porque usted entiende que esto es sinónimo de bruto, no sufra más, los productos Ramón Cortines tienen la solución" ("If you're black and you don't like to be identified as such, if you're Indian and don't like that they call you that because you know it's synonymous with stupid, don't suffer any longer, Ramón Cortines's products have the solution"; 5). The cosmetic change in hairstyle affords Dominicans a more privileged social status by liberating them from being labeled in racial categories they reject and distancing them from an uncivilized indigenous past. Like the space of the Dominican beauty salon in New York City studied by Candelario, Cortines's pop-up shop becomes "a discursive site ordered by Dominican ideological codes . . . that operate across a transnational social field with its particular relations of power" (180).

At the same time Cortines reproduces Dominican racial hierarchies, he is subjected to racialization as a Latino in the United States. This becomes apparent when he is harassed, perhaps by the police, for setting up shop on sidewalk. He rebuffs whoever is trying to shut down his business by insisting: "This is America, I can put my business wherever I want. This is a free country, we give freedom and liberty to the rest of the world, if you don't want it we give it to you anyway. We are like that pal carajo to el mundo and God bless America" (8). The code switching in his response suggests that Cortines occupies a complicated insider (English-speaking American) and outsider (Spanish-speaking Latino) subject position. He both embraces and critiques the freedom the United States supposedly offers. By assuming he is free to pursue his informal business practices, Cortines embodies the naïve point of view of the immigrant who has been sold the American dream of economic success, a tall tale that does not include the realities of what it means to navigate law, citizenship, and racism in a new country. By contrast, Cortines's cynicism about imperialist interventionism suggests a more sophisticated understanding of the supposed freedom his host country offers. As in numerous instances throughout the play, Mir humorously incorporates the lyrics and rhythms of famous songs in the speech of his characters to facilitate a message of protest: "This is a free country, America the beautiful, the beautiful America, I am a citizen I have rights where are my rights" (8).

Ramón asks a good question: where are the rights afforded to him as a citizen? Even though he enjoys the coveted status as citizen Casiano lacks, Ramón is not a full citizen because he does not possess the same rights white Americans take for granted. He is harassed by the police as he pursues his American dream of economic success. The fact that Ramón must operate as an informal entrepreneur suggests he does not have the same opportunities as others to secure the support he needs to formalize his business. As William Flores observes, "In the United States, discourse on citizenship is too often limited to concepts of 'legal' status and formal membership in the nation-state. This country's anti-immigrant hysteria deflects our attention from a simple reality: being a citizen guarantees neither full membership in society nor equal rights" (255). Mae M. Ngai would argue that Latinos, along with Asian Americans, are "cast as permanently foreign and unassimilable to the nation" (8). As an "alien citizen," Ramón embodies an impossible subject position as a US citizen yet racialized as "alien." Casiano's quest to regularize his citizenship status is thus stymied from the start, for his experiences embodying black, white, and Latino identities reveal that nonwhite racial groups are routinely denied equal rights and full citizenship even when they possess the legal status of citizen.

To some extent, impersonating others also suggests the loss of Casiano's Dominican identity. For example, he states that the day he became Ishmael Rosenthal, "I knew I wasn't him, at the beginning, then after a week or two, I started to have problems recognizing myself, I didn't know who I was, but I knew that I wasn't Casiano anymore. I started eating Bagels with cream cheese" and wearing a yarmulke at home (2). But Casiano's Dominican identity, which is already seen as hybrid through his many references to the presence of American popular culture and material goods in his home country, is never entirely obliterated. For example, as Ishmael, he cannot resist attending a party hosted by Dominicans in New Jersey where the national specialty, *mondongo*, is to be served, and to which he brings both Caribbean rum and kosher Manischewitz wine.[14] On more than one occasion, Casiano's voice seeps through the language of his adopted character, revealing that his Dominican self is always present. For example, in the raucous sermon he delivers as the Pentecostal preacher George Aponte Solano, Casiano's entreaties to pray and to rise up and sing turn into a politicized sermon that takes up the cause of immigrants: "We need more people like you and you and you, people that believe in justice, we need more people, people willing to stand up against those whose actions have caused a lot of pain to our people, those who have pointed their fingers at us an accused us for all the sins and illness of society. God is showing us the way today, Jesus will demonstrate that we are humble, hardworking, tax paying, law obeying, family oriented and church going people" (5). By this point in the sermon, the voice is predominately that of Casiano in the role of self-appointed defense lawyer as he shifts into cross-examination mode. Likewise, the plural *you* of his flock/theater audience assumes the role of jury/theater audience and is asked not just to pray, but to stand up for the rights of others.

All the characters Casiano plays perform an address that is extrascenic, for they call upon the audience to perform the role of jury. Discussing the theatricality of court scenes, Rabih Mroué writes: "By definition, the trial gathers two opposing parties to confront one another verbally in front of a judge, each of them exposing their own point of view, defending it through various speeches and statements, presenting evidence and alibis, in the presence of a public intent on listening and witnessing, and awaiting the final decision of the judge who officiates in the name of law and justice" (x). On trial here is the criminalization of immigration in an epoch in which the economic global world order has encouraged the mass movement of people across national borders. Like the trial, in the theater there is a public "intent on listening and witnessing" and capable of discerning between the amusing stories of the personas who "occupy" Casiano and the voice of Mir (via Casiano) making a case for undocumented immigrants. As a lawyer, Casiano again shows his trickster qualities and bicultural adroitness by letting the judge know he is confident in presenting his own case since he has watched many legal shows on television. Casiano also tells the judge, "if you are a lawyer then I can be a lawyer too, this land is your land? This land is my land from California to the New York City highland, therefore nadie nobody is a stranger, foreigner, an alien" (5). Not only does Casiano switch from English to Spanish words and pronunciation—"highland" for "island" and the redundant "nadie" "nobody"—he also integrates lyrics from one of best-known folk songs in the United States, Woody Guthrie's 1940 "This Land is Your Land." The song's theme of inclusivity and celebration of America's capacious geography have a truly ironic ring in the context of a trial against an "illegal alien," a term that puzzles a world view like Casiano's that understands the Americas as fluid space of continuous cultural exchange.

Mondongo, the Dominican stew referenced when Ishmael Rosenthal attends a Dominican party and in the play's title, like the ethnologist Fernando Ortiz's description of the Cuban stew *ajiaco*, evokes the mixture of ingredients that compose a Dominican identity in a constant state of transculturation.[15] Using the bilingual neologism *mondongal*, Casiano delivers an amusing closing statement that pleads for the jury to embrace the good and the bad that comes with the processes of transculturation:

> Ladies and Gentlemen of the Jury: by taking the stand I stand a chance, a chance to stand off instead of standing aside or what is worse stand back. I choose to stand by to protect the things that we stand for and remember that to stand forth is to stand in, [it] is not standing in line or to stand in the way, it is to stand out, reach a conclusion by standing to reason and then and only then get up and stand up and stand up for your rights. It might sound confusing, but this is the way the world goes, the good mix in a big pot with the bad in an eternal mondongal relationship. (8)

In spite of his play with prepositional phrases, Casiano's circuitous call for social justice comes through clearly when spectators detect the rhythm and phrasing of Bob Marley's reggae classic "Get Up, Stand Up." Mroué suggests that while the scenarios in the theater and the courts share many similarities, the theater tends to put the burden of judgment on the audience rather than the judge. The theater presents the case at hand and leaves "enough breathing space for the audience to build their own opinions and decisions. . . . It is the place where questions are asked, without reaching conclusions or judgments" (x). The question *Mondongo Scam* asks of its audience is whether it will stand up for immigrant rights and understand that multiple cultural and national affiliations do not constitute a crime.

María Isabel Bosch's *Las viajeras* similarly places audiences in an ethical position of having to respond to a migration problem, but in this case the crime is clear: trafficking women for sexual exploitation. While Bosch's piece also encourages audiences to "stand up" for the rights of undocumented migrants, the tension between emotional identification and intellectual distancing at play in *Las viajeras* produces a hybrid aesthetics that affords the spectator an ethical position that differs from traditional political theater. *Las viajeras* is important for making visible the transnational lives of Dominicans in host countries other than the United States. As Ninna Nyberg Sørensen notes, "while the story of Dominican migration has in many ways become the story of New York City, we should not anticipate that Dominican migration to other places produces the same outcomes"—moreover, she argues that Dominican migration has become increasingly complex "in the substitution of 'old' migration destinations by new ones, the growing class diversification and informalisation of migration (increasing numbers travel and work in undocumented ways), and the feminisation of particular streams" (223). At the end of the twentieth century, Argentina, Spain, Italy, and the Netherlands became important destinations for female Dominican migrants.[16] Sørensen's work on Dominican migration to Spain contributes to a growing body of research on migration streams that documents the upsurge of women from the Global South supporting their families and homeland economies by migrating to the Global North to take on domestic, caretaking roles.[17]

Dominican women, like other female migrants from the Global South, often work as nannies, maids, and sex workers. *Las viajeras* raises awareness about the large number of Dominican women migrants trafficked to Argentina for sex work beginning in the mid-1990s.[18] Marjan Wijers, a specialist in international law and human rights, defines trafficking "as the process in which migrant women are brought into prostitution through the use of coercion, deceit, abuse or violence and in which they are denied fundamental human rights and freedoms" (69). Unexpectedly, it was Bosch's position as a cultural attaché in the Dominican embassy in Buenos Aires that gave rise to her awareness of the sex-trafficking problem, and, subsequently, her conception of *Las viajeras*, which was her first major solo project.[19] What began as benign curiosity became outrage when Bosch learned that the clusters of cold, disoriented, and hungry Dominican women gathering at the embassy daily were the victims of sex trafficking. Bosch states that she was haunted by the stories and scenes she witnessed at the embassy long after she left her position there, and that her sense of helplessness turned into the first step in creating *Las viajeras*. Bosch wrote letters from the points of view of composites of women she had met and had read about in the media, in legal documents, and in nongovernmental reports on migration. As denunciatory as these means of communication may be, Bosch, in order to empathize with her compatriot's plight, shifted her position from witness to the suffering to adopting their voices and points of view. The texts became dramatic scenes when she began to improvise with the material with the Argentine director Jorge Merzari. Choreographed dance-movement sequences, music, lighting, and minimalist props were added, transforming *Las viajeras* into a theater work. The title was suggested by Bosch's mother, who told her that in the southern part of the Dominican Republic *Las viajeras* was the name used for women who migrated in search of a better life.[20] The term is a euphemism that belies the open secret that these "women travelers" are often recruited to become prostitutes.

The epistolary monologues have the extrascenic effect of positioning spectators as the letter's addressees, which forces them to recognize their complicity in the silence surrounding the social problem. Disconcertingly, both the sending and receiving societies benefit from human trafficking. As Saskia Sassen explains, in the era of globalization, the growing impoverishment of the countries in the Global South "enables and even promotes the migration and trafficking of women as a strategy for survival. The same infrastructure designed to facilitate cross-border flows of capital, information, and trade also makes possible a range of unintended cross-border flows, as growing numbers of traffickers, smugglers, and even governments now make money off the backs of women. Through their work and remittances, women infuse cash into the economies of deeply indebted countries, and into the pockets of 'entrepreneurs' who have seen other opportunities vanish" (273). While the presence of Afro-Caribbean women is easily noticeable in the mainly white, European culture of Buenos Aires, the women are, in more than one sense, stripped of their rights and made legally invisible. Like Casiano in *Mondongo Scam*, the women legally arrive in their destination country with passports and tourist visas and become undocumented when their visas expire. Unlike Casiano, they remain abroad because they are trapped, victims of a transnational crime ring. In the Dominican Republic, a recruiter convinces the women that it is worthwhile mortgaging their homes or securing a loan (often from the recruiter) to migrate to Argentina where she can earn a better salary to support her family. The women pay these brokers for their services in securing passports, visas, and documents such as false "invitation letters" that guarantee airport transportation, housing, and help finding employment. Upon arrival, the women discover they must pay for their room and board and that the work promised them never materializes. With no return trip ticket and now indebted to traffickers in both their home country and Argentina, they are forced to follow the suggested path of prostitution. The women are denied their basic human rights such as "the right to work as a prostitute or not, the right to decide on the conditions of work, the right to enter and leave the sex industry, the right to refuse certain customers, the right to refuse certain sexual acts, the right to freedom of movement, the right not to be exploited" (Wijers 69). They are not protected by migrant worker laws because they are undocumented; in fact, their irregular status trumps their sexual exploitation, "turning these women into criminals instead of victims" (70). Their dependency on the recruiter-pimp, lack of citizen rights, and unfamiliarity with legal and other institutional resources leave these women extremely vulnerable.

In the Dominican Republic, *Las viajeras* are "forgotten" or made invisible through passive acceptance or denial of their experiences. When two of the characters in *Las viajeras* slip away from the tenement where they are housed and seek help at the Dominican embassy, they are given a plate of raviolis to eat, leading one of them to naively say, "Pa'eso e que silven la embajadases, ¿no e' veldad?" ("This is what embassies are for, right?" 5). The phrase is then pointedly repeated in standard Spanish as a direct address to the audience by Bosch. Clearly, *Las viajeras* suggests that providing an occasional plate of pasta constitutes an insufficient response. As representatives of the Dominican Republic in Argentina, the embassy employees appear to do very little to protect the rights of their compatriots. When the women are asked why they came to Argentina, their answer—to take a trip—is laughable even to them, yet the staff member passively accepts the explanation and digs no deeper. *Las viajeras* critiques both the sending society for failing to resolve the conditions that force their departure and the receiving society that fails to help them. As mentioned previously, the letters read by the woman have the extrascenic effect of addressing the spectators, but they also serve to constantly evoke the physical surroundings and everyday experiences that make up their world in the Dominican Republic, which helps maintain a constant bifocal view of the two societies implicated in the sex trade.

The transnational nature of the problem of sex trafficking led Bosch to perform *Las viajeras* for audiences in numerous countries, making it the play with perhaps the greatest international reach included in this study. She has performed it over two hundred times in both the Dominican Republic and Argentina, as well as in other nations that have been impacted by human trafficking. In addition to performing *Las viajeras* at international theater festivals to a wide cross-section of theater enthusiasts, Bosch received funding from the Dominican government for a tour that performed *Las viajeras* at schools and community centers at ten towns on the island known as sources for women destined for commercial sexual exploitation. On some occasions, the audience included sex trafficking victims. For example, in performances in Switzerland and the Netherlands, Bosch recalls that "casi un 80 por ciento de la audiencia estuvo integrada por viajeras de carne y hueso. Me preguntaba, en medio de la función, quién era yo para contarles a ellas, lo que sabían y conocían mejor que yo. Estas funciones resultaron una especie de catarsis colectiva en donde ya no sabía qué era lo que me causaba las lágrimas" ("almost 80 percent of the audience was made up of real-life women travelers. I asked myself in the middle of the performance, who was I to tell them what they knew and experienced better than I? These performances ended up being a kind of collective catharsis in which I no longer knew what it was that made me cry"; "María Isabel Bosch"). As the theater scholar Randy Martin reminds us, one of the operations of art is to make publics (5). The women gathered by the performance may lack rights of citizenship and recognition by the state, but "unlike political citizenship, which asks that we take state authority for granted, art compels us to seek in ourselves the authority by which we are obliged to one another in the fleeting, discretionary occasions for publics to gather together" (Martin 12). By Arendt's terms, the theater conjures the public realm by summoning people together. If for many political citizenship is taken for granted, for others it is out of reach. *Las viajeras* brings a marginalized population made invisible in the sphere of politics to a seat in the audience and to the center stage, creating an ephemeral sense of citizenship and belonging.

While the transnational circuit of audiences obviously experienced the performance in different ways and the nuances of Bosch's performances shifted in tune with spectator response, there are formal elements that remain constant and that structure the audience relationship with the play. *Las viajeras* alternates between narrative monologue scenes in which Bosch performs four different characters and visual dramaturgy scenes in which she performs dance movements. The spoken narratives abide by the aesthetics of traditional realist theater in the sense that although the structure is one of episodic montage lacking causality, taken together the episodes tell a complete and chronological story of the circumstances leading a woman to migrate to Argentina; to the discovery that she has been duped and must work as a prostitute to repay the recruiter who lent her money for the journey and for documents (that turn out to be false); to despair; and, ultimately, to suicide. Although *Las viajeras* eschews the conventional three-dimensional setting of dramatic realism, the carefully drawn character psychology and wealth of details about the sex trafficking industry create a world on stage that gives rise to empathy and identification on the part of the spectator.

The narratives include the stories from four women from different geographical points of the Dominican Republic and carefully reproduces their regional dialects. The performance begins with Bosch playing the role of Yuberkis, a naïve campesina from the interior of the Dominican Republic who is trapped in the patriarchal web of her husband, father-in-law, and the generous, but duplicitous, don Tulio, who offers to help them get out of debt by paying for her trip abroad. In this scene, we witness Yuberkis's heart-wrenching departure—she leaves behind her small son—and the brutal process of coming to terms with the reality of being held hostage in a Buenos Aires *conventillo* (tenement). Initially, Yuberkis is clouded by naïvety, believing the man who met her at the airport was protecting her from robbery by taking her passport and money and that the job as a dancer secured for her would be enjoyable (2). Yuberkis's perception takes an abrupt turn when she is raped by her soon-to-be *chulo* (pimp). Reytania, by contrast, is a hairdresser and experienced prostitute from the south of the Dominican Republic. Her modest desire to have enough money to build back home in San Cristóbal a sturdy house of "blo' y cemento" ("blocks and cement"; 4) that might withstand hurricanes, and her more ambitious dream of owning a beauty salon where she will expertly straighten the hair of her clients are sidelined by the fear and hunger she suffers in Buenos Aires.

Different from the violence of entrapment, coercion, and debt bondage, the third *viajera*, Inés, suffers the cruelty of being shunned. Her scene portrays her annual return visit to her middle-class home in Santo Domingo. Her family is aware that she never used her father's money to study computing as planned, but they never question how she manages to support herself, let alone send home monthly remittances. Inés repeatedly asks, "¿Por qué no hablan? . . . ¿por qué no hacen algo? . . . Si saben . . . Bastante que saben" ("Why don't they speak? . . . Why don't they do something? . . . If they know . . . They know quite a bit"; 6). In one of the many instances of direct audience address in the play, Inés shares what her family denies knowing: "Tengo que contarle lo que me pasa a alguien" ("I have to tell somebody what's happening to me"; 7), and she narrates how male clients were brought to her in the back of a nail salon. The hypocrisy of the family's repudiation of Inés is that of an entire society that passively accepts money from the illegal sex trafficking industry but fails to act to protect, locally and transnationally, both voluntary and involuntary sex worker's civil, labor, and human rights. However, as I detail below, the shifting relationship the performance establishes with the audience challenges passive reactions to the social problems portrayed.

The final story is Elsa's, a middle-aged laundress steeped in Afro-Caribbean spiritual practices from Punta Cana. Elsa answered an advertisement offering domestic work in Argentina and soon found herself thrown out to sea once the traffickers realized they had netted a woman passed her prime. Homeless and hungry, Elsa tells of absurd and poignant cultural misunderstandings that leave her with no chance for employment, and therefore no possibility of returning home. As we have seen throughout this study, transnational Dominican theater highlights how the marginalization of Dominicans as immigrants leads many to better understand the operations of racism and xenophobia in their own country. For example, when the recruiter determined that Elsa would not do as a prostitute, she states, "Me botó, como botan allá a lo' haitiano" ("He threw me out, like they throw out the Haitians back home"; 8). Much like a Haitian servant in an upper-class Dominican household, Elsa is constantly insulted and fired for not understanding the domestic practices expected in a modern, appliance-filled Argentine urban household. In the same vein, Elsa's racialized otherness is exacerbated by her difficulty understanding the Spanish dialect of Buenos Aires, and the miscommunications that arise are akin to those experienced between Spanish-speaking Dominicans and Creole-speaking Haitians back home. Elsa receives racial insults and laments that trying to follow her employer's instructions "te hacen sentir má vieja . . . má bruta . . . má atrasada"; ("makes you feel older . . . more stupid . . . more backward"; 9). In another instance of linguistic miscommunication, when a man on the street yells "cuero barato," Elsa takes offense, only to realize after smashing him on the head—and landing in jail for the attack—that in Argentinean Spanish he was hawking inexpensive leather, not identifying her in Dominican Spanish as a "cheap prostitute." Out of place and misunderstood, Elsa's tale ends with her committing suicide. As she leaps in front of a train, Elsa's final wish is for her children not to learn of her fate, though she does hope that her story might serve as a warning for women back home about the dangers of human trafficking.

Though the character sketches performed by Bosch are intended to generate affective recognition and solidarity, the pull between psychological realism and stylized distancing techniques in her performance produces an ethical encounter rather than simply a didactic message. Ridout notes that "increasingly, the relationship between theatre and ethics comes to be a question of form rather than content. It is how you make it, and what relationships you establish in making it (between producers, consumers, actors, spectators, participants), that matters, not what message or ideology you are trying to communicate" (49). *Las viajeras* places audiences in an ethical relationship with the performance through the fluctuation between aesthetics that seek different relationships between spectator and actor. In some regards, the performance answers Brecht's call for music, lighting, and choreography to stand as discrete elements alongside the drama as a means of creating alienation and intellectual empathy.[21] *Las viajeras*'s visual and auditory dimension, the body in movement to music, undoubtedly breaks with the illusory dramatic world of the monologues. The lengthy dance interludes in between each story and at the beginning of the piece are marked off by a change in lighting and an abrupt swelling of dramatic symphonic music. The audience no longer listens to a character but observes a nearly naked body execute slow dance movements while manipulating a number

5.2. María Isabel Bosch in *Las viajeras*. Photo credit: Diego Schiavini.

of lightweight white cuts of cloth, the play's only items for costuming and props. Dramatically speaking, we might read the body as stripped of character and, as a result, focus on the social problem targeted by *Las viajeras*, the female body deprived of basic human rights and the circumstances that brought about this situation. However, for some viewers this sort of emotional distancing might be thwarted by the creators' musical selection, Henryk Górecki's Symphony No. 3 (*Symphony of Sorrowful Songs*).[22] The plaintive soprano voice and long, smooth legato string sounds create an atmosphere that emotionally draws in spectators, likely causing them to lose sight of the play's moral argument.

Another tension between identification and distancing can be perceived in the construction of character. As I have noted, first writing letters and then embodying the voices of *Las viajeras* is an act of actor-character empathy and identification, and there is no question that Bosch's performance also seeks audience identification with character. However, *Las viajeras* demands an alert spectator and denies the passive experience of being caught up vicariously in the drama because it constantly makes spectators aware of the distinction between actor and character. This awareness is heightened primarily in the visual dramaturgy scenes in which the dancer's initially

5.3. Yuberkis in *Las viajeras*. Photo credit: Diego Schiavini.

free form dance movements begin to approximate the distinct physicality of the different characters. As Bosch assumes the postures and expressions of each new character, she wraps and unwraps the gauzy cloths. At times she manipulates them in such a way that they suggest a form of protective covering or, conversely, an immobilizing restraint and, at others, they are shaped to form concrete costuming and props, such as a bundle that stands for Yuberkis's baby, Elsa's head wrap, and Reytania's dress. It is as though we are witnessing the Stanislavski system of an actor preparing her character. Paradoxically, staging the normally offstage imaginative work of building actor-character empathy has the effect of blocking spectators from identifying with the characters and invites them instead to observe an actor taking up a social problem through art.

In a similar way, a distancing effect is produced when the illusion of the fourth wall dividing the fictional world of the performance and the real world of the audience is broken through direct audience address. Each of the transitions between the dance interludes and the narrative monologues is marked by the actor, not the character, rehearsing in contrasting vocal styles, the recitation of verses from the social poem *La luna con gatillo* by the Argentine poet Raúl González Tuñón (1941). Each time the actor recites the poem, she begins with its refrain, "No quiero ser la mosca aplastada" ("I do not want to be the squashed fly"). As she repeats the poem throughout the performance, she adds a series of verses that begin "Tengo derecho al . . ." ("I have the right to . . ."), which are followed with a series of basic human rights, such as the right to physical and intellectual sustenance and the right to free movement through and enjoyment of the amenities offered by an urban environment. These poetic interventions conclude by reiterating "¡Tengo derecho!" ("I have rights!"; 10). As Bosch's repetition of the poem's refrain become increasingly sharp and accusatory, the audience becomes even more conscious of the performer's awareness of being observed and of the fact that she is returning the gaze to them, no longer in the character of a prostitute, but as an actor that demands visibility for women without rights of citizenship. In short, the use of a variety of performance modes in narrating and embodying stories about *Las viajeras* demands shifting interpretative strategies on the part of the audience, and it also suggests that only multiple representational modes can capture the complexity of the social problem explored. Indeed, as I further develop in the next chapter, multiple strategies such as metatheater, intertextuality, and a restless search for dramatic forms mark the unique transnational aesthetic qualities of Frank Disla's plays about migration.

There is no doubt that the central objective of *Las viajeras* is to raise consciousness about sex trafficking, a global issue affecting women's rights, and that *Mondongo Scam* similarly advocates for the rights of undocumented immigrants. In both pieces, however, the didacticism of the political message is less intriguing than the politics of the forms used in representing the stories. In the same vein as Ridout, Lehmann argues that it is not the direct political content that makes theater political—rather, it is "through the implicit substance and critical value of its mode of representation" (178). Theater intervenes politically by offering a forum that links perception to experience. In the society of the spectacle, Lehmann writes, the bombardment of images of human suffering in the media "creates a radical distance for passive viewing" and dissolves "the bond between perception and action, receiving message and 'answerability'" (184). Theater works like *Las viajeras* and *Mondongo Scam* confront spectators with the problem of having to react to what is being performed in their presence. The audience is engaged in the theatrical production of meaning, which for Lehmann is an experience that "would not only be aesthetic but therein at the same time ethico-political"

(185). In the theater, moreover, there is no comforting distance of *aquí* and *allá* that one experiences in viewing global media—rather, there is a "mutual implication of actors and spectators," which offers an "aesthetic of responsibility (or response-ability)" (185). The ethical encounter in *Las viajeras* is created through its epistolary framing and through a hybrid dramaturgy that mixes aesthetics of accessibility with aesthetics of estrangement, while in *Mondongo Scam* the court scene framework and constant metatheatrical shift in roles place spectators in active interpretative roles. Moving between music, dance, and narrative, these theater works provoke both emotional empathy and intellectual distancing, allowing Mir and Bosch to resist settling for the shock tactics of ripped from the headlines sensationalism (the media) or the one-sided delivery of a didactic message (political propaganda).

On the contrary, the shifting modes of representation trigger the spectator's awareness of his or her capacity to respond, in Casiano's words—"to get up, stand up, stand up for your rights"—a responsibility and "response-ability" that, for Lehmann, is lacking in other contexts of image production (185). Returning by way of conclusion to the public sphere imagined by Arendt as a dinner table that locates people in proximity with one another, both relating and separating them in such a way they are able to engage in civil speech and action, so too does the theater event structure a forum of collective address in which people interact through speech and persuasion in the roles of actors and observers. In the *convivio* of the theater event, stories of Dominican migration are given form and witnessed, activating discussions, remembrances, and future imaginings crucial for claiming identity, space, and a political voice for communities that live across borders without the full rights of citizenship. Not only do *Mondongo Scam* and *Las viajeras* evoke the "mutual implication" of the *aquí* and *allá* of the stories represented onstage and the real-world space of the auditorium, their vision also speaks to both a local and a global audience and imagines a common, yet multi-sited Dominican polis inclusive of the constantly shifting *aquí* and *allá* of transnationalism. This theater practice constitutes a transnational Dominican public, and, as I argue in the following chapter, it also embodies a unique style and focuses our attention on the margins of both the US Latino and Latin American theater traditions.

Chapter 6

The Aesthetics of Minor Transnationalism in the Theater of Frank Disla

> Hi . . . digo hola . . . Hola o Hello, he ahí el dilema . . . ¿Qué es más importante, vivir la crisis agobiante que despedaza eternamente a mi pueblo o seguir en esta cárcel corriendo el riesgo de caer preso? Oh Hamlet, príncipe de Dinamarca."
>
> **—Poncia, from *Un búfalo de El Paso, Texas* (40–41)**

In this chapter, I argue that the insistent formal experimentation in Frank Disla's plays about migration is suggestive of the transnational artist's pursuit of new forms of political and artistic belonging. Not only do Disla's characters explore the ontological condition of belonging to more than one society (or perhaps none), his own dramatic oeuvre occupies an unsure space in literary history as well. The creative practices of Dominican theater artists like Disla take place in a network of relationships that simultaneously links them to two nation-states, and like the characters in their plays who enact the social scenarios of migration, transnational playwrights and their artistic endeavors cross borders. Consequently, their work can go unnoticed, since it does not fit easily into either a minority US Latino or a national Dominican theater paradigm. Instead, the cosmopolitan and creolized aesthetics of Frank Disla's work, its engagement with difference and exclusion, and its challenge to hegemonic notions of citizenship most productively might be understood within the cultural orientations of what Françoise Lionnet and Shu-mei Shih call "minor transnationalism." By reading Disla's work as an instance of minor transnationalism, I hope to invite further analysis of transnational performance as an important site for new thinking about how twenty-first-century theater artists intervene in a globalized cultural politics that traverses national boundaries.

As I have argued throughout this book, the work of Dominican theater practitioners who move between the Dominican Republic and the United States addresses a multi-sited social field, fostering the imagination of a transnational Dominican community. "By becoming mobile and making narratives out of this mobility," the literary scholar Andrew Smith suggests, "people escape the control of states and national borders and the limited, linear, ways of understanding themselves which states promote in their citizens" (245). As we have seen, the staging of scenarios of migration, together with other forms of cultural production, represent "cultural remittances" that pressure both the sending and receiving societies to form more inclusive notions of national identity and belonging.[1] It is important to remember, nevertheless, that for many Dominicans "becoming mobile" is neither a choice nor is inspired by a conscious desire to experience a new mode of constructing identity or legal category of citizenship; rather, it is the result of the state's failure to provide social and economic security for much of its citizenry.

At the same time, Dominican transnationalism is symptomatic of the increasing economic, technological, political, and cultural interconnectedness of global society. The discourses of globalization and transnationalism, however, differ importantly with respect to "the key assumptions they make about the role of the state in the production of meaning, identity and social outcomes" (M. Smith 17). Whereas globalization discourse tends to depict social processes in spaces unmoored from national territories, transnationalism, Michael Peter Smith argues, "insists on the continuing significance of borders, state policies, and national identities even as these are often transgressed by transnational communication circuits and social practices" (18). Indeed, mobility does not free transnational subjects of regulatory regimes such as the state and the market, and, in fact, they are exposed to "new modes of subjectification that cut across political borders" as well (Ong 18). For example, many of the literary characters in the plays and performances analyzed throughout this book underscore how the hybrid identities embodied by Dominican transnationals are minoritized by the dominant cultures in both nation-states and how they "are perceived as foreigners in both societies: Dominicans in New York City and dominicanyorks in Santo Domingo" (Guarnizo 52). Furthermore, when citizenship is determined by location in sovereign territories and membership to a body politic, the rights of transnational subjects are not guaranteed (see chapter 5). The studies of Dominican transnationalism mentioned in the introduction identify a trend of transmigrants using the host nation-state as an economic resource while maintaining a psychic and cultural connection with the home country. Dominican transnationals are not apt to assimilate, even though they may remain permanently in the United States. Therefore, they are in continual negotiation with discourses of citizenship and identity in both locations, and their real-time engagement with these discourses in different cultures impacts how they shape their concepts of self and society, unlocks hegemonic notions of *dominicanidad*, and, in the case of Frank Disla, adds a cosmopolitan quality to his cultural production.

While imagining an audience across borders helps theorize new, transnational publics, there is no guarantee that a transnational aesthetics will achieve the basic objective of any theater artist: acknowledgement of their art by an audience. The works of Disla, author of more than a dozen plays, are central to my understanding of Dominican transnational theater, and they constitute a compelling case for Latin(o) American theater studies to theorize a category of transnational theatrical activity. Disla is a transmigrant theater practitioner in the sense that although he has resided in the United States since 1987, he continues to write in Spanish and to identify himself as Dominican.[2] On the one hand, vehicles for promoting his work link Disla to a transnational Dominican literary field that exceeds the insular territory of the nation, but, on the other hand, Disla's transnational positioning limits him from making many inroads in the US Latino literary market or the international Spanish-language literary market. Torres-Saillant has critiqued the lack of a publishing industry in the Dominican Republic due to writers' reliance on self-publishing and connections to the state publishing apparatus, which creates "una situación en la que quien publica no es necesariamente el que debe, sino el que puede" ("a situation in which he who publishes isn't necessarily who should, but rather he who can"; "Similitudes" 103). Consequently, the market is dominated by books written by a handful of established and well-connected authors and with works of questionable merit, most of which are sold only in a limited, local market. As Torres-Saillant points out, since authors or the state front the publishing costs, printers are not motivated to operate as true publishing houses that would invest in marketing and distribution to recoup their expenses ("Similitudes" 102). Dominican writers in the diaspora face similar challenges, particularly since many write exclusively in Spanish. Torres-Saillant and Hernández note that "these literary artists have very few publication opportunities. Normally, they have to finance, supervise production, and distribute their own books. They have hardly any chance of becoming included in mainstream literary markets or at least attaining a level of prestige outside their immigrant enclaves" (*Dominican Americans* 120). More recently, however, authors such as Julia Álvarez and Junot Díaz have been incorporated in the mainstream US Latino literature market and are read in translation in the Dominican Republic, whereas authors like Viriato Sención and Rey Emmanuel Andújar, who have written in Spanish and resided in the United States, have gained a readership in the Dominican Republic.[3]

To date, although his migration was motivated in part by a search for new personal and artistic horizons, Disla's exclusive use of Spanish and links with the theater establishment in the Dominican Republic has maintained his strong profile at home (personal interview). His sustained connection with homeland Dominican theater, in spite of living in the United States for thirty years, is nurtured by his lifetime collaboration with his brother, Reynaldo Disla, who has long held positions in the Dominican Ministry of Culture and has authored and directed over thirty-five theater pieces. The work of the Disla brothers, who are among the most productive and innovative Dominican theater practitioners of the past fifty years, represents a noteworthy gap in Latin American theater history and criticism.[4] Throughout childhood, adolescence, and young adulthood, together and in independent projects, the Disla brothers created plays and founded theater publications and performance collectives, playing a key role in the development of Dominican popular theater in the 1970s and 1980s. Frank Disla's work has been consistently validated in his home country, and four of his plays have been anthologized in the Dominican Casa de Teatro series for having won prizes in its annual competition.[5] Even more telling, in terms of reconceptualizing the field of Dominican literature as transnational, is the fact that Disla has twice won the Dominican Republic's Cristóbal de Llerena national theater prize while living abroad—first in 1992 for *Desarraigados* (Uprooted), and in 2005 for *Un búfalo de El Paso, Texas* (A Buffalo from El Paso, Texas), which is the main focus of my analysis in this chapter. In my view, Disla has used his home country as a resource for staging, critiquing, and publishing his work, while his residence in the United States has fed his artistic imagination, resulting in plays that bring new styles and themes to both the Dominican national stage and a much wider implicit audience.

Although in the United States Disla's plays have not yet been edited by publishers or staged in professional theaters, several of his pieces have received dramatized readings and full performances in small venues. His work has also been validated in his country of residence in a way that suggests the institutionalization of a transnational Dominican literary field. In addition to the Cristóbal de Llerena national theater awards, Disla has recently received the Letras de Ultramar prize for *Ascenso y caída de Andresito Reyna* (The Rise and Fall of Andresito Reyna) (2013) and *Un romance andaluz* (An Andalusian Romance) (2016). This literary competition for Dominican authors residing abroad demonstrates how Dominican cultural institutions have responded to the development of a transnational society—it is sponsored by the Ministry of Culture of the Dominican Republic and is administered by the Dominican commissioner of culture in the United States. The winning texts are included in a series published by Editora Nacional, and the authors are celebrated in Santo Domingo at the International Book Fair. In the introduction, I remarked on some of the flaws of this system of selective publishing, and it could be argued that the privilege of having an editorial outlet for Dominicans in the diaspora simply repeats in the United States the same inadequacies of the state-dominated Dominican publishing industry. Nonetheless, extending the Ministry of Culture to serve Dominicans abroad represents a literary infrastructure other Latino groups are not able to count on. In an essay on the arrival of Latino literature to the US market in the 1990s, as an "accepted, English-language component of the multicultural canon," Juan Flores makes the point that Puerto Ricans lack the institutional support that other Latino groups with consulates in the US enjoy ("Life" 187). Flores is cautious about celebrating the politics of hyphenated, assimilationist Latino cultural production when it fails to recognize the "differential access to literary and cultural capital as a result of direct colonial relations" (196). Referencing Gustavo Pérez-Firmat's *Life on the Hyphen: The Cuban-American Way*, Flores claims that the internal colonialism lived by Puerto Ricans in the United States positions them "off the hyphen" and that Nuyorican literature is a "lowercase literature" that fits neither the paradigm of national literature nor the paradigm of US Latino literature (196). By contrast, the Dominican Republic has developed a cultural politics to support the interests of the diasporic community in recognition that the nation's literary field spans two nation-states, but also for pragmatic reasons: this overseas population is inextricably linked to the economic well-being of the nation. While writers such as Díaz and Álvarez are identified with US Latino literature, Dominican authors residing in the United States (like Disla) are positioned in a transnational framework that seeks a homeland audience, as well as a Spanish-speaking audience in United States and abroad. Therefore, transnational Dominican literature does not fit well in an either/or model; rather than viewing writers like Disla as "on" or "off" the hyphen, the prefix *trans* in *transnational*, meaning "across" or "through" allows us to think of a pendular, multi-sited literary practice.

Lionnet and Shih's notion of minor transnationalism is in line with the idea of a "lowercase literature" operating in the margins, and it offers a productive starting point for theorizing the theatrical activity of artists that cannot be simply located in either national or ethnic paradigms. They draw their theory of minor transnationalism from ethnic, transnational, and postcolonial cultural studies, and from concepts developed by the French philosophers Jacques Derrida, Gilles Deleuze, and Félix Guattari, and from the postcolonial thinker Édouard Glissant, among others. By "minor transnationalism" they refer to minority subjectivities and discourses that create networks within and across national boundaries as well as to a cultural mood that differs from the more jubilant "major" key: "'minor transnationalism' is perhaps the mode in which the traumas of colonial, imperial, and global hegemonies as well as the affective dimensions of transcolonial solidarities continue to work themselves out and produce new possibilities" (Lionnet and Shih 21). Lionnet and Shih aim to avoid the binary framework into which postcolonial, globalization, and transnational studies critiques often fall when they approach minority cultural formations as vertical engagements of assimilation and opposition. They write: "What is lacking in the binary model of above-and-below, the utopic and the dystopic, and the global and the local is an awareness and recognition of the creative interventions that networks of minoritized cultures produce within and across national boundaries. All too often the emphasis on the major-resistant mode of cultural practices denies the complex and multiple forms of cultural expressions of minorities and diasporic peoples and hides their micropractices of transnationality" (7). As we have seen earlier in this study, Luis Guarnizo argues that Dominican transnationals occupy subaltern positions in both the United States and the Dominican Republic. In the same way, Disla's dramaturgy is made minor by its translocal space of enunciation. In the context of the United States, his Spanish-language plays form part of a minoritarian cultural discourse, while in the Spanish-dominant Dominican Republic, Disla's works, written and conceived abroad, are deterritorialized and become minor in the context of the majoritarian culture of the nation. Therefore, in my estimation, Disla's dramatic production cannot be read exclusively in relation to either Dominican national or US Latino ethnic cultures. It moves between and transcends both cultural landscapes, posing important questions about minor transnational cultures that live across borders and the possibilities of creating art that represents them.

Disla's minor transnational sensibilities are made visible in part because his dramas about Chilean, Cuban, Mexican, and Puerto Rican migrants insert Dominican migration in a wider framework of global mobility.[6] That is, Disla's work can be studied in the context of Dominican migration to the United States and within a specific debate on changing representations of Dominican cultural identity, but as Lionnet and Shih caution, it is important not to essentialize the cultural practices of minority diaspora cultures and limit them to a homogeneous major-resistant mode. Thus, we might view Disla's dramaturgy as representative of a US-Dominican transnational dynamic on the one hand, and, on the other, as an example of minor transnationalism in the lateral linkages his plays make with other nomadic, border crossing cultures. In this way, Disla's work can be read along with Dominican *teatristas* who have developed their theater projects transnationally, as well as in a wider context of Latin American playwrights in the United States whose texts and productions are in conversation with their nations of origin. Disla's creative practices, dramatic themes, and styles reflect a distinctive aesthetics that is at once "minor" in its focus on minority diaspora cultures and cosmopolitan in terms outlined by the cultural anthropologist Ulf Hannerz: "Cosmopolitanism is first of all an orientation, a willingness to engage with the Other. It entails an intellectual and esthetic openness toward divergent cultural experiences, a search for contrasts rather than uniformity" (103).[7] One might argue, then, that Disla's inclusive approach to the theme of migration and, on a formal level, his experimentation with different genres and use of metatheatrical role-playing and intertextuality are apt artistic strategies for creating an aesthetics of minor transnationalism useful for understanding a broad array of theater practitioners working across borders.[8]

In the plays included in *Desarraigados*, along with *El Barbero de Saint Ann Street* and *Chicken Cordon Blue*, Disla tells stories of migration through self-reflexive experimentation with genre, intertexts, and metatheater, developing an aesthetics of minor transnationalism that is later fully realized in *Un búfalo de El Paso, Texas*. For example, *Desarraigados* shows Disla's search for a genre to approximate the theme of migration—it consists of four pieces that range from a monologue, a compact multi-character domestic drama, a dramatic dialogue, and a one-act ensemble piece set, tellingly, on a boat. The migrant characters in these stories are literally and figuratively adrift—lost in memory, alcoholism, urban violence, and loneliness.[9] In another piece that treats the theme of migration, *El Barbero de Saint Ann Street*, the characters perform multiple roles that are mainly provided by other texts. As might be expected, the title serves as a paratextual, framing reference for the play, for it evokes other theatrical barbers: *The Barber of Seville* and *Sweeney Todd: The Demon Barber of Fleet Street*. The paratext cues the reader to anticipate a mix of amorous intrigue, murder, and, above all, musical performances. In *El Barbero de Saint Ann Street*, confronting a betrayal brings to the forefront the disillusions of a seventy-four-year-old Puerto Rican barber, Philip, and his longtime Dominican client and friend, Erasmo. Both live frustrated by unrealized life aspirations: Philip was lured to the United States long ago by the bright lights of Broadway and is tormented by his failure to make a career in show business; the former military man Erasmo is too haunted by the Trujillo and Balaguer regimes to return home. Philip has discovered that Erasmo betrayed him with his wife, and their encounter turns out to be their last when, after a delirious series of scenes in which Philip directs Erasmo in playing different roles, Philip reveals he knows the truth and kills himself (and his wife). Astonishingly, the modes of performance and the specific texts performed by the two men range from Greek tragedy and Henrik Ibsen to zarzuela, cabaret, and Broadway musicals. Incorporating intertexts creates a constant shift in style and tone within the play, which marks an intensification of this same restless search for form from one piece to the next in the collection of one-acts in *Desarraigados* and, as we will see, in the monologue pieces in *Chicken Cordon Blue*. These qualities, which might be described as textual migration—crossing textual borders—and metatheatrical migrancy—moving from one role to another—are most fully articulated as a minor transnational aesthetics in Disla's more recently published play, *Un búfalo de El Paso, Texas* (2005).

Migrant Identities in *Chicken Cordon Blue*

In the development of Disla's unique artistic style, *Chicken Cordon Blue* represents one of his best-known pieces because it has reached a relatively wide audience, having been being published and staged in multiple venues.[10] The play is composed of four vignettes, monologues voiced by migrants from different Latin American countries that are connected by an entertaining emcee, Miss Cordon, and performed on a bare stage. The stage directions indicate a minimalist staging "sin coacción de ningún género" ("without the imposition of any genre"; 75) and highlight the task of the players and spectators in imagining the harsh realities the lives of *pollos* in the United States. Literally, *pollos* are chickens, but the term is used figuratively to refer to newly arrived migrants and/or their irregular status. The multiplicity of stories, ambiances, and performance styles offered in the monologues challenge audiences to reflect on the experience of migration more thoughtfully than the charged discourses on migration circulating in politics and the media. Furthermore, the various national origins of the characters—Puerto Rico, Mexico, Cuba, and Dominican Republic—remind Dominican audiences that the minoritized cultures produced by global mobility are many, shifting the play from mainly engaging with nationalist discourses of identity and instead locating Dominicans in a larger context of minority diaspora cultures.

As if to soften the uncomfortable task of witnessing the raw stories of migrants, Miss Cordon empathizes with the spectators' discomfort, at one point seating herself in the auditorium and admitting that she does not understand the stories unfolding on stage in which "todo es pollo y los asuntos, conflictos y acciones son tratados como en un gallinero y no como en el

6.1. *Chicken Cordon Blue* handbill. Photo credit: Juan José Saleta.

teatro, donde todo debe ser bello, tocado por *el pencil* mágico de este arte . . . pero los tiempos cambian y quizás esté equivocada" ("where everything is chicken and the issues, conflicts, and actions are treated like in a chicken coop and not as in the theater, where everything should be beautiful, touched by the magic pencil of this art . . . but times change and I might be wrong"; 84).[11]

In the monologues, the characters raise chickens, eat chicken dishes, and frequently compare their life circumstances to being "consumed" by *la olla* (the cooking pot) or *la gallera* (the chicken coop or cockpit) that is the US labor machine. The chicken metaphor is extended to include Miss Cordon, whose role it is to serve as the evening's host and as a "cord" linking the monologue pieces. In her first entrance, Miss Cordon arrives holding dead chickens and dramatically tells the audience how she saved them from being wasted after their sacrifice in a *santería* ceremony. She jokes that she is an "entremés andante" in more than one sense of the word: both an appetizer and an entertaining dramatic interlude (76). The play's title becomes clear when Miss Cordon sets about preparing chicken cordon bleu to be shared with the audience.

The English spelling of *blue* rather than the French (*bleu*) evokes the US context of the story and the melancholy, or "minor" key of the monologues.

6.2. Miss Cordon hands out chicken cordon bleu. Photo credit: Juan José Saleta.

The changed spelling also suggests the revitalization of a recipe, and perhaps by extension, of a society, when new ingredients, or cultures, are introduced. Miss Cordon produces a transculturated chicken cordon bleu prepared with sweet cheese and *queso blanco* (white cheese): "Tengo mi propio estilo, no hay nada mejor que la originalidad y no es solamente eso, es que sabe bien" ("I have my own style, there's nothing better than originality and it's not only that, it tastes good"; 80). Ultimately, Miss Cordon's role is less important for connecting the stand-alone monologues as it is for connecting the universe of *Chicken Cordon Blue* with the audience and calling for empathy and recognition. Although her role is to interact with the real-life audience, Miss Cordon repeatedly reminds us that she is following the author's script (yet she often questions it and improvises) and that she remains within the fiction of the play, just as imaginary as any of the other characters and therefore invisible, or nonexistent, outside the fictional world of the play. Moreover, Miss Cordon outs herself as a *pollo* when she makes her appeal to the audience: "El planeta es de todos, hasta de los pollos, por más que no nos quieran ver, más tendrán que vernos" ("The planet belongs to everyone, even the undocumented, no matter how much they don't want to see us, they will have to see us"; 95). Here Miss Cordon includes herself as a *pollo*, relating earlier references to her status as an imaginary and invisible character to the "nonexistence" of an undocumented immigrant. In the context of the

Sala Ravelo of the Dominican National Theater, the play's call for the stories of migrants to be seen and heard constitutes a departure from a pattern of marginalization and rejection of the culture of the diaspora.

Each monologue includes a performance motif that suggests the conscious and unconscious ways immigrants negotiate their identities in new contexts. Similar to *Mondongo Scam* (see chapter 5), in *Chicken Cordon Blue* the metatheatrical trying on of different personas constitutes a translation strategy that does not result in assimilation—replacing one nationalist attachment with another—but in hybrid minority diaspora identities that embody multiple identifications. In Brenda González's monologue, for example, we learn that her mask is youth. While getting drunk during a poignantly solitary birthday celebration, the aging Puerto Rican woman becomes increasingly truthful about her age. Motivated by the fear that "a una anciana no le dan trabajo en ningún sitio" ("they don't give jobs to old ladies anywhere"; 79) and that she will never earn enough money to retire, the frustrated performer wears a wig and makeup to disguise her true age. From the story of internal colonialism and the failed *sueño americano* (American dream) for Puerto Ricans, *Chicken Cordon Blue* shifts to the story of illegal migration across the US-Mexico border. Equally inebriated, Jorge Múñiz downplays the terrifying experience of crossing the border by spinning a tale in the self-conscious style of a Mexican telenovela actor or romantic singer. Accompanied by the bar's soundtrack of mariachi and ranchera music, the image Jorge presents of himself as a tenderhearted macho, justified in killing his best friend who betrayed him with his wife, contrasts with the reality that he is completely adrift and vulnerable in what he calls "este inmenso gallinero que es la vida" ("this immense cock pit that is life"; 84).

While the first two vignettes expose the disorientation experienced by migrants as they attempt to inhabit immigrant identities, the third and fourth monologues go a step further and show hybrid transnational subjectivities in the process of construction. In a one-way telephone conversation with a male friend in Cuba, it becomes clear that for Angélico, Elizabeth, New Jersey, forms part of the Cuban political and cultural imaginary just as much as Havana does.[12] As the overabundance of phones in his home suggests, Angélico is constantly connected to Cuba. He performs his Cuban identity in the diaspora by driving a vintage Cadillac, raising roosters for illegal cockfighting and *santería* ceremonies, and, most importantly, by asserting his machismo. Over the phone, Angélico metes out sexist advice about how to handle women, but a call on the other line reveals that he is completely dominated by his demanding wife. Angélico returns to his macho performance when he picks up his conversation with his friend, but the visual image of him with a skirt accidentally stuck to his pants as he moves about frantically cooking, cleaning, and ironing, all the while chatting on the phone, show that he has adapted to quite a different role in his life in the United States. Play with gender categories here does not necessarily denaturalize the culturally constructed binaries of male and female, although the monologue does signal that there are different ways and spaces in which to be Cuban. That is, while Disla lampoons machismo, a component of Cuban identity that Angélico fails to reproduce, he stops short of presenting a new male Cuban diasporic subject.

For his only tale of Dominican migration, Disla imagines a monologue delivered largely to an invisible psychiatrist by a young woman, Esperanza Suárez, who is white, American-born, and Dominican-adopted. Her monologue suggests the dissolution of nativist identity categories that emphasize territorial and biological concepts of national identities. Esperanza is adopted by a Dominican family in New Jersey, but she spends her childhood and adolescence in Santo Domingo, returning to the United States with her family as a young adult. In this family, transnational migration and adoption disassociate *dominicanidad* from blood ties and geography. Esperanza's national identity is established by the legal framework of adoption, and regardless of place of residence, she is culturally Dominican because her household raised her in accordance with Dominican values and customs.[13] However, in adolescence, being tall and light-skinned, her neighborhood friends began to note her physical difference and nicknamed her "La Polla Gringa" (87). As Esperanza notes, this was an insult because "gringo chicken" referred to imported, high-yield poultry that Dominicans mocked for supposedly being riddled with worms, causing AIDS, infertility, and hormonal changes that could impact one's sexual orientation (Disla 87; Derby, "Gringo Chicken" 452). The historian Lauren Derby has shown that in the early 1990s the poultry industry became a battleground for asserting Dominican national identity, and she argues that the gringo chicken debate "symbolized the ambivalence of national identity in the Caribbean, as the mediating nexus between foreign and homegrown (lo extranjero vs. lo criollo), cash and food crops, money and morality, market and family, and the United States and the Dominican Republic" ("Gringo Chickens" 452). The "Polla Gringa" label makes Esperanza feel like an outsider and she finds refuge in her friend Leonel's household, where she enjoys spending time speaking and reading in English, her native language. This is a humorous touch, because the name of her friend evokes Leonel Fernández, the first New York City-raised Dominican to become president of the republic. On one level, Esperanza is alienated from her Dominican identity by having a foreign physical appearance and being adopted, and, on another level, by being raised by a family that has resided in the United States and is marked as Dominicanyork. Like the imported gringo chicken, Esperanza's identity and life experience "raises a key issue every Dominican must contend with: that is, what defines nationality in the U.S.-directed world system? What is 'Dominican' in a context in which the external and the internal have for centuries been thoroughly interpenetrated and have rendered ambiguous the boundaries separating the foreign and the national?" (Derby, "Gringo Chickens" 452–53).

The consumption of popular culture disseminated by the mass media represents a non-food product that similarly signals the porousness of national boundaries brought about by globalization. Throughout the monologues in *Chicken Cordon Blue* the distinct soundtracks for each character underscore how popular culture in the form of music supplies images and scenarios that feed the imagination, a key source of agency in the global world, according to the globalization theorist Arjun Appadurai (32, 55). Feeling rejected by Santo Domingo locals, Esperanza finds a peer group among African American expatriates: "No me sentía dominicana, ni norteamericana blanca, así que me coloqué entre un grupo de morenos de Newark que vivían retirados en Santo Domingo en una congregación de Hare Krishna" ("I felt neither Dominican, nor white American, so I situated myself among a group of blacks from Newark who lived amongst themselves in a Santo Domingo Hare Krishna congregation"; 88). During this period Esperanza deeply identifies with African American hip-hop culture and begins to see her life through the prisms of possible lives offered through video culture: "El mundo de fantasía de los videos, las luces, el escenario, los chicos y chicas bailando, fue mi escape, mi refugio, porque la realidad todavía estaba llena de basura" ("The fantasy world of videos, the lights, the set, the boys and girls dancing, was my escape, my refuge, because reality was still full of garbage"; 89). Esperanza suspends her university studies and sets aside her political poetry and focuses instead on her relationship with an African American man and joining a rap music group. When her family moves back to New Jersey, she further retreats from reality and settles in the basement of their home, where she endlessly rehearses to become a video DJ. Esperanza's "homeland" is rap music and video clips, not a national territory. Her identifications are informed by a transnational youth black culture, a "stylish solidarity," or politics based on body and style described by Paul Gilroy: "Clothing, objects, things, and commodities provide the only entry ticket into stylish solidarities powerful enough to foster novel forms of nationality found in collectivities like the Gangsta Nation, the Hip hop Nation, and, of course, the Nation of Islam" (268). Racially white, culturally Hispanic,

6.3. Esperanza Suárez in *Chicken Cordon Blue*. Photo credit: Juan José Saleta.

and acting black, Esperanza Suárez's movement between cultures embodies a transcultural identity in flux.

While *Chicken Cordon Blue* does not invite celebration of Esperanza's or any of the other character's hybrid identities—this is particularly so in Esperanza's case, since her immigrant identity is pathologized by framing her monologue as a psychiatric session—it performs the experiences of diasporic minorities and seeks the audience's recognition of the complexities of such lives. In *Chicken Cordon Blue* and his other plays about migration, Disla transcends a major-resistant mode that is limited to responding to Dominican nationalism and as an alternative locates diasporic *dominicanidad* in a network of minoritized transnational cultures. This shifts the discussion from how Dominican identity has been enriched or eroded by the processes of migration to what Dominican transnational identities have in common with other twenty-first-century cultures that have become unmoored from national territories.

Border Crossing in *Un búfalo de El Paso, Texas*

It should not surprise, then, that in *Un búfalo de El Paso, Texas*, Disla's most complete display of the tenor and techniques representative of minor transnationalism, only one of the narrative threads contains a specific tale of Dominican migration and El Paso (the US-Mexico border) does not figure prominently in the text. However, in both form and content *Un búfalo* displays myriad forms of border crossing. In the play, two actors, Pancho and Poncia, play multiple roles in ten episodic scenes involving two central storylines. In one story, the Cuban-American Vietnam War veteran Emilio Ramírez laments the horrors of war and the loss of his true love, Tais Pérez, who has fallen into a seedy world of erotic dancing, drugs, and prostitution. Emilio is the play's titular buffalo, a type of heroic loner. His past relationship with Tais links him to her sordid family saga in which she was sexually abused by her uncle, Mateo Horowiz, and her cousin, Tony. Mateo Horowiz is a Jewish factory owner from Brooklyn who marries Elena, a Dominican immigrant who worked in his factory as a cleaner. The play's other narrative thread is Pancho and Poncia playing actors creating and rehearsing scenes from several plays. Throughout, Pancho and Poncia constantly switch character roles and at times the different spaces and epochs intersect, presupposing the active intellectual participation of the audience. As the editors note on the book's back cover, distancing techniques in this work paradoxically serve as "una pesquisa interior, psicológica y profunda" (a deep, psychological interior examination). In my estimation, Disla's rejection of straightforward psychological realism in favor of ludic experiment with dramatic conventions represents the culmination of the author's search for an aesthetics that convey the compound qualities of transnational subjectivities.[14]

Perhaps the most striking feature of the structure of *Un búfalo* is the repetition of buffalo stampedes that connect the fragmented narratives. In the first eight scenes, Pancho and Poncia, regardless of the story and characters they are performing, escape a buffalo stampede simulated by body movement and sound effects. In the final scenes, they join the stampede and the play ends with Pancho and Poncia turning the buffalo away from heading over a precipice and guiding them, along with the spectators, to the auditorium exit. Earlier in the play, however, herds roaming across the plains as a collectivity evoke a less benign reading of the buffalo image. In at least two instances, the buffalos are figured as fascist hordes, first as Nazis persecuting Mateo Horowiz, who portrays himself as a wandering Jew, and second as Falangist Spaniards pursuing Federico García Lorca during the Spanish Civil War. Thus, the buffalo herds suggest forced migrations, or fleeing, as well as the ideological movements that give rise to such geographical dislocations.[15] In a monologue on the equalizing effects of mortality, Pancho, playing an actor, explains, "Por eso odio las multitudes que como cuadrilla de bovinos se desplazan en movimientos colectivos sin fin, movidos por cualquier idea común y que también irremediablemente desaparecerán sin rastro" ("That is why I hate multitudes that travel in endless collective movements like herds of cattle, moved by any common idea that will also inevitably disappear without a trace"; 40). Although twentieth-century fascist movements may have come and gone, *Un búfalo* makes evident that rather than disappearing without a trace they have reappeared in new guises.

While the world economy may demand that workers cross national borders, post-9/11 security anxieties and an economic recession have fed an anti-immigration movement in the United States that aims to criminalize migration and close borders. This threatening mood resonates when Mateo likens being a Puerto Rican in the United States to being a Jew in Nazi Germany: "Tiempos éstos en que hablar de bomba es un atentado. A mi vecino de Puerto Rico se lo llevaron preso, como a un judío por la Gestapo. Le preguntaron por qué tenía la música tan alta, que era tiempo de luto y él les dijo que la Bomba y La Plena la escuchaba a ese volumen por costumbre" ("What kind of times are these, in which talking about *bomba* is a bomb attack. They took my Puerto Rican neighbor to jail, like a Jew taken away by the Gestapo. They asked him why he had the music on so loud, that it was a period of mourning, and he told them that it was customary to listen to *bomba y plena* at a loud volume"; 21). In the War on Terror, what formerly might have been a clash over cultural difference becomes a threat to national security meriting the beating and incarceration of the Puerto Rican neighbor. As the repeat stampedes at the end of each scene suggest, collective movements continue to thunder through humanity, the question is whether to join them, run in the opposite direction, or be trampled.

In addition to the motif of roaming buffalo herds, the characters and action of *Un búfalo* evoke a deterritorialized sense of belonging by constantly crossing spatial and temporal borders. The unexplained shifts in time and space give the impression of the characters existing not so much in a specific space and time as in different places and epochs all at once. Through the dialogue, the audience might surmise that the action is taking place in a go-go bar in the United States, a Spanish *mesón* (bar) in the Dominican Republic, or on a stage. These spaces suit a transnational dramaturgy that straddles borders, for they are public spaces through which anonymous patrons pass rather than the static, domestic spaces of nationalist drama.[16] The characters, who are marked by their uprootedness and ethnic difference, are situated in the United States, but their life experiences and social networks span small towns in New Jersey, megacities like New York City and Caracas, and distant locales such as Vietnam and Romania. It is difficult to situate temporally the dizzying array of episodes narrated by the characters, but two main points of reference are the present post-9/11 era and the 1960s. The allusions to the 1960s and the height of the Cold War—the Cuban Missile Crisis and the US military interventions in the Dominican Republic and Vietnam—remind us that it was a time when ideological lines divided the planet in a bipolar tension between superpowers. In the Ramírez family, raised on a diet of his Cuban father's anti-Communist rhetoric, Emilio enlists to fight in the Vietnam War, whereas his brother—an admirer of Che Guevara—stays home. *Un búfalo* betrays some longing for this clearly divided world when Emilio's brother is remembered as "un búfalo más que guarda un fragmento del muro de Berlín como recuerdo de sus sueños . . . se cercenó el ala izquierda" ("another buffalo who keeps a fragment of the Berlin wall like a memento of his dreams . . . his left wing was clipped"; 12). The fall of socialism cut short leftist dreams, and one of the questions posed by the play is what kind of beliefs and values will form the basis of new social movements in a world drawn with more permeable boundaries and divided into multiple spheres of power.

The characters frequently frame their comments with variations on the phrase *en estos tiempos* (in these times), showing an acute consciousness of new global sensibilities and disorientations.[17] Pancho, speaking in the role of actor, observes that the characters in *Un búfalo,* "buscan como todos desesperadamente a qué asirse, aunque sea a un témpano de la guerra fría. Ay, Iván Illianov, qué falta haces" ("desperately seek, like all of us, for something to hold on to, even if it's an iceberg from the Cold War. Ah, Iván Illianov, how much we miss you"; 35). The nostalgia Pancho expresses for Vladimir Lenin (Vladmir Ilyich Ulyanov) comes off as humorous, as does his litany of ideologically confused cheers: "Viva Hitler, carajo, la doctrina Monroe, la Enmienda Platt, la Ley Torricelli, los campos de concentración, el despotismo, el nepotismo, el libre albedrío y la liberación de las féminas, el clonaje y el aborto" ("Long live Hitler, dammit, the Monroe Doctrine, the Platt Amendment, the Torricelli Law, concentration camps, despotism, nepotism, free will, the liberation of women, cloning, and abortion"; 36). According to Pancho, these are confusing times no longer governed by dualities: "Hay que nadar contra la corriente y a la vez arrastrarnos con ella . . . retroceder y avanzar son sinónimos . . . la gobernabilidad . . . la libre empresa . . . el comercio internacional . . . el mundo una aldea global donde ya no puedo ocultarme . . . las dualidades no existen" ("You must swim against the current and at the same time be dragged along by it . . . to retreat and to advance are synonyms . . . governability . . . free enterprise . . . international trade . . . the world, a global village where I can no longer hide . . ."; 41). The roaming herds of buffalo hint that ideologies come and go, and that yesterday's fascism looms on today's horizon in a new embodiment, but the play's ending also indicates hope that herds/social movements will join people in new affiliations and causes. Rather than allowing the buffalos to plummet over a precipice, the actors, who unmask and show their true faces, leave their fictional world onstage and step into the auditorium to guide the herd—spectators and buffalos—to the exits: "Salgamos de nuevo al ruedo, y a empezar . . . No importa que sea de nuevo, a correr búfalos, a correr . . . Otras llanuras nos aguardan" ("Let us enter the arena and begin again . . . It doesn't matter that it's again, run, buffalos, run . . . other plains await us"; 73).

Prior to the ending, however, *Un búfalo* crosses the invisible wall between the stage and the auditorium in numerous self-reflexive moments. In a metatheatrical fashion, *Un búfalo* frequently transgresses the border between fiction and reality, and, through intertextuality, it migrates from one text to another. In the context of Latin American theater, Gail Bulman argues, intertextuality often serves "to establish unique definitions of nation and to depict national identities, while, at the same time, it creates a literary game that highlights both texts, thus uncovering new artistic meanings as well. Intertextuality moves these dramatic texts beyond dialogue, and establishes multiple dialogues with the past, present and future, with other cultures, with other nations, or with multiple paradigms within self and nation" (27). Since, as Bulman points out, intertextuality helps imagine multiple models of literature, nation, and identity, I find it to be a fitting literary strategy for expressing the hybridity and cosmopolitanism of minor transnational collectivities. Again, it is important to qualify that while living across cultures may spark new creative forms, Dominican transnationals face the struggle of subaltern status in two nation-states. The intertextual reference to Shakespeare in the quote that heads this chapter exemplifies both the creativity and the plight of the transnational artist. It is voiced by a male author character played by Poncia: "Hi . . . digo hola . . . Hola o Hello, he ahí el dilema . . . ¿Qué es más importante, vivir la crisis agobiante que despedaza eternamente a mi pueblo o seguir en esta cárcel corriendo el riesgo de caer preso? Oh Hamlet, príncipe de Dinamarca" ("Hola . . . I mean Hi. Hi or Hola, that is the question . . . What is more important, to live the overwhelming crisis that eternally tears apart my people or to continue in this jail and run the risk of falling prisoner? Oh Hamlet, prince of Denmark"; 40–41). Here, Hamlet's existential dilemma is coded as having to choose between living in a system that fails its people (Dominican Republic), and living in a society that increasingly criminalizes immigrants (United States), though I would argue that the quote's bilingual opening offers a third option—the author character, like Disla, can opt to be located transnationally in both places.

Intertextual references in *Un búfalo* range from allusions to figures from Greek mythology and contemporary comic-book heroes, to the integration of the words and dramatic situations imagined in the songs of singer-songwriter Juan Luis Guerra, the works of theater practitioners such as Bertolt Brecht, Federico García Lorca, and Grupo Yuyachkani, to name a few examples.[18] With its multiplicity of stories, it is easy to forget that at the heart of *Un búfalo* is the narrative of a hero, Emilio, who roams in search of his lost love, Tais Pérez. Their story is parodied by the self-reflexive awareness with which the pair plays the part of ill-fated lovers, the parallels drawn between their actions and those from classical and pop cultures, and the degradation of the standard notion of "hero" in their characterization as a damaged Vietnam War vet and an erotic dancer. If the receptor of the play initially did not recognize Tais's name as an allusion to the famously destructive Greek courtesan, they will, when Tais, in an opium-induced haze, announces that she will model herself on the Greek concubine: "Pisaré las huellas de Thaïs . . . Tendré poder, los hombres se rendirán a mis pies . . ." ("I will follow in the footsteps of Thaïs . . . I will have power, men will surrender at my feet"; 18).[19] Like Thaïs, Emilio and the other male characters are conscious of playing the role of a larger-than-life persona. In the scene-ending buffalo stampedes, for example, they resign themselves to the duty of saving the female character: "Si no te arrastro te barren, maldito papel de héroe" ("If I don't grab you, they'll run you down, damn hero role"; 44).

The models of heroism for the male characters, Batman (66), Speedy González (34), Superman (53), and Ulysses (52), collapse distinctions between ancient and modern, and high and low culture. Similarly, in the following quote in which the hero sweeps in to save the day, the characters allude to both the Greek mythological figure Helen of Troy and the character Elena from the popular song "Elena" by the contemporary musician Juan Luis Guerra: "Ulises, the strong, the smart, llega. ¡Oh Elena, tu honor salvado! Móntate en el barco, ya sea en un furgón . . . Si te va bien escribe, Elena, la del Higüerito o de Troya, da lo mismo . . ." ("Ulysses, the strong, the brave, is here. Oh Elena! Your honor is saved! Get on the boat, even if it's in a freight car . . . if things go well for you, write, Elena of Higüerito, or Troy, it's all the same"; 52).[20] The postmodern pastiche of intertexts has a comic effect partly due to the comic book-like exaggeration of gender stereotypes. On the one hand, the men possess unattainable superhero qualities, while the women are only known for their dangerous beauty and sexuality and thus need "saving" to restore their honor. Perhaps more intriguing is the connection made between the Dominican town Higüerito and Troy in the phrase *da lo mismo*. By drawing attention to their sameness, Disla compares Dominican migration with one of the great heroic journeys of all time—Ulysses's return home from the Trojan War—and implicitly places the contemporary exodus from his country in the context of universal migrations.

However, unlike Helen of Troy, who had a face so beautiful that it instigated the Trojan War, the Elena of Higüerito in Disla's play loses face—namely, her dignity and identity. The title of Disla's scene, "Elena, la criolla" (Elena, the Creole), nevertheless, emphasizes that Elena was native to somewhere, that she had roots. In Guerra's song, and in the play, the narrative is as follows: Elena, a Dominican immigrant, arrives in New York City via Caracas with money she earned selling her body. In New York City, Elena lives in the Bronx with a Jewish factory worker. Captivated by consumer items temptingly gracing every storefront in the city, Elena takes risks and naïvely becomes a pawn in a drug-dealing operation, which results in her murder on a train. The entire content and most phrases of "Elena" are incorporated verbatim into *Un búfalo*, including the song's famous phrase, "si te va bien, escribe," (if it goes well, write), to which the play character responds: "Nunca escribí, ni para el sello de correo aparecía . . . En Caracas era un pez nadando en su propia agua . . . En Nueva York, el abandono, la soledad y la incertidumbre . . ." ("I never wrote, I never even had enough for a stamp . . . In Caracas I was a fish in water . . . In New York City, abandonment, loneliness, and uncertainty . . ."; 24).[21] In many ways, Disla's dramatization of the song echoes Guerra's fatalistic message about migration, which was typical of the negative Dominican discourse on migration in the late 1980s and early 1990s, a period in which the country grappled with the sudden impact of migration on so many aspects of national life. A crucial difference, however, is that Guerra sings the story of Elena whereas Disla grants Elena a voice, which gives her the opportunity to explain—for example, why she never wrote. In both Guerra's song and Disla's scene, Elena's migration is a tale of her progressive loss of roots, ideals, and morals. For example, the description of Elena moving through the streets of Manhattan with her *pie de arcilla* (clay foot) might be read as a country girl out of her depth in New York City's urban jungle, or, in relation to her increasing consumerist desires, as having "feet of clay," an idiomatic expression denoting a weakness or flaw. In *Un búfalo*, Disla expands upon these meanings by including Elena's personal history. In this context, the reference to clay links Elena to her homeland, and to her artisan father, who made *muñecas sin rostro*, faceless clay dolls that have come to be ubiquitous representations of Dominican folk art. The poetic passage in which Elena describes her sentiments when she sees these dolls in Dominican homes in Washington Heights adds depth to her shallow characterization in the song: "Me transporto al Higüerito, a mi padre lustrando el barro y pienso que nunca debimos salir de allí, la vida era como un río, simple en su discurrir, como un árbol asentado sobre sus raíces o la lluvia rauda y pertinaz en su contacto con la tierra como un eterno acto de amor sin pagos ni recompensa" ("I am transported to Higüerito, to my father polishing the mud, and I think that we should have never left there, life was like a river, simple in its flow, like a tree resting on its roots, or the rain, swift and persistent, in its contact with the earth, like an eternal act of love without payment or reward"; 25). Elena's New York City experience diametrically opposes this depiction of a life of honest manual labor and natural harmony. Ironically, in New York City and divested of her cultural roots, Elena of Higüerito comes to embody one of its famous faceless dolls when she dies anonymously on the train.

In addition to providing Elena with a backstory, *Un búfalo* develops the character Mateo Horowiz, mentioned in the song as "el judío de la factoría." In the song, this detail seems to be a simplistic mode of signifying that New Yorkers are ethnically and culturally different from Dominicans, whereas in the play, Mateo has a dramatic and thematic function. He serves as a Brechtian narrator who alternates between narrating and representing Elena's story: "Vivo en el Bronx y vengo a contarles la historia de Elena, una emigrante como yo" ("I live in the Bronx and I've come to tell you the story of Elena, an emigrant like me"; 21–22). Disla not only exploits a Brechtian style of performance, his character Mateo also recalls one of Brecht's lesser-known pieces, *Round Heads and Pointed Heads* (1936). Throughout *Un búfalo*, Mateo's pointy-shaped head is both referenced in the stage directions and mentioned in the dialogue: "*Mira la estrella. Se toca la punta en su cabeza.* No la quiero redonda . . . Prefiero estos cuernos de búfalo . . . Es lo que me distingue de un alemán o un palestino . . . les tengo fobia" ("*He looks at the star. He touches his pointy head.* I don't want a round head, I prefer my buffalo horns . . . It's what distinguishes me from a German or a Palestinian . . . I hate them"; 26). In Brecht's satirical parable about Nazi Germany, the leaders of the fictitious land called Yahoo maintain control via the ethnic strife between the immigrant, pointy-headed Czichs, and the native, roundheaded Czuchs. Dressed as a Jew from Nazi Germany and situated in a story taking place in the twenty-first-century United States, Disla's pointy-headed character Mateo highlights how persecutions and exclusions based on racism cut across cultures and epochs. His portrayal as a wandering Jew also has the effect of situating Dominican migration in a broader historical context of global diasporas. Thus, what began in Guerra's song as a stereotype is creatively transformed in Disla's story to support some of his play's major themes.

The focus on Federico García Lorca in *Un búfalo* also dovetails with the themes of migration, difference, and the status and creative vision of the transnational artist. The inclusion of Lorca, an artist marked by difference, brings into relief that homosexuality and political affiliation, like racism and xenophobia, give rise to forces of exclusion. In citing Lorca, Disla again employs a strategy of multiplicity by integrating an intertext that in turn leads to numerous other texts, including dramas and poetry by Lorca, poetry by Pedro Mir, and a Greek tragedy. For example, Pancho, a puppeteer reluctantly working with an actor he repeatedly refers to as crazy, rehearses scenes from Lorca's play *Bodas de sangre*: "Es un unipersonal con *Bodas de Sangre*. Ella me lo propuso . . . Vio un grupo peruano en Nueva York y se enamoró de su técnica, de sus formas definidas" ("It's *Blood Wedding* as a solo piece. She proposed the idea to me. She saw a Peruvian group in New York City and fell in love with their technique, with their precise forms"; 30). Aside from the amusement of imagining how they might pull off a story about a love triangle as a solo piece, some spectators will chuckle as they make a second intertextual connection and recognize that the New York production admired by Poncia is Peruvian Grupo Yuyachkani's well-known solo performance adaptation of *Antigone*. Most of the intertexts in the theater rehearsal scenes will entertain the literature aficionado and thus serve to highlight the playwright's sophistication.[22] But more crucially, I think the intertextuality is representative of the open intellectual and aesthetic orientations of cosmopolitanism described by Ulf Hannerz. Indeed, Disla appears to parody any notion of originality or genius when Poncia, speaking as an author character announces that she steals ideas and draws from "cualquier fuente" ("any source"; 40).

Intertextual moves from one text to another in *Un búfalo* draw attention to the fact that two actors are constantly playing of multiple roles. I call metatheatrical migrancy the moments in which the characters flow from one identity into the next so quickly that traces of previous characters peep through. For example, in a brief instance while rehearsing her new solo performance version of *Bodas de Sangre*, we are simultaneously shown the actor, the intertext, and another character from *Un búfalo* when the actor shifts without warning from her character as an actor reciting a line from *Bodas de Sangre* to speaking as Tais Pérez: "Con un cuchillito que apenas cabe en las manos . . . hubiera matado al maldito judío, ese animal, y a mi primo también, heme ahora aquí, víctima de mí misma, sin identidad precisa, hija de esos tiempos modernos . . ." ("With a small knife that scarcely fits the hand . . . I would have killed that damn Jew, that animal, and my cousin, too; here I am now, a victim of myself, without a sure identity, daughter of these modern times"; 33). Similarly, Pancho, speaking simultaneously as Emilio Ramírez, Mateo Horowiz, and the puppeteer, exclaims, "no sé quien soy" ("I don't know who I am"; 32–33). The characters are creolized like the fluid identities of migrants in the sense that the multiple layers of their identities show through in different contexts in ever-changing combinations. This metatheatrical overload and subsequent identity confusion supports the play's characterization of today's modern times as a confused morass of peoples and ideologies roaming about the globe. But as the end of *Un búfalo* suggests in the hopeful act of herding the buffalo away from the cliff and onto new plains for exploration, in this globalized world of unprecedented mobility, some individual identities will be lost only to form new, hybrid ones, and new ideologies and collective affiliations will join people in new "herds," or social movements. It would follow that art, too, reconfigures itself into new movements and styles. Following Brecht's comments on changing aesthetics, one element of Disla's "newness" is the hybrid text that results from intense metatheatrical and intertextual migrations: "Methods wear out, stimuli fail. New problems loom up and demand new techniques. Reality alters; to represent it means of representation must alter too. Nothing arises from nothing; the new springs from the old, but that is just what makes it new" ("Popular" 110).

The stories, themes, and aesthetics performed in *Un búfalo* reject the sensibilities of monolingualism, root, and territory in favor of errantry, relation, rhizome, and creolization. Glissant uses these terms to describe a "poetics of relation, in which each and every identity is extended through a relationship with the Other" (11). Cultures and identities are always already mixed, and they continually enter into contact zones in which processes of relation further creolize them.[23] For Lionnet and Shih, "the transnational is our language to designate this originary multiplicity or creolization, which foregrounds the formative experiences of minorities within and beyond nation-states" (9). The strategy of intertextuality in *Un búfalo* illustrates how, in the cultural orientations of minor transnationalism, "The idea of a self-contained national literary tradition seems anomalous, time-bound, and hopelessly nostalgic" (A. Smith 245). Instead, Disla's textual migrancy exposes transnational cultural works as drawing from multiple traditions and constructing audiences with cosmopolitan rather than national outlooks. Unlike the pedagogical imperative of constituting an imagined nation that characterizes much of the Latin American nineteenth- and twentieth-century dramatic canons, Disla's dramaturgy speaks to an unbounded audience, the transnational community of mainland *and* insular Dominican audiences, as well as other minoritarian collectivities that live across borders.

While the generous borrowing of texts and exuberant experimentation with interpretive styles provide some of *Un búfalo*'s most entertaining moments, they also stage Disla's claim for a space in world theater history. The authorial voice is filtered through Poncia, who plays a male character called "the author." In this self-ironic portrait of an artist, the author is presented as a starving artist who admits that he has sold his soul to a "Globalized Faustus" and that he is dependent on stolen imported products, Dutch cheese, and Argentine sausages for his sustenance (39), just as the authors/actor characters in the play "steal" from texts from the universal theater canon to sustain their artistic creativity. Among the texts mentioned by the fictitious author, however, is a play that sounds suspiciously like *Un búfalo*: "Últimamente he estado bregando en el submundo de los aplastados, mi objetivo es hacer una sinopsis de la miseria humana de estos tiempos, en la que se refleje todo, la mezquinidad de los héroes cotidianos, sus luchas y sus triunfos, sus derrotas y frustraciones . . . Pero nadie invierte en proyecto semejante" ("Lately I've been struggling in the underworld of losers, my objective is to create a compendium of the human misery of these times, in which everything is reflected, the paltriness of the common heroes, their battles and triumphs, their defeats and frustrations . . . but nobody invests in a project like this"; 42–43). On more than one occasion a character in *Un búfalo* mentions the lack of funding for the arts in current times. Ironically, while the fictitious author has been commissioned to produce a hackneyed melodrama called *Te regalo mis sueños* (I Give You My Dreams), which was probably inspired by another source, the homonymous romantic ballad popularized by the Dominican crooner Fausto Rey, he is aware that an experimental and intellectually challenging text in a "minor key" like *Un búfalo* will struggle to find backing.[24] Part of the politics of cosmopolitanism is its insistence on recognizing "multiple (and sometimes) contending allegiances" (Gilbert and Lo 7). The creative works of Frank Disla and other transnational Dominican artists speak to communities and political bodies that straddle national borders, and implicit in *Un búfalo* is a call for imagining how to support these cultural practices. A minor transnational theater imagines new styles, new audiences, and it calls for new critical approaches and new practices in arts subsidy. Just as real life transmigrants labor to be recognized as full citizens and exert pressure to form new understandings of political and personal belonging, the creative projects of transnational theater practitioners oblige us to reconsider the national and ethnic categories that have traditionally defined art and to take into account the complex, Janus-faced quality of transnational cultural production that seeks to link communities across state borders.

Coda

> We are in a complete new world. . . . There are still plenty of people who come and never go back. There are still plenty of people who stay and never can leave. But there's also this other dimension . . . that's completely unstable, where people are back and forth all the time, and I think that is something that, as artists, as writers, that is really cool to deal with because it's new, because no one's really seen it before, a community that can kind of just jump back and forth . . . constantly exchanging information and experiences both from home and carrying them from home to the United States and back, people who jump back and forth kind of like the shuttles on a loom because they're really strengthening and reinforcing connections between two places.
>
> **—Junot Díaz**

As Junot Díaz suggests in the above-mentioned quote, the "new world" of the twenty-first century is marked by migration patterns that have inspired artists to explore new senses of collective belonging.[1] In today's context of transnational migration, the possibility of dual citizenship and of return migration, and the accessibility of air travel and of the internet allow migrants to cultivate social, political, and economic relations across borders to a degree heretofore unseen. Díaz captures the networks created by this cross-border movement in the vivid metaphor of a weaving produced by a loom, invoking the ease with which people move—"people who jump back and forth like the shuttles on a loom"—and the strong fabrics created by the exchange of "information and experiences" between home, in this case, the Dominican Republic and the United States. In line with Díaz and recent scholarship on Dominican culture and migration, this book suggests that the dramatic increase in Dominican migration to the United States in the second half of the twentieth century and the ensuing economic and cultural flows linking the two nations has made it impossible to conceive of Dominican culture and identity as territorially anchored. These days, "Dominicanlandia dot com," a Spanglish neologism coined by the character Dennis in *Barceló con hielo*, alludes to both the Dominican Republic and the Dominican enclaves in the United States.

Clustered at the end of the twentieth century through the first two decades of the twenty-first century is a noticeable quantity of performance texts that address the theme of migration by playwrights who envision and often create their art across borders. I call this new direction in Dominican theater and performance transnational because it encompasses the work of dramatists situated *aquí* and *allá*, which is variously the United States and the Dominican Republic, depending on the author's permanent or temporary location.[2] The lives and artistic practices of the authors analyzed here have spanned the United States and the Dominican Republic in various ways and to different degrees and their plays address a multi-local audience of island-based and diasporic Dominicans with stories of characters whose life choices and world views are informed by both places. Accordingly, I view all the plays discussed in this study as transnational, whether they be about the journey of illegal migration (chapters 1 and 5), the experience of (mis)adaptation (chapter 2), the dream and reality of return (chapter 4), or the development of a transnational Dominican American identity and literary aesthetic (chapters 3 and 6). By performing close readings of fifteen solo performances and ensemble dramas from both *aquí* and *allá* in conversation with scholarship on theater and performance; migration theory; and literary, cultural, and historical studies, I uncover a transnational performance practice in which the gathering of authors, actors, and audiences create momentary spaces for displaying bodies and discourses often obscured by the hegemonic culture of the nation-state in both the United States and the Dominican Republic. The bifocal ontology dramatized in these works, produced by intense socioeconomic and political transnationalism, uniquely marks their contribution to the Latin(o) American theater tradition, and my hope is that this study kindles further research and critique on the overlooked Dominican theater arts.

The body of plays I have examined does not fit neatly into national and ethnic literary categories. In a world profoundly altered by mass migration and globalization, these traditional divisions stifle conversations over art produced by minority diaspora cultures that are on the move and may settle (or not) and assimilate (or not) in ways distinct from earlier waves of migration. Thus, rather than locating the plays examined in this book in either a US Latino or a Latin American theater tradition, this study has hypothesized the usefulness of the framework of transnationalism. Given the social, economic, and political networks woven by transnational migrants, the Dominican diaspora is still linked to the fate of the homeland—thus, at this juncture a transnational view that looks across and beyond the nation-state is indispensable. Borrowed from the social sciences, the pendular, both/and lens of transnationalism helps elucidate not only new forms of citizenship and collective belonging but also artistic production that complicates national and ethnic categories because it takes place across borders.[3] In some ways, *Aquí and Allá: Transnational Dominican Theater and Performance* answers Susan Stanford Friedman's call for literary scholars to avail themselves of the terminologies and typologies of migration developed in social science theories, while at the same time attend to the ambivalences and "the nuanced psychological dimension of migration so often explored in literature" (283). The plays analyzed in this book enable us to see how Dominicans can claim an ethnic identity and space in the United States and at the same time remain very much in dialogue with long-held racialized and gendered perceptions of identity promoted by authoritarian discourses deeply rooted back home. Plays such as *Yoleros*, *Miches: Ponle Esperanza*, *Por hora y a* Piece-Work, and *Nuyor/Islas* have more in common with the nation-based discourses of resistance to cultural changes brought about by migration than they do with the emergent Dominican American identities featured in *Dominicanish*, *Mondongo Scam*, *Barceló con hielo*, and *La luz de un cigarillo*, while pieces such as *Ciudadano Cero*, *P.A.R.G.O: Los pecados permitidos*, *Las viajeras*, and *Un búfalo de El Paso, Texas* are concerned with identities and claims of belonging in a context of globalization more broadly. Regardless of their different perspectives on migration, each of the plays encourages readers and audiences to expand notions of Dominican identity by acknowledging a transnational public that is multi-sited and inclusive of Dominicans of the diaspora.

Throughout this study, I have sought to explore the unique ways in which the activity of theater both chronicles and facilitates new understandings of collective identity. My interest has been, first, to unpack the ways in which Dominican theater, an artistic practice largely neglected in literary and cultural criticism, makes visible transnational discourses of identity that seek recognition not only in the place of migration but also in the homeland. Second, critical interpretations of the plays and performances have elucidated how they highlight transnational subjectivities as well as complicate and often defy negative representations of Dominican migrant identity. Lastly, the fruitful combination of the concepts stemming from the social sciences with humanistic approaches has helped me to posit the historically grounded, embodied, and collective endeavor of theatrical performance as a powerful community-making practice. The cultural anthropologist Richard Flores's research on the Mexican dramatic tradition of Los Pastores asserts the public, processual, and historically situated nature of cultural performance and its link to cultural citizenship, defined as "those enactments and practices that forge a sense of community and belonging, lead to renewed experiences of identity, and provide a social space for the formation of collective practices and its concomitant forms of power" (125). In an era dominated by mediatized social relations, the theater continues to offer embodied and sensorial gatherings that temporarily make "members from strangers" (R. Flores 146) and that activate communal thinking and feeling. Although staging the stories of migrants in itself constitutes a political act, the efficaciousness of the theater lies in the repetition and perpetual reconstitution of the ephemeral community implicit in theatrical performance—the playwright, the production, and the spectators. In the face of the shrinking public sphere, Dominican transnational theater claims an alternative space to rehearse together new forms of conviviality in a world transformed by global migration. In this space, the narratives of migration embodied in theatrical performance powerfully counter the many forces at work in undermining the development of critical ideas, inclusive social relations, and the values that sustain democratic life.

Notes

Introduction

1. Unless otherwise indicated, all translations are my own.

2. Van Hear includes technological advances in global communications, the collapse of the Soviet Bloc, the resurgence of ethnic, religious, and nationalist interests, and the development of human rights movements as dimensions of globalization that are precipitating large movements of people in a series of "new diasporas" (2–3).

3. In response the Cuban Revolution, the end of the Trujillo dictatorship, and the establishment of Puerto Rico as a free associated state, migration from the Hispanic Caribbean to the United States surged during the latter half of the twentieth century. Scholars such as Vanessa Pérez Rosario, however, remind us that the roots of migration from the Hispanic Caribbean reach back to the nineteenth century. As United States imperialism came to economically and politically dominate the region in the late nineteenth century, increasing numbers of people began migrating to the north (3).

4. For various accounts of Dominican migration, see studies by Glenn Hendricks (1974), Eugenia Georges (1990), Sherry Grasmuck and Patricia R. Pessar (1991), Peggy Levitt (2001), Milagros Ricourt (2002), Ana Aparicio (2006), and Frank Graziano (2013), among others.

5. New York City has the largest population of Dominicans in the United States, but there are also large enclaves in Florida, New Jersey, Connecticut, Rhode Island, and the Boston area.

6. In his 2011 study, Duany mentions that 14.1 percent of the population of the Dominican Republic lives in the United States, and I am estimating that an updated figure would reach 15–20 percent (169).

7. Grasmuck and Pessar (1991), Levitt (2001), and Duany (2011) strongly characterize Dominican migrants as acting transnationally, whereas Hernández and Torres-Saillant (1998), Ricourt (2002), and Aparicio (2006) focus on migrants becoming local Dominican American actors seeking to build community and empowerment in the United States. In my view, these positions need not be considered mutually exclusive. Accordingly, throughout this book, I use the term *Dominican* inclusively to refer to people of Dominican descent both residing in the homeland and abroad. When I use *Dominican American*, I am specifying the group born to immigrant parents in the

United States. Some Dominican Americans might also identify as Latino/a to signify a strong orientation toward life and politics in the United States, while others might display a strong identification with the homeland.

8. Glick Schiller elaborates on the process of assimilation: "Until the 1960s immigrants were expected to assimilate by abandoning their own cultures and identities and merging into or helping to forge the mainstream culture. This process was thought to take several generations. Ethnic communities might be formed along the way, but assimilation was the ultimate outcome and political goal" (24).

9. Duany cites Michael Kearney in his use of the terms *border* and *boundary.* A boundary is the official delimitation of a state while a border is a more fluid geographical and cultural zone between states (1).

10. In addition to her own work, Glick Schiller mentions Linda Basch, Georges Fouron, Karen Olwig, Patricia Pessar, Ninna Sørensen, and Joyce Toney as examples of scholars attentive to foundational Caribbean research.

11. I also identify with Torres-Saillant's politics of denouncing the lack of Dominican scholars because it calls attention to the systemic discrimination Dominicans and other minorities face in academia. However, I hope Torres-Saillant welcomes research produced by both Dominicans and non-Dominicans (like myself) that seeks to correct the relative absence of Dominican lives and voices in scholarly debates. I believe that by analyzing a largely ignored cultural phenomenon, Dominican theater and performance, this book can shed light on how theatrical performance serves as a site of transnational community building.

12. There are manifold overviews that outline the facets of the term *diaspora.* See, for example, Clifford (1994), Khachig Tölölyan (1996), Robin Cohen (1997), and Steven Vertovec (2009).

13. A good start to producing committed scholarship in service of the Dominican community is Torres-Saillant's *The Dominican Americans* (1998), co-edited with Ramona Hernández.

14. Current literature on migration tends to favor the term *incorporation* over *assimilation.* Immigrants can identify with their country of residence, adopt a new language, develop new civic and social ties, and participate in politics without losing their ethnic identity. Some scholars have emphasized the stratified and ethnoracial dimensions of incorporation. This theory is a modified version of the "segmented assimilation" approach elaborated by scholars such as Alejandro Portes and Min Zhou. The race and class stratification faced by many immigrant groups may result in non-assimilation to mainstream US culture, but rather, the adoption of the oppositional lifestyle characteristics of urban minorities such as Afro Americans and Puerto Ricans (Itzigsohn 8–17).

15. Here Itzigsohn follows Nina Glick Schiller's understanding of simultaneity: "Many migrants simultaneously become incorporated into a new land while preserv-

ing forms of transnational connection that connected them to daily life and decision making in other locations. I mean by simultaneity simply that people can live in more than one locality at the same time and be connected to the political processes of more than one state" (35).

16. Research by Itzigsohn (2009), Kasinitz et al. (2008), and Duany (2011), for example, substantiates the claim that Dominicans are particularly transnational in their orientation, while the essays included in *The Changing Face of Home: The Transnational Lives of the Second Generation*, edited by Peggy Levitt and Mary C. Waters (2002), show a variety of second-generation transnational practices across a wide array of cultures.

17. See "Diasporic Disquisitions: Dominicanists, Transnationalism, and the Community" for Torres-Saillant's critique of transnational approaches to Dominican migration that do not adequately address the painful realities of forced migration.

18. Scholars such as Frank Moya Pons, Christian Krohn-Hansen, Lauren Derby, Ana Liberato, Silvio Torres-Saillant, Néstor Rodríguez, and Maja Horn offer historical, sociological, political, and cultural analyses of the historical roots of authoritarianism in the Dominican Republic and its effects on Dominican culture in the present.

19. Studies by Ginetta Candelario (2007), April Mayes (2014), Lorgia García-Peña (2017), and Ernesto Sagás (2000) offer nuanced discussions of the historical origins and the continued impact of anti-black racism in the Dominican Republic.

20. "Fictive" must be understood "by analogy with the *persona ficta* of the juridical tradition in the sense of an institutional effect, a 'fabrication.' No nation possesses an ethnic base naturally, but as social formations are nationalized, the populations included within them, divided up among them or dominated by them are ethnicized—that is, represented in the past or in the future *as if* they formed a natural community, possessing of itself an identity of origins, culture and interests which transcends individuals and social conditions" (Balibar 96).

21. See also Ernesto Sagás on the political manipulations of *antihaitianismo* in the Dominican Republic.

22. Daisy Cocco De Filippis is the first Dominican to receive a PhD at the City University of New York. She was professor of Caribbean and Latin American literature at York College (CUNY) and is currently the president of Naugatuck Valley Community College in Connecticut. She is a prolific critic whose pioneering research has helped establish the field of Dominican literature in the diaspora and has brought visibility to women writers.

23. See Franklin Gutiérrez's 2004 *Literatura dominicana en los Estados Unidos: Historia y trayectoria de la diáspora intelectual* for details on these activities. New research is also uncovering Dominican literary roots in the United States before the 1980s. Daisy Cocco De Filippis, Franklin Gutiérrez, and others have broken new

ground in their research on Dominican literature from the late nineteenth century through the first half of the twentieth century. See, for example, *Literatura dominicana en los Estados Unidos: Presencia temprana, 1900–1950* (2001).

24. Julia Álvarez published the novels *How the García Girls Lost their Accent* (1991) and *In the Time of the Butterflies* (1994), and Junot Díaz published his collection of short stories, *Drown* (1996). Three oft-cited novels that followed the 1990s "boom" of US-Dominican writers include *Geographies of Home* by Loida Maritza Pérez (1999), *Song of the Water Saints* by Nelly Rosario (2003), *Let it Rain Coffee* by Angie Cruz (2005), and, of course, Díaz's Pulitzer Prize–winning novel, *The Brief Wondrous Life of Oscar Wao* (2007). Until recently, the author Rhina P. Espaillat, a poet and teacher born in the Dominican Republic, who has spent all her adult life in the United States, has been overlooked. She is the winner of the 1998 T. S. Eliot Prize and author of *Lapsing to Grace* (1992) and *Where Horizons Go* (1998), among other works.

25. The editors of a special issue of *Callaloo: A Journal of African Diaspora Arts and Letters* devoted to Dominican literature and culture, echo this sentiment. They write: "Among the literatures of Latin America and the Caribbean, that of the Dominican Republic, despite being the oldest in the New World, is nonetheless the least familiar to international audiences" (Paravisini-Gebert and López-Springfield 819).

26. This period coincides with the rise of the politician Leonel Fernández, who dominated Dominican politics from the mid-1990s through the first decade of the twenty-first century. He was born in Santo Domingo, but he spent his formative years in New York City. Fernández is known for reaching out to the diaspora community, partly to court its vote (Dominicans with dual citizenship could vote for the first time in national elections in 2004; an estimated two-thirds of the votes from abroad went to Fernández), but also to develop social and economic projects mutually beneficial to islander and expatriate Dominicans. In the cultural arena, the Fernández government created the Dominican Commission of Culture in the United States, an organization dedicated to supporting Dominican artists in the United States in hopes that they promote national values and become influential among other Latino communities (see the commission's mission statement on their website).

27. *Voces de ultramar: Literatura dominicana de la diáspora*, edited by José Acosta, anthologizes the authors celebrated at the 2005 Feria del Libro.

28. To get a sense of how the tenor of the discussion the development of Dominican studies has evolved over time, see Torres-Saillant and Hernández, "Editors' Preface: Dominican Quiddities in the U.S. Academy" and Hernández and Stevens-Acevedo, "Dominican Studies: A Field in Its Own Right." See also the useful analysis of dissertations on Dominican topics produced in the United States by Sarah Aponte.

29. Aponte reports that 6 Dominican-related dissertations were produced between 1939 and 1956, 13 in the 1960s, 47 in the 1970s, 123 in the 1980s, 199 in the 1990s, and 285 between 2000 and 2009 (48).

30. See, for example, excellent and wide-ranging studies such as Caridad Svich and María Teresa Marrero's *Out of the Fringe: Contemporary Latina/o Theater and Performance* (2000), Alicia Arrizón and Lillian Manzor's *Latinas on Stage* (2000), Alberto Sandoval-Sánchez and Nancy Saporta-Sternbach's *Stages of Life: Transcultural Performance and Identity in U.S. Latina Theater* (2001), Luis A. Ramos-García's edited volume *The State of Latino Theater in the United States: Hybridity, Transculturation, and Identity* (2002), Jon D. Rossini's *Contemporary Latino/a Theater: Wrighting Ethnicity* (2008), and, most recently, Patricia Ybarra's *Latinx Theater in the Times of Neoliberalism* (2017).

31. Studies by the Mumford Center indicate that since 1990, the number of "New Latinos" has more than doubled, from three million to over six million (Logan 1), and that this population is growing more rapidly than Mexicans, Puerto Ricans, and Cubans, historically the largest groups. The total Dominican population, for example, grew from 596,700 in 1990 to over one million in 2000, representing an 89 percent growth rate (Grieco 4). In the context of New York City, this meant that one in five new immigrants to the city was Dominican, which represented a 50 percent increase over the rate of the previous decade (Torres-Saillant and Hernández, *Dominican Americans* 150).

32. It should be noted that in the late 1990s, the Dominican theater practitioner Roy Arias founded the company Teatro Estudio Internacional (International Studio Theater), which was housed in the Times Square Arts Center. One of the stages was named after the Dominican actor and activist Ilka Tanya Payán, Arias's former mentor, and the theater did produce some works with Caribbean themes (A. B. Lugo). However, as the name might have foreseen, Teatro Estudio Internacional never became a Dominican theater. The space is now advertised online as Roy Arias Stages, which offers dance classes and rents the stage venues for rehearsals and performances. Arias was honored at the VI Hispanic Theater Festival, sponsored by the Dominican Cultural Commission in New York City in 2016 ("Homenajeados").

33. For important historical accounts of Dominican theater on the island, see articles and monographs by scholars such as Danilo Ginebra (Teatro Gratey), Jaime Lockwood, José Molinaza, Manuel de Jesús Goico Castro, Ángel Mejía, and Pedro Vergés. More recently, Carlos Mota and Howard Quackenbush have made important contributions to anthologizing Dominican plays.

34. Following the two volumes, Molinaza published *Historia del teatro dominicano* (1998), which summarizes the periods covered in the first two books and chronicles Dominican theater from the 1930s to the 1980s.

35. Since 1997 the Festival Internacional de Teatro (FITE) has taken place generally every two years in Santo Domingo. The festival mission statement reiterates the perception that Dominican theater is still developing: "La misión de este importante festival es consolidar el movimiento teatral del país creando la plataforma de desar-

rollo, la valoración y la difusión de los grupos, las compañías y teatristas nacionales más relevantes y emergentes" ("The mission of this important festival is to consolidate the country's theatrical movement by creating a platform for the development, assessment, and promotion of the emerging and most relevant national collectives, companies, and theater practitioners"; "Festival").

36. Another Dominican piece, *En el nombre de Salomé*, has been included in the theater's repertoire since 2016. The play focuses on a Dominican historical figure, the nineteenth-century poet Salomé Ureña de Henríquez, and is an adaptation by Marco Antonio Rodríguez of Julia Álvarez's novel *In the Name of Salomé*. See the Repertorio Español website for details regarding the productions by the company since 1968.

37. Dominican actors have found recent success in Hollywood; actors such as Dascha Polanco, Dania Ramirez, Zoe Saldaña-Perego, Ramses Jimenez, and Manny Pérez are frequently seen on the small screen and big screen alike.

38. In response to the lack of institutional support for producing and publishing Spanish-language theater in New York City, three Dominican dramatists—José M. de la Rosa, Claudio Marte, and Álex Vásquez Escaño, along with Pablo García Gámez (who is Venezuelan)—have staged their works and published their dramatic texts in their own production company called Teátrica (Morón Espinosa 95). Independent groups like Teátrica seek funding in myriad ways, including using crowdfunding platforms like Indiegogo. In their Indiegogo fundraising statement for the play *Yoleros*, the company writes: "We seek to serve communities that lack access to cultural arts programs and to spread the importance and benefits of theater to often under-served Spanish-speaking audiences." At the same time, Teátrica also aims "to engage English-speakers in the tradition of Latino theater to deepen their understanding of the experiences of their close neighbors who often live across language barriers" ("Yoleros"). See also their website.

39. Jáquez addresses what I identify as a transnational artistic method in an interview entitled "La soledad me da tiempo de crear" (Ronzino).

40. In general terms, Sagás and Molina describe how Dominican identity is impacted by transnationalism: "The crossover of norms and values between countries or societies permits migrants to expand and integrate, without reservation, other people's reality and culture into their native one" (8). In particular, exposure to different forms of racism and racial politics in the United States has opened discussions on this formerly taboo topic in the Dominican Republic. See, for example, studies by Pessar (2003), Silvio Torres-Saillant ("Tribulations") and Jorge Duany (2004).

41. With regard to the corpus of authors in this study, the phrase *living transnationally* signifies that they have all experienced some form of migration (temporary in some cases, permanent in others), and not simply that they live in social field that has been transformed by transnational connections.

Chapter 1: The Drama of *Yola* Migration and the Biopolitics of Disposability

Epigraph: Puerto Rico is close / but take a plane / and if you get a visa / there aren't problems in immigration / But don't go in a *yola* / don't get your hopes up / because in the Mona Canal / the sharks eat you (Vargas).

1. Jorge Duany, the leading scholar of Dominican migration to Puerto Rico, reports that "Between 1990 and 2009 the U.S. Coast Guard (2009) intercepted 35,471 undocumented Dominicans at sea; many more were not caught and entered Puerto Rico clandestinely" (*Blurred Borders* 59). He also notes that previously, between 1982 and 2009, the US Coast Guard intercepted the sea voyages of nearly 37,000 undocumented Dominicans (193). Migrants clearly do reach Puerto Rican shores, however, by air or boat, for Dominicans have become the largest minority on the island. Duany writes: "Census data confirm the spectacular growth of Puerto Rico's Dominican population, multiplying nearly forty times between 1960 and 1990" (*Blurred Borders* 189). See also Duany's earlier work: *Los dominicanos en Puerto Rico: Migración en la semi-periferia* (1990).

2. Álex Vásquez Escaño has lived in New York City since 1986. He has trained as a dramatist at the New School, at the Ollantay Center for the Arts, DANISARTE, and the Abdón Villamizar Dramaturgy Workshop. His *Cama para dos*, which he developed in the Villamizar workshop, won the Instituto Arte Teatral Internacional (IATI) prize in 2008 and was published in *Máscaras errantes: Antología de dramaturgos en los Estados Unidos* (2011). Julissa Rivera Céspedes works in the Dominican Republic and has trained as an actor, puppeteer, and dramatist. She teaches in the Faculty of Arts at the Universidad Autónoma de Santo Domingo, and, since 1999, she has worked with one of the country's most dynamic independent theater collectives, La Cuarta Espacio Teatral. She has participated in many productions directed by top Dominican directors such as Dionis Rufino, and her works have been staged in a variety of important venues.

3. In addition to studying the sociocultural imaginaries depicting boat people in search of modern freedom and citizenship, Michaeline Crichlow's article "Making Waves: (Dis)Placements, Enganglements, Mo(ve)ments" helpfully reviews the history of the less dominant narrative of intra Caribbean migration, as well as details the comparative racialization and invisibilization of Haitians in the Dominican Republic and Dominicans in Puerto Rico.

4. In light of the human rights abuses in Haiti, during the 1994 boat migration crisis President Clinton briefly reversed the policy of "direct return" and permitted screenings to ensure political refugees would not be automatically returned to the island. By contrast, the Cuban *balsero* crisis of the same period was the beginning of the

end of Cold War policies that granted Cuban migrants the privileged status of political refugee. Under the 1995 "wet-foot, dry-foot" policy, Cubans were not automatically granted asylum when interdicted at sea. In 2017, just eight days before leaving office, President Obama tightened the "dry-foot" clause of the policy that enabled Cubans who had reached the United States by land or sea to stay and remain eligible for a green card after one year. Like other foreign nationals, Cubans are now subject to deportation if they do not possess a visa.

5. In line with Giroux's position on how the state has abandoned its disadvantaged citizens, the well-known Dominican journalists Minerva Isa and Eladio Pichardo write: "Los viajes marítimos clandestinos, denigrante, ignominiosa y espeluznante dimensión de la emigración dominicana, son expresión de la insensibilidad social, develan la ineptitud de las élites políticas y empresariales para crear condiciones y oportunidades que garanticen el empleo, la salud y la educación a los ciudadanos en su tierra" ("The clandestine sea voyages, a denigrating, ignominious, and horrifying dimension of Dominican emigration, are an expression of social insensitivity and reveal the ineptitude of political and business elites to create conditions and opportunities that guarantee employment, health, and education for citizens in their own land"). By Giroux's terms, Dominican boat people form part of a population that occupies "a political space that effectively invalidates the categories of 'citizen' and 'democratic representation' that are integral to the nation-state system" (*Stormy Weather* 22). In this new form of biopolitics, referred to as a "necropolitics" by Achille Mbembe, the Dominican migrants I am calling "human flotsam," occupy the status of "the living dead" (qtd. in Giroux, *Stormy Weather* 22).

6. The creation of the Caribbean Border Interagency Group in 2006 has made a significant impact on stemming the flow of yola migration by coordinating the efforts of the US Customs and Border Protection's Office of Air and Marine Operations, the Office of Field Operations, the Office of Border Patrol, the US Coast Guard, Immigration and Customs Enforcement, and the US Attorney's Office, District of Puerto Rico. These agencies are working together to deter the victimization of undocumented people by smugglers, prevent loss of life at sea, and criminally prosecute repeat offenders. The 2006 implementation of the US Coast Guard's at-sea biometrics program, which takes fingerprints and digital photographs of the intercepted migrants, has also been credited with the decline in illegal trips. As Graziano notes, in addition to the increased border enforcement, the weak US economy and political stability in the Dominican Republic have also had an effect in the decline in yola migration ("Why" 4). However, while 3,612 boats were interdicted in 2006, depending on the number of passengers per boat, the far fewer 307 interdictions at sea in 2012 still mean that large numbers of Dominicans continue to leave the island by boat. If interdicted at sea, today's migrants are likely to be criminally prosecuted, whereas in the past tens of thousands of travelers were sent home with few consequences.

7. While the Dominican police and navy appear to cooperate with US Coast Guard efforts to thwart illegal migration, it is well-known that even at the highest levels Dominican officials receive payments from smugglers and are more invested in individual profit than putting an end to yola smuggling operations.

8. Founded in 2003, Colectivo Shampoo is a multidisciplinary art collective. Their projects have been exhibited at the Bienal del Caribe in Santo Domingo (2003), San Juan Trienal Poligráfica (2004), Brooklyn Museum of Art (2007), and the Santo Domingo Museo de Arte de Moderno (2008) (Mena). See the amusing Colectivo Shampoo video montage presenting the project and showing the reaction of the print media and newscasters: "D' La Mona Plaza."

9. Giroux's "disposable" populations, in which I include Dominican boat people, "are largely invisible in the global media or, when disruptively present, defined as redundant, pathological and dangerous" (*Stormy Weather* 22).

10. Seeing footage of sharks attacking shipwrecked boatpeople prompted Torres-Saillant to ponder the currency of the sentiments expressed in Pedro Mir's classic poem, "Hay un país en el mundo (Poema gris en varias ocasiones)" ("There is a Country in the World [Grey Poem on Various Occasions]") (1949): "Ahí comprendimos visceralmente el funesto fin a que habíamos llegado, cosa que ya entendíamos a nivel conceptual. Un país que cancela la esperanza y que condena a sus hijos a tan tenebrosas salidas es un país del cual se puede verdaderamente decir: 'Este es un país que no merece el nombre de país / Sino de tumba, féretro, hueco o sepultura'" ("Then we viscerally realized the fateful end to which we had arrived, which we already understood at the conceptual level. A country that cancels hope and condemns its children to such dark departures is a country about which one can truly say, 'this is a country that does not deserve the name of country / But rather, coffin, hole or grave'"; "Redimir" 230).

11. Not surprisingly, the most extreme stories are picked up by the Associated Press and, consequently, reach a large audience. In one such story, a fisherman, one of five survivors of the thirty-three migrants who set out to Puerto Rico by yola, tells gruesome details of the process of eating human flesh ("Dominican Migrant").

12. One blogger writes: "No, no es que consideremos que este film, este docudrama original de Jorge Lendeborg sea una gran película, un monumento cinematográfico o algo por el estilo. Pero, para comenzar, tiene algo que ya de por sí nos gusta: no se parece a ninguna otra película dominicana que hayamos visto" ("No, it's not that we consider that this film, this original docudrama by Jorge Lendeborg, is a great film, a cinematographic monument or something like that. But, to begin with, it has something that we already like: it does not look like any other Dominican movie we've seen"; "60 millas").

13. *Yoleros* has been staged by Teátrica, a theater company cofounded by Vásquez Escaño. It was the first Spanish-language production at the Bushwick Starr Theater in Brooklyn and won the 2015 outstanding performance by an ensemble cast by the His-

panic Organization of Latin Actors (HOLA) ("Yoleros"). My analysis references the play script published in Teátrica's collection, *Palabras acentuadas: Antología de cuatro dramaturgos en Nueva York*. *Miches* won honorable mention in the 2005 International Theater Competition sponsored by Casa de Teatro and was published with the other prizewinning texts of that year. La Cuarta Espacio Teatral premiered a reworked stage version titled *Al garete* at the VI Festival Internacional de Teatro de Santo Domingo in 2009. *Al garete* was also produced in New York City, where it won the New York Latin ACE award for best foreign production and its director, Dionis Rufino, won for best visiting director. My analysis focuses on the original *Miches* text included in the Casa de Teatro collection.

14. Casa de Teatro is a nonprofit cultural institution in the colonial zone of Santo Domingo. It was established by the writer Freddy Ginebra in 1974 as an alternative space for emerging Dominican artists. Casa de Teatro hosts workshops, performances, concerts, and exhibitions of all kinds, and it sponsors literary contests annually for poetry, prose, and theater. The anthology publications of the prizewinning pieces are a welcome resource for readers and scholars seeking texts published outside the government publishing industry. See the Casa de Teatro website for a current calendar of events.

15. The male-centered focus of the play is odd given that trafficking of Dominican women for prostitution is a real problem. See chapter 5 for more on human rights and human smuggling.

16. Similarly, in *Yoleros*, the ship captain is associated with the devil when a passenger complains, "¡Esto no es más que un crucero del infierno . . . !" ("This is just a cruise to hell . . . !"). Capitán replies, "¿Quién soy yo?" ("Who am I?"), to which the passenger responds, "Dimelo tú a mí" ("You tell me") (106).

17. For Taylor, the archive consists of elements such as documents, texts, buildings, museums, and bones, just to name a few—components that reflect institutional practices that are resistant to change. The repertoire, of an ephemeral and transformative nature, involves embodied practices and nonreproducible knowledge (20). The archive is resistant to change because the process of archiving entails fixing practices, classification, identification, and selection; however, it is not immune to change (19). In fact, Taylor notes how the archive is mediated by the living, corporeal bodies and memories that engage it through performance.

18. The character Muchacha in *Miches* echoes this very same observation: "Saben de los que salen pero nada de los que llegan" ("They know of those who leave but nothing of those who arrive"; 199).

19. Embarazada is a pregnant woman, Rebelde is a female rebel, Loquita is a gay man, Deportado is a male deportee, Maestro is a male teacher, Estudiante is a male student, Capitán is a male captain, Ayudante is the captain's male assistant, and Boricua is a Dominican male nicknamed "Boricua," the indigenous name for Puerto Rico.

20. The scholar Manuel Guzmán now goes by Manolo Estavillo—the article I cite uses his former name.

21. The captain in *Miches* laments, "Hay que dar la cara . . . y dar cuentas . . . pero no puedo pensar en todo lo que he visto, me vuelvo loco, desquiciado, de rabia, de culpa, de pena, de vergüenza" ("You have to face it . . . and be held accountable . . . but I can't think of all I have seen, I go crazy, with anger, guilt, sadness, shame"; 236), while the captain in *Yoleros* asks in anguish, "Mamá: ¿es esto todavía es un viaje de valentía o lo he convertido en un acto de desesperación?" (Mom: is this still a journey of courage or have I turned it into an act of desperation?" 119).

22. Robin Miskolcze argues that the maritime captains who saved women and children "defined a new masculine individualism, one that was morally minded, rooted in Christian principles, and dedicated to preserving virtue" (xi).

23. Agamben comes to understand the subjectivity of "bare life" through the *homo sacer*, "an obscure figure of archaic Roman law, in which human life is included in the juridical order . . . solely in the form of its exclusion (that is, of its capacity to be killed), has thus offered the key by which not only the sacred texts of sovereignty but also the very codes of political power will unveil their mysteries" (8).

24. On the motif of breastfeeding and seventeenth-century English national imagination, Rachel Trubowitz writes: "Mothers who heed the natural urge to breast-feed their children can thus be integrated fully into the nation and empire building activities of the state; but those who repress or ignore the nursing instinct are shown to deny nature" (43). Similar discourse is seen in journalistic accounts of Faustina's experience; see Florentino Durán.

Chapter 2: Alternate Belongings

1. Peterson critiques the politics of heterosexual, male, and white identity in solo performances by artists such as Eric Borgosian, Spalding Gray, Denis Leary, and Wallace Shawn, among others, and asserts that while he hopes this identity "is already destined for dissolution, monologue performance seems almost inevitably to conserve and reiterate it" (vii).

2. For Butler, there is no stable or unified identity that exists outside its performative acts. Instead, the demand for repeat performances to reaffirm the norms that regulate identity not only reveals its own instability and citationality, but also allows for subversive repetition that exposes the norms as arbitrary and inefficacious (26).

3. Born in Santo Domingo in 1977, Andújar is the award-winning author of the novels *El hombre triángulo* (2005), *Candela* (2007), and *Los gestos inútiles* (2015), and the short-story collections *El factor carne* (2005), *Amoricidio* (2007), *UGDU y otros relatos* (2011), and *Saturnario* (2013), among other texts. Andújar's short stories and novels have won many prizes. *Candela* was awarded the 2008 Best Novel prize by the PEN International Puerto Rican Centre (and is being turned into a film directed by

Andrés Farias), while *Los gestos inútiles* won the 2015 Premio Alba Narrativa. Andújar has long been interested in the connections between body, language, and literature and is also well-known as a performer. He has performed solo pieces in the United States, Dominican Republic, Puerto Rico, and France, and he has developed projects with his artistic collective MaRe Unidadperformance (with Mabel Mazano) and is an associate of the Aguijón Theater in Chicago. Andújar completed a doctorate in literature at the Centro de Estudios Avanzados de Puerto Rico y el Caribe in 2013, and his dissertation on the Dominican poet Aída Cartagena Portalatín was published by Editorial Isla Negra and APEC University in the Dominican Republic. He lives in Chicago, where he teaches language, literature, and history courses at Governors State University.

4. Andújar's work is in line with Jo Bonney's observation on the connection between current culture and solo work: "The language and attitude of solo artists have often paralleled that of their contemporaries in the music scene, whether it's the 'hipster' rhythms of black jazz musicians, the voice distortions of techo-rock, the in-your-face rants of punk rockers or the street cadences of hip-hop" (xiv).

5. The image of young people casually dressed in hip-hop styles break dancing and lined up to enter the formal space of the Teatro Nacional contrasts strikingly with Santo Domingo's theatergoing public of the past (see the video "Ciudadano Cero en la Sala Ravelo Teatro Nacional," directed by Loraine Ferrand).

6. For more on Ferrand's methodology, see her audiovisual presentation "La Dramaturgia del cuerpo en Jornada extra."

7. *Ciudadano Cero* was first performed on August 31, 2005, in the Sala Patrick Hudson at the Instituto Cultural Dominico Americano. In the summer of 2006, Andújar again performed the piece on May 5 in the Sala Ravelo del Teatro Nacional as a part of the V Santo Domingo International Theater Festival and again at the Casa de Teatro on August 23. In 2007 *Ciudadano Cero* was chosen as the inaugural performance at the new Teatro Victoria Espinosa in Santurce, Puerto Rico, at the 43rd Puerto Rican International Theater Festival, sponsored by the Instituto de Cultura Puertorriqueña.

8. The term *postdramatic* is associated with Hans-Thies Lehmann and will be explored further in chapter 5.

9. Both videos are directed by Ferrand. In addition to the videos and the hybrid narrative/poetic performance text, there are two additional narratives in *El factor carne* in which the Ciudadano Cero character appears that provide important clues for understanding the fragmented theatrical text and the project overall.

10. Carlos Goico (1952–2009), described by some as the Dominican Vincent van Gogh for his bold use of color and his battle with mental illness, lived on the margins of Dominican society. His work will most certainly receive more acclaim posthumously than it did during his lifetime.

11. Facing a dearth of managers and disc labels willing to promote hip-hop in the land of merengue, Tony Hasbun founded the Cooperativa Empresarial Lo Correcto,

the first hip-hop company in the Dominican Republic, in 1998. The group is comprised of various rap groups and personalities including Bethoven Villaman, Ovni, Crooklyn, Sin Fin, Facundo and Básico, who together form Lo Correcto. For more on the origins and goals of this project, see the documentary film *Lo Correcto Hip Hop Dominicano.*

12. For a much fuller description of his neighborhood, see the narrative fragment *aquí vivo* (I live here) from the Ciudadano *Fábulas* preceding the performance text.

13. My direct citations are drawn mainly from the text published in *El factor carne.* As explained by Andújar, the arrangement of the text and the use of italics and bold refer in a general way to vocal inflections and gestures in the performance (personal e-mail communication).

14. For more on masculinity and queer identities in Andújar's narrative works, see essays by Yolanda Martínez-San Miguel and Elena Valdez.

15. The term *tíguere*, spelled the way most Dominicans pronounce *tigre*, has formed part of the mythology of Dominican masculinity since the 1930s, and is one of the most recognized *Dominicanismos.* In his study of Dominican political authoritarianism, Christian Krohn-Hansen describes the *tíguere* as a "man who was both astute and socially intelligent; both courageous and smart, both cunning and convincing; and a gifted talker who got out of most situations in a manner acceptable to others, while himself at no moment stepped back, stopped chasing, or lost sight of his aim (be that women, money, a job, a promotion, etc.)" (148). I would add that in the context of the contemporary urban jungle, *tíguere* has a more aggressive connotation.

16. In his essay "Similitudes y un ancho mar de diferencia: La experiencia literaria de aquí y allá" (Similarities and a Wide Sea of Differences: The Literary Experience Here and There) Torres-Saillant declares that the Dominican Republic lacks a true publishing industry independent of the state (102).

17. The premiere of *P.A.R.G.O.* helped launch Jáquez's career. For his performance he was named Best Actor by the Hispanic Organization for Latin Actors (HOLA) and the New York Latin ACE awards during the 2002–2003 season. *P.A.R.G.O.* has been performed hundreds of times in various theaters in the Dominican Republic and in New York City, Washington, DC, Miami, Havana, Buenos Aires, and Mexico City. In 2012 Jáquez returned to Santo Domingo for a revival of the popular show. After his success with *P.A.R.G.O.*, Jáquez has consistently collaborated across borders as a writer, director, and actor in dozens of productions, becoming a visible presence in the commercial and noncommercial performing arts worlds of both Santo Domingo and New York. The Dominican Republic Ministry of Culture named Jáquez Cultural Personality of the year in 2011, and he has won over a dozen Cassandra Awards, the nation's top prize for artists in the entertainment industry. Recent high-profile projects for Jáquez that involve working in both New York City and Santo Domingo include co-writing (with David Maldonado) and directing a new salsa musical, *I Like*

It Like That, starring Tito Nieves, at the Puerto Rican Traveling Theater (September 2016), and serving as artistic director of a Santo Domingo production of *Mamma Mia!* (November 2018).

18. Among numerous other factors, such as racial discrimination, many scholars attribute the struggle for sociopolitical and economic advancement and lack of assimilation of Dominicans in the United States in the 1980s and 1990s to a "permanently temporary" transient mentality and consequent slow rates of naturalization. For example, the 1990 US Census shows that only 18 percent of Dominicans residing in the United States had been naturalized, whereas immigrants from many Asian countries had naturalization rates above 50 percent (Pessar, *Visa* 73). Paradoxically, though migrants proudly assert their *dominicanidad* in New York City and reproduce many of the cultural practices brought from home, upon returning to the Dominican Republic they are often stigmatized by island residents as not-authentically Dominican and as social climbers with ties to the criminal world.

19. Jáquez reproduces Caribbean variants of Spanish pronunciation throughout, and even distinguishes Pasión's Puerto Rican accent and vocabulary from the Dominican characters. The unpublished manuscript shows some inconsistencies in his use of standard Spanish and phonetic spellings in imitation of Dominican speech. In addition to the manuscript, my analysis is based on a DVD recording of the play.

20. *Quisqueya* signifies the Dominican homeland and was the indigenous Taino name of the island of Hispaniola. Papichío's story of arriving to the United States in a shipping container recalls Agliberto Meléndez's 1988 film *Pasaje de ida* (*One Way Ticket*), which is based on a real trip from the early 1980s during which Dominican stowaways in a cargo ship, the *Regina Express*, die asphyxiated in a ship container.

21. For more on the "queerness" of Puerto Rican identity, see the fall 2003 volume of *Centro Journal*, edited by Alberto Sandoval-Sánchez, which is dedicated, in great part, to the analysis of transnationalism and transvestitism in the Puerto Rican writer Mayra Santos-Febres's popular novel *Sirena Silena vestida de pena* (2000). See also the journal's excellent 2007 special issue on Puerto Rican queer sexualities (edited by Luis Aponte-Parés, Jossiana Arroyo, Elizabeth Crespo-Kebler, Lawrence La Fountain-Stokes, and Frances Negrón-Muntaner).

22. For criticism on P.A.R.G.O., see also essays by Maja Horn and Mónica Volonteri. With regard to recognizing Jáquez as a transnational artist, my work has points of contact with Horn in particular.

23. The incorporation of the audience into the fiction of the play is but one of the many links *P.A.R.G.O.* shares with *Quíntuples* (1984) by the Puerto Rican author Luis Rafael Sánchez. Like the support group context in *P.A.R.G.O.*, in *Quíntuples* spectators become the audience for a conference on family affairs. Both plays feature tour de force, multiple-role solo performances (one actor plays four roles in *P.A.R.G.O.* and two actors play six roles in *Quíntuples*), they share an atmosphere that borders on

a circus-like parading of "freaks," and they both bombard the audience with references to popular culture. Finally, even though Jáquez is best known as a performer and a director, and Sánchez as a writer, similar to *Quíntuples*, the stage directions in *P.A.R.G.O.* are miniature narratives in their own right and contain amusing information not available to the viewers.

24. The word *pargo* also means fish, a snapper, and, like *pájaro* (bird) in Cuba and the Dominican Republic and *pato* (duck) in Puerto Rico, it is used as a signifier for homosexuality. These animal metaphors signal effeminate masculinity, whereas as we saw in *Ciudadano Cero*, *tíguere* signals a macho, or tough-guy male identity.

25. In print publications and online articles, the spelling of Dió-genes Abréu appears in three variations. I follow the style used in his self-published essay collections and in his publications in the Letras de ultramar series of the Dominican Editora Nacional. Abréu was born and raised in the Dominican Republic. He studied art at the National School of Fine Arts in Santo Domingo, the State University of New York (SUNY), and earned an MFA from the City College of New York. His artwork has been exhibited in museums and galleries in Santo Domingo, New York City, and Tokyo, and he has published two collections of poetry: *Poemas para los vivos* (1983) and *Para mujeres sin maquillaje* (1985). His play *La Jom Atenda* won the 2011 Letras de Ultramar theater prize and was nominated for 2014 playwriting awards by ACE and HOLA. The play starred Mateo Gómez and Susanna Guzmán and was directed by Nelson Landrieu at Teatro LATEA and Teatro Las Tablas. *La cosa nostra dominicana* was directed by Maitreyi Villamán Matos and staged at the New York Centro Cultural Cívico Dominicano (New York Dominican Civic Cultural Center) in 2009. My analysis refers to the play script published in Dinorah Coronado's collection of Dominican playwrights in the United States. In addition to his involvement in the arts, Abréu has served as a community organizer at Northern Manhattan Improvement Corporation, a nonprofit organization serving Dominican enclave neighborhoods such as Washington Heights and Inwood.

26. The title *Perejil: el ocaso de la "hispanidad" dominicana* refers to a controversial book entitled *El ocaso de la nación dominicana* (*The Decline of the Dominican Nation*) by Manuel Núñez (1990). As is well-known, for speakers of Haitian Creole, *perejil* is difficult to pronounce. During the border massacre of 1937, officials, unable to distinguish Haitians from Dominicans, administered an oral test to single out the Haitians. Núñez's book contributes to a history of racist nationalist discourses articulated by intellectuals such as Arturo Peña Battle and Joaquín Balaguer that blame the "decline" of the Dominican Republic on the influence of Haiti. Controversy erupted when, a decade after the first edition was released, an esteemed panel of judges awarded the racist tome the Best Book Prize at the 2002 Dominican International Book Fair. Abréu's *Sin haitianidad no hay dominicanidad* rejects the nationalist maneuver of defining Dominican identity in opposition to Haiti.

27. See the meme generator "El Dominican-York" for an endless supply of stereotyped attitudes associated with male Dominican migrants.

28. Alberto Sandoval-Sánchez writes that in the late 1950s, "illegal aliens, criminals, gangsters, and drug addicts were used to stereotype Latinos/as. Cisco Kid, Speedy Gonzalez, and Tonto were displaced and replaced by juvenile delinquents and dysfunctional gang members in the ghettos of cities with large Latino/a populations" (*José Can You See* 28). Plays and films have long characterized Latinos in typecast gangster roles. Consider, for example, *West Side Story* (1961), *Scarface* (1983), *Carlito's Way* (1988), and *American Me* (1992). By contrast, plays like *Zoot Suit* by Luis Valdez (1979) and *Short Eyes* by Miguel Piñero (1974) attempt to recast these perceptions of Latino stereotypes.

29. The Dominican actor Roberto Larancuent played the role of the three drug dealers in the play.

30. The stage notes state that the projected images "debe manejarse como contrapartida a la imagen negativa (estereotipo) que el jodedor representa sobre su comunidad como totalidad" ("should be used as a counterpoint to the negative image (stereotype) that the drug dealer projects over his community as a whole"; 18).

31. The popular cable weekly television program *Nueva York de Noche*, presented by Fermín Luna, began in 1978, and ran for over twenty years (Rodríguez de León 173).

32. See the Centro Cívico Cultural Dominicano website.

Chapter 3: Breaking the Silence of Heteronormativity in the Theater of Marco Antonio Rodríguez

1. In addition to writing drama, Rodríguez is a prolific screenwriter, actor, and director. His plays have garnered many prizes and productions. *La luz de un cigarillo* was produced in New York City at Teatro LATEA and Lehman College Stages, in Santo Domingo at Teatro Las Máscaras, in Buenos Aires at Teatro La Mueca, and in Chicago at the Urban Theater Company at Batey Urbano. The play received five HOLA (Hispanic Organization of Latin Actors) awards and four ACE (Association of Latin Entertainment Critics of New York) awards, including Outstanding Achievement in Playwriting and Directing, along with an array of acting and production design awards. *Barceló con hielo* was selected among seventy-five entries as the winner of the 2012 MetLife Nuestras Voces Playwriting competition at New York City's Repertorio Español, where it was produced in 2014. The play won four HOLA awards: Iván Camilo and Javier Fano won Outstanding Performance by a Featured Male Actor, Rodríguez won Outstanding Achievement in Playwriting, and Gilbert Zaldvívar won for Outstanding Production. In 2017 the Comisionado Dominicano de Cultura in New York City granted Rodríguez special honors and dedicated its seventh annual International Theater Festival to him. Rodríguez was also designated as an honoree at the 2017 New York City Dominican Day Parade.

2. He is a graduate of New York City's famed La Guardia High School of Performing Arts and holds an MFA from Southern Methodist University. He spent formative years as an actor and playwright in Dallas and currently resides in New York City. His connection to Dallas is echoed in *La luz de un cigarillo*, since Julio César, the principal male character, is an actor who works in Dallas. However, Rodríguez states that the stories dramatized in his plays are are inspired by people, situations, and events he has observed—they are not autobiographical (personal email communication).

3. *La luz de un cigarillo* and *Barceló con hielo* premiered in Spanish, thus in this chapter I cite the Spanish text first and follow with Rodríguez's English translation. *La luz del cigarillo* and *Ashes of Light* were published as separate volumes while *Barceló on the Rocks/Barceló con hielo* was published as a single, bilingual edition. See also Rodríguez's bilingual website.

4. For example, the space of the kitchen in *La luz de un cigarillo* strongly recalls the setting of the 1982 Cuban American family drama *Sanguivin in Union City* (Union City Thanksgiving) by Manuel Martín Jr. (see Cuban Theater Digital Archive).

5. Here I refer to Teresa de Lauretis's well-known assertion that gender is constructed via social technologies such as visual representations, "institutionalized discourses, epistemologies, and critical practices, as well as the practices of everyday life" (3).

6. Balaguer (1906–2002) was in Dominican public life for seven decades. He served in various positions under the Trujillo regime, 1930–1961, and was president 1966–1978 ("The Twelve Years") and 1986–1996 ("The Return Years"). As noted in the introduction, Liberato suggests that Balaguer was the most powerful politician in the post-Trujillo era to reinforce Dominican nationalism "through pride in Spanish-Catholic ancestry and anti-black sentiment" (63).

7. Balaguer employed the same "authoritarian pedagogies" imparted by Trujillo and many other authoritarian leaders since the birth of the Dominican nation, but Ana Liberato claims that Balaguer is more than a mere "heir" of the authoritarianism of the Trujillo regime and that his long stay in power "established his own legacy through the deployment of specific methods and styles of governing as well as distinct ways of dealing with the military, the opposition, the poor, organized labor, and the privileged classes" (1–2).

8. Rodríguez's mother was pro-Balaguer and his father opposed him. His uncle was assassinated under the Trujillo regime ("Hermandad en el Teatro").

9. Liberato argues that memory work in the Dominican Republic has been low intensity and episodic: "There have not been sustained and heightened confrontations by different communities of memory over competing narratives of the recent past," (12) and that "heightened awareness of the past has come in waves without setting in motion processes of active, permanent, and inclusive mourning and deep examination of the truths of Trujillo and Balaguer legacies" (12).

10. L. Howard Quackenbush notes that Efraím Castillo's play *Los lectores del ático* (1998) features a character named El Doctor, clearly based on Balaguer, and suggests that play was published only after Balaguer left office, and, even then, out of fear, the editors did not identify on the back cover the historical figure on whom the protagonist is modeled (96).

11. In line with recent scholarship on Dominican identity that places the nation in a geopolitical relationship with not only Haiti but also the United States, Horn argues that in addition to the traditional colonial Hispanic patriarchal culture, Dominican gender norms have been influenced since the first decades of the twentieth century by US imperial and racialized ideas of masculinity.

12. Based on his ethnographic work on second-generation Dominicans in Providence, Rhode Island, José Itzigsohn claims that the second generation employs a transnational symbolic framework to construct a sense of identity but is less involved in concrete forms of border crossing transnational activities (142).

13. In September 2013 the Dominican Constitutional Court issued judgment TC0168/13. Covering 1929–2010, it retroactively divested hundreds of thousands of Dominicans of Haitian descent of their Dominican nationality, leaving them stateless. The writers Edwidge Danticat and Junot Díaz, of Haitian and Dominican origin, respectively, were among the prominent voices in the diaspora to critique this legislation. See, for example, their conversation published by Richard André.

14. *Barceló con hielo* premiered at Repertorio Español in New York City. The plays in repertory at this theater cater to a somewhat conservative audience base, though in recent years the theater's productions of new playwrights have attracted a more diverse audience. When the actor playing Nino dropped out of the production, Rodríguez unexpectedly wound up playing the part because he was able to tackle the tricky role of appearing as both a young man and an older man and using very colloquial forms of speech. Rodríguez states that Nino is a composite of father figures in his life but is not an autobiographical character (personal email communication).

15. In perhaps a nod to the loaded significance of these roles, it should be noted that Jaston played the cowboy role while Nino played the Indian.

16. It seems that the primary impact Rodríguez seeks is for Nino to threaten Jaston with "outing" his sexuality, since he does not invoke race in the English translation (in both play translations, there are many instances in which Rodríguez does not produce a word-for-word translation). It is as though his supposed racial inferiority is a given and that the real wounding would occur by relaying the secret of his sexuality.

17. The mother's rejection of the painting is the only suggestion in the play that she is aware of the nature of the relationship between Nino and Jaston. The first page number in the parenthetical reference refers to the text in Spanish; the second refers to Rodríguez's English translation.

18. Documentary films, for example, have been an important arena for reviving collective memory in the Dominican Republic. See, for example, René Antonio Fortunato's documentaries, *Trujillo: El Poder del Jefe* (3 volumes), *Balaguer: La herencia del tirano*, and *Balaguer: La violencia del poder.* Liberato writes that to varying degrees, today's wave in memory work in the Dominican Republic have been influenced by "nonprofit organizations, private donors, international NGOs, the Dominican state, Dominican historians, public intellectuals, filmmakers, cultural groups, and elite victims' families" (13).

19. Each play provides some details of Nino's relationship with Norma and Luz, but Rodríguez does not flesh out this backstory into a coherent whole. Nino knew both women back in the Dominican Republic and in accordance with his performance of a hegemonic male identity, he appeared to be exclusively heterosexual and to embody the virility of a macho with offspring from multiple partners (de Moya 83).

20. In the English version, to maintain the humorous play with the *ch* sound, *chimichanga* is substituted for *chancleta*, which would be translated as "flip-flops."

21. De Moya provides a long list of rearing practices by mothers that socialize boys to perform hegemonic masculinities. He gathered the list from observations of mother-child interactions, informal conversations, and interviews with men and women over the course of three years (73).

Chapter 4: "Home Is Where Theatre Is"

1. See chapter 1 for a discussion of plays about yola migration and chapter 2 for more discussion of the Dominicanyork label.

2. Torres-Saillant explains that his title references Max Henríquez Ureña's 1930 essay, "El retorno de los galeones" (The Return of the Galleon Ships), which pointed out how the modernist movement paradoxically "llevó su fuerza renovadora de América a España a aquella imperial Iberia que había venido a la región con sus poderosas naves durante la conquista (1963:25)" ("brought its renovating power from America to Spain, to the Iberian empire that had come to the region with its powerful vessels during the conquest [1963:25]"; 393).

3. Other plays that merit mention in connection to the theme of return include texts published in Dinorah Coronado's 2011 anthology of Dominican plays: *Ya viene abuela* by Dinorah Coronado, *Me lo dijo Adela* by Claudio Marte, and *Antesala de la muerte* by Lucía Tavaras. Rather than the many dramas about migration that treat the experiences of arrival and adaptation, these plays explore various kinds of return and focus on how affective and material ties are maintained over a lifetime.

4. Since graduating from the Escuela de Arte Dramático de Bellas Artes in Santo Domingo in 1987, Elizabeth Ovalle has had a productive career as an actor, director,

and playwright. Author of over a dozen plays, her work addresses current social problems. She was nominated for a Cassandra Award for her performance in *Alerta roja* (2001), a monologue she authored about women with AIDS; she wrote and performed in *Conmigo no* (2007), a piece about domestic violence; and in 2014, she won the Cristóbal de Llerena national theater prize for *A la espera*, a play about human trafficking that has been staged internationally. Ovalle has held leadership positions in the theater section of the Dominican Secretaría de Estado de Cultura.

5. Torres-Saillant critiques how popular media outlets such as *Última Hora*, *Sucesos*, and *El siglo* have stoked uneasiness about Dominicans in the diaspora by depicting them as stereotyped, criminalized "others" who, upon return, bring violence and alien values to the Dominican Republic. He writes that "la criminalización de los ausentes constituye un acto de agresión contra la diáspora dominicana, una difamación rampante contra una población que ha evitado el colapso funesto de la economía nacional" ("the criminalization of Dominicans abroad constitutes an act of aggression against the Dominican diaspora, a rampant defamation against a population that has prevented the disastrous collapse of the national economy"; "Retorno" 47). Torres-Saillant similarly notes that intellectual discourses in books like Manuel Nuñez's 1990 *El ocaso de la nación dominicana* (The Decline of the Dominican Nation) contribute to these perceptions by positing the cultural hybridity of Dominicanyorks and Dominican-Haitians as corrosive to Dominican national identity ("Retorno" 49). In its one-sided portrayal of the experience of migration, we will see that *Por hora y a* Piece-Work resonates with some of the negative discourses on the figure of the migrant.

6. *Por hora y a* Piece-Work is published in the Casa de Teatro series and in Quackenbush's anthology of Dominican women playwrights, which is the version I cite.

7. As Ramona Hernández and others have documented, in the 1980s and 1990s Dominican migrants arrived en masse to the United States just as the labor market was restructuring and New York City was transforming into a postindustrial city. The declining manufacturing industry, particularly the garment sector, was the largest employer of Dominicans—of women in particular—during this period. For more details, see Ramona Hernández, "On Dominicans in New York City's Garment Industry."

8. On one occasion, Juana describes the lack of medical services and schools in her rural town, and the battle against hunger as motivations for her migration (258), but the play focuses on depicting the maladaptation of Dominicans to life in New York City and Juana's subsequent return. The story of departure, set in the Dominican Republic, is relatively rare in the transnational playwrights studied in this book.

9. For example, any ethnographic study of Dominican immigrant laborers would provide nuance to Ovalle's bleak story. See, for example, *Between Two Islands: Dominican International Migration* by Sherri Grasmuck and Patricia R. Pessar, which

analyzes undocumented Dominican immigrants and their changing household structures and gender roles without criminalizing them.

10. *Dominicanos ausentes* (absent Dominicans) is frequently used in the Dominican Republic to refer to Dominicans in the diaspora. García-Peña favors the term because of its transnational quality since it references "Dominicans who are not living on the island yet still presumed to be part of the nation" (172). She also observes that the notion of absence is apt for capturing the vulnerable positions migrants occupy in both nation-states (172).

11. The piece premiered in 1994 at the Dance Theater Workshop in New York City with Corniel playing the part of Fefa. It formed part an emerging minority artist project called "Out of the Shadows," directed by George Emilio Sanchez. Corniel is an actor, creative writer, journalist, and professor. She lived in New Jersey from 1991 to 1994, where she was involved in a job interviewing Hispanics and African Americans about health-related topics. During this period, she collaborated with other transnational theater practitioners included in this study, Claudio Mir and Frank Disla, on several projects. In the mid-1990s Corniel returned to the Dominican Republic, where she taught theater classes and worked as a journalist, reporting in notable arts periodicals, *Contemporánea*, *Mirada al Arte*, and *Ventana*, *Listín Diario*'s cultural supplement, for which she also served as editor. Corniel currently lives in the United States, where she completed a doctorate in Hispanic Languages and Literature at Stony Brook University. She teaches in the City University of New York system and continues to work as an actor in both New York City and Santo Domingo. In 2003 she was nominated for a Cassandra Award for her role in *René: Para despertar la memoria*, staged by Teatro La Cuarta in Santo Domingo, and in 2014 she was nominated for an ACE award for her role in Pablo García Gámez's *Noche tan Linda*, staged by Pregones and the Puerto Rican Traveling Theater.

12. As noted in chapter 1, the large amounts of luggage that have become a ubiquitous image of Dominicans in airports has been the subject of caricature. Torres-Saillant proposes instead that they be seen as the social burden the migrants carry for their nation-state's failings ("Retorno" 30).

13. Any citations in English are in the original. The Spanish portions of this bilingual piece are translated.

14. For an in-depth study of US imperial designs in the Dominican Republic and Haiti and the resultant exclusionary racial discourses, see García-Peña, *The Borders of Dominicanidad: Race, Nation, and the Archives of Contradiction*.

15. Race is referenced only when Juana identifies the factory inspector (in reality, a migration agent) as *el hombre blanco* (the white man), distinguishing him from Dominican factory workers.

16. The sociologist Luis Guarnizo describes Dominican migrants as "subaltern to and excluded by the dominant cultures in the nation-states involved" (52). See his

study documenting the many ways returnees suffer discrimination, such as their exclusion from prestigious business and social associations.

17. On the changing attitudes toward Dominican migration, Guarnizo details a shift from "a positive consensus across classes about migrants" (46) in the 1960s and 1970s to the 1990s, when, "the dominant classes had drastically recast their perception; from quasi heroes in the 1970s, migrants had become villains who were the cause of all evils affecting the country—from inflation to crime, violence, and drug addiction" (46).

18. The most established of the four authors included in this chapter, Luisa Angélica Sherezada "Chiqui" Vicioso, has dedicated her life's work as an ambassador, sociologist, educator, and creative writer to the vindication of women's rights. She is the author of the first piece of feminist literary criticism in the Dominican Republic, *Algo que decir: ensayos sobre literatura femenina* (Something to Say: Essays about Feminine Literature) (1981), and, more recently, *El teatro dominicano: Una visión femenina del género* (Dominican Theater: A Feminine Vision of the Genre) (2003). In the late 1990s, Vicioso made her first forays into the theater, winning the National Theater Prize in 1997 for *Wish-ky Sour*, a play about women and alcoholism. Vicioso has also written the theater pieces *Salomé U: Cartas a una ausencia* (1998), *Perrerías* (2001), and *Nuyor/Islas* (2003). Vicioso is also an activist and has worked for several UN agencies, including UNICEF, and as a consultant for UNESCO, among other organizations. She was appointed ambassador for Women's Children's and Youth Affairs for the Foreign Relations Ministry, and in 2012 she was the national vice presidential candidate for the Alianza País Party.

19. Margo Milleret notes in her study *Latin American Women On/In Stages* that the Latin American theater canon has offered few roles for older women (159).

20. *Nuyor/Islas* was first performed at the Festival Internacional de Teatro in Santo Domingo in 2003. Descriptions of the productions of *Nuyor/Islas* in articles by Vivian Martínez-Tabares and Beatriz Rizk have facilitated my analysis of the 2006 published playscript.

21. This is a biographical detail. In a blog describing the unique hospitality of Santiago de los Caballeros, Vicioso states that she wrote *Ay Fefa* after her mother moved to a returnee community there. She writes that "the typical *marchantas* (women street vendors) of Santiago still existed and one in particular would arrive at my mother's house on her donkey and they would watch the *telenovela* together. Mami would offer her juice or coffee and if it was noon she would invite her to stay for lunch" (Dominican cooking).

22. Rizk notes that in the New York production the mute bill collector is physically present throughout *Ay Fefa*, but opines that the production in Santo Domingo was more theatrically compelling by locating the character on stilts, looking over the top of the walls enclosing Ramona, with his silent reactions projected onto one of the walls (45).

23. Flores writes that the encounter between nonmigrant nationals and "othered" migrants who have returned to the homeland is intense and that "rejection and resentment alternate with acceptance and inclusion" (*Diaspora* 45).

24. Vicioso misspells Vicini, an Italian Dominican family of sugar barons. The documentary *The Price of Sugar*, directed by Bill Haney (2007), depicts the political power of this family and the repression of Haitian sugar workers on their plantations. The Báez name references Ramón Buenaventura Báez Figueroa, descendent of two Dominican presidents, infamous for his involvement in a billion dollar banking fraud scandal while president of Banco Intercontinental.

25. Silvio Torres-Saillant explains why Dominicans in the diaspora have developed empathy with Haitians: "A nosotros en la diáspora se nos hace fácil identificarnos con los de abajo porque nuestra dura realidad en el margen social que habitamos nos recuerda constantemente que somos de abajo. De ahí que nosotros allá no seamos tan antihaitianos como ustedes aquí, pues allá de alguna manera nosotros somos los haitianos" ("Those of us in the diaspora easily identify with the underdogs because our harsh reality in the social margins we inhabit constantly reminds us that we are from below. As a result, Dominicans in the diaspora are not as anti-Haitian as you are here, because over there we are in a certain way Haitians"; "Retorno" 107).

26. Josefina Báez is a poet, dancer, teacher, activist, and founder and director of Ay Ombe Theatre (1986). She immigrated from La Romana, Dominican Republic, to New York City in 1972, when she was twelve years old. Since the 1990s she has been performing around the world in experimental pieces such as *Dominicanish*, *Apartarte/Casarte*, *Comrade Bliss ain't Playing*, and *Levente no.Yolayorkdominicanyork*. Báez presents a unique case of transnationality because her work adds a layer of hybridity from her extensive experience studying dance in India and Cuba. Her performances and workshops around the world—New Zealand, Russia, Denmark, Cuba, Chile, and Mexico—have made Báez one of the best-known contemporary Dominican artists.

27. My analysis of the piece is based on the published text, live readings of excerpts, and a digital recording of the 1999 premiere performance directed by Claudio Mir at the Dance Theater Workshop in New York City. Mir directed, adapted, and arranged Báez's poetic texts for this performance.

28. All quotes reproduce the spacing and style of the original.

29. Escuela's statement about baseball being "good" to him was coined by Miñoso. For more on the problematic notion of gratitude expressed by a minority player in an often abusive and colonial-like professional sports league, see the essay "Speaking Black Latino/a/ness: Race, Performance, and Poetry in Tato Laviera, Willie Perdomo, and Josefina Báez" by La Fountain-Stokes.

30. García-Peña claims that Dominicans are racial exiles who "are expunged from the Dominican nation because of their race yet they remain inadmissible in the United States for the same reason" (173).

Chapter 5: Borrowed Identities

1. International migration is a defining characteristic of our times. Seyla Benhabib highlights the uptake in migration since 1965: "Strikingly, more than half of the increase of migrants from 1910 to 2000 occurred in the last three and a half decades of the twentieth century, between 1965 and 2000. In this period 75 million people undertook crossborder movements to settle in countries other than that of their origin (United Nations, Department of Economic and Social Affairs 2001)" (5).

2. Brysk and Shafir argue that "new rights make the possession and exercise of former rights more effective, and accession to new rights removes fences between groups previously separated by legal barriers or social custom. Each time citizenship is expanded or extended, it becomes stronger and richer" (277).

3. These universal rights are noted in the United Nations Declaration of Human Rights in articles 19, 27, and 27(1) ("Universal Declaration").

4. The cultural practices of María Isabel Bosch and Claudio Mir are transnational. Bosch resides in Argentina, but her theater company, Tibai Teatro (Argentina-República Dominicana), has consistently performed in Santo Domingo and Buenos Aires. Although Bosch has made her home in Argentina, in one article she is lauded by a Dominican theater critic as "la mejor actriz dramática del país" (the country's best dramatic actress) ("Las viajeras" 6). Bosch's best-known works engage Dominican themes, such as *Las viajeras* and *Contando a mi abuelo*, a solo piece that performs short stories written by her famous grandfather, the author and politician Juan Bosch. Fellow Dominican performer Claudio Mir has been living in the United States since the 1990s. As a theater and visual artist, musician, filmmaker, and educator, Mir's artistic training has been transnational and transdisciplinary: in addition to participating in prestigious acting and directing workshops hosted by Eugenio Barba, Jerzy Grotowsky, Miguel Rubio, and Teresa Ralli in Italy and Spain, he holds a degree in acting from the Escuela Nacional de Arte Escénico in Santo Domingo. Mir has also earned degrees in the United States in photography and visual arts (currently he is a candidate for an MFA in creative writing at Rutgers-Newark). A community artist, Mir has long employed the arts to raise awareness of HIV/AIDS prevention, domestic violence, racism, and drug abuse in advocacy projects developed in summer camps, hospitals, and theaters. He works at Rutgers-New Brunswick as a program coordinator in the Collaborative Center for Community-Based Research and Service.

5. For Arendt, abilities and talents identify what a person is; while only through action and speech do people disclose who they are. Theater is a form of the storytelling or narrative making Arendt invokes as necessary for people to disclose to the world who they are (184–88).

with Geirola, Frank Disla's brother Reynaldo names *Un búfalo* as one of the pieces he most desires to direct and mentions that he once began the project and worked for a time with the actors Wallis Uribe (who played Esperanza Suárez in *Chicken Cordon Blue*) and Arturo López (296–97). In the United States, *Un búfalo* received a dramatized reading at the Barco de Papel bookstore in Queens, New York.

Coda

1. Junot Díaz made these remarks in a September 14, 2007, podcast interview with Christopher Lydon; they are quoted in Paul Jay, *Global Matters: The Transnational Turn in Literary Studies* (177).

2. The exception is the playwright and performer María Isabel Bosch, who lives in Buenos Aires.

3. My work at the intersection of Spanish language and literatures, ethnic studies, and theater and performance studies also complicates labeling my research and disciplinary affiliation. See my article "Hispanic Caribbean Theatre on the Move: Crossing Borders, Redefining Boundaries" for a discussion of the opportunities and challenges of interdisciplinary teaching and research.

Works Cited

Abréu, Dió-genes. *La cosa nostra dominicana. Máscaras Errantes: Antología de dramaturgos dominicanos en los Estados Unidos*, edited by Dinorah Coronado, Editora Nacional, 2011, pp. 16–29.

Abréu, Dió-genes. *Engañifas, Discurso y Práctica Social*. Caliope, 2007.

Abréu, Dió-genes. *Perejil: El ocaso de la hispanidad dominicana. Celebración de la multiplicidad cultural desde New York*. Editora Mediabyte, 2004.

Abréu, Dió-genes. *Sin Haitianidad no hay Dominicanidad: Cartografía de una identidad que se bifurca*. Editora Nacional, 2013.

Abréu, Dió-genes. "What up, Nigga? El Dominicanyork como terrorista cultural." *Perejil: El ocaso de la "hispanidad" dominicana. Celebración de la multiplicidad cultural desde New York*. Editora Mediabyte, 2004, pp. 165–200.

Acosta, José. *Voces de ultramar: Literatura dominicana de la diáspora*. Ediciones Ferilibro, 2005.

Agamben, Giorgio. *Homo Sacer: Sovereign Power and Bare Life*. Translated by Daniel Heller-Roazen, Stanford UP, 1988.

Aldama, Frederick Luis. *Latino/a Literature in the Classroom: Twenty-First-Century Approaches to Teaching*. Routledge, 2015.

Álvarez, Julia. *How the García Girls Lost Their Accents*. Algonquin Books, 1991.

Álvarez, Julia. *In the Name of Salomé*. Algonquin Books, 2000.

Álvarez, Julia. *In the Time of the Butterflies*. Algonquin Books, 1994.

André, Richard. "The Dominican Republic and Haiti: A Shared View from the Diaspora." A Conversation with Edwidge Danticat and Junot Díaz. *Americas Quarterly*, Summer 2014, www.americasquarterly.org/content/dominican-republic-and-haiti-shared-view-diaspora.

Andújar, Rey Emmanuel. "Ciudadano Cero: La antropología de un seppuku caribeño." *El factor carne*. Isla negra, 2005, pp. 41–51.

Andújar, Rey Emmanuel. *Ciudadano Cero: Pieza teatral, una dramaturgia del escritor a partir de la dramaturgia del cuerpo. El factor carne*. Isla negra, 2005, pp. 75–82.

Andújar, Rey Emmanuel. "Fábulas del Ciudadano Cero: Mono-logando." *El factor carne*. Isla negra, 2005, pp. 52–74

Andújar, Rey Emmanuel. *El factor carne*. Isla negra, 2005.

Andújar, Rey Emmanuel. "Re: Tus fotos." Received by Camilla Stevens, 10 Dec. 2018.

Aparicio, Ana. *Dominican-Americans and the Politics of Empowerment*. UP of Florida, 2006.

Aponte, Sarah. "Dominican Related Dissertations in the U.S.: An Analytical Approach (1939–2009)." *Camino Real*, vol. 3, no. 4, 2011, pp. 21–51.

Aponte-Parés, Luis, et al., editors. "Puerto Rican Queer Sexualities." Special issue of *Centro Journal*, vol. 19, no. 1, 2007, pp. 1–422.

Appadurai, Arjun. *Modernity at Large: Cultural Dimensions of Globalization*. U of Minnesota P, 1996.

Arendt, Hannah. *The Human Condition*. U of Chicago P, 1998.

Arias, Roy. "Roy Arias Stages." www.royariasstages.com/777-theatre.

Arrizón, Alicia, and Lillian Manzor, editors. *Latinas on Stage*. Third Woman Press, 2000.

Austerlitz, Paul. "Cimarrones urbanos: la música como contranarrativa de la negritud dominicana." *Global* 61, editorialfunglode.com/index.php/perfil-revista-global/448-cimarrones-urbanos-la-musica-como-contranarrativa-de-la-negritud-dominicana.

Báez, Josefina. *Dominicanish: A Performance Text*. New York: Josefina Báez, 2000.

Báez, Josefina. *Levente no. Yolayorkdominicanyork*. I.Om.Be Press, 2011.

Balibar, Etienne. "The Nation Form: History and Ideology." *Race, Nation, Class: Ambiguous Identities*, edited by Etienne Balibar and Immanuel Wallerstein, translated by Chris Turner, Verso, 2002, pp. 86–106.

Basch, Linda, et al. *Nations Unbound: Transnational Projects, Postcolonial Predicaments, and Deterritorialized Nation-States*. Gordon and Breach, 1994.

Benhabib, Seyla. *The Rights of Others: Aliens, Residents, and Citizens*. Cambridge UP, 2004.

Benhabib, Seyla, and Judith Resnik. *Migrations and Mobilities: Citizenship, Borders, and Gender*. New York UP, 2009.

Bidó, Carlos, director. *Viajeros*. Tropical Films, 2006.

Bollaín, Icíar, director. *Flores de otro mundo*. Image Entertainment, 1999.

Bonney, Jo. "Preface." *Extreme Exposure: An Anthology of Solo Performance Texts from the Twentieth Century*, edited by Jo Bonney, Theatre Communications Group, 2000, pp. xi–xvi.

Bosch, María Isabel. "Las viajeras." 2003. Theatrical Script.

Bosch, María Isabel. "'Las viajeras,' motivaciones para un espectáculo teatral." 2003. Essay.

Brah, Avtar. *Cartographies of Diaspora: Contesting Identities*. Routledge, 1996.

Brecht, Bertolt. "The Popular and the Realistic." *Brecht on Theatre: The Development of an Aesthetic*, edited and translated by John Willet, Methuen, 1974, pp. 107–15.

Brecht, Bertolt. *Round Heads and Pointed Heads: Bertolt Brecht Collected Plays, Vol. 4*, edited by Tom Kuhn and John Willet, Methuen, 2001, pp. 1–114.

Brecht, Bertolt. "A Short Organum for the Theatre." *Brecht on Theatre: The Development of an Aesthetic*, edited and translated by John Willet, Methuen, 1974, pp. 179–205.

Brecht, Bertolt. "Theatre for Pleasure or Theatre for Instruction." *Brecht on Theatre: The Development of an Aesthetic*, edited and translated by John Willet, Methuen, 1974, pp. 69–77.

Bulman, Gail A. *Staging Words, Performing Worlds: Intertextuality and Nation in Contemporary Latina American Theater*. Bucknell UP, 2007.

Butler, Judith. "Critically Queer." *Gay and Lesbian Quarterly*, no. 1, 1993, pp. 19–32.

Campos Sagaseta de Ilúrdoz, Juan Carlos (Koldo). "Las Viajeras y María Isabel Bosch." Cronopiando. *El Nacional* (Santo Domingo), 12 Mar. 2002, p. 6.

Candelario, Ginetta E. B. *Black Behind the Ears: Dominican Racial Identity from Museums to Beauty Shops*. Duke UP, 2007.

Carvajal, José. Interview. "Viriato Sención, 18 años después del Premio Nacional de Novela." http://escritorjosecarvajal.blogspot.com/2010/08/viriato-sencion-18-anos-despues-del.html.

Caro, Otto. *"RR" Tragedia Musical. Concurso de Teatro de Casa de Teatro 1983*. Casa de Teatro, 1985, pp. 343–585.

Casa de Teatro. https://www.casadeteatro.org/.

Castles, Stephen, and Alastair Davidson. "Preface." *Citizenship and Migration: Globalization and the Politics of Belonging*. Routledge, 2000, pp. vii–xiii.

Centro Cívico Cultural Dominicano. http://cccdominicano.org/.

Chambers, Iain. "Maritime Criticism and Theoretical Shipwrecks." *PMLA*, vol. 125, no. 3, May 2010, pp. 678–84.

Clifford, James. "Diasporas." *Cultural Anthropology*, vol. 9, no. 3, Aug. 1994, pp. 302–38.

Cocco De Filippis, Daisy. *Desde la diáspora: A Diáspora Position*. Alcance, 2003.

Cocco De Filippis, Daisy. "Palabras para rescatar existencias: De diáspora, nacionalidad, escritura y marginalidad." *La literatura dominicana al final del siglo: diálogo entre la tierra natal y la diáspora*, edited by Daisy Cocco De Filippis, Dominican Studies Working Paper Series 2, 1999, pp. 4–11.

Cocco De Filippis, Daisy, and Emma Jane Robinett, editors and translators. *Poemas del exilio y de otras inquietudes/Poems of Exile and Other Concerns*. Alcance, 1988.

Cocco De Filippis, Daisy, and Franklin Gutiérrez, editors. *Literatura dominicana en los Estados Unidos: Presencia temprana de la literatura dominicana*. Editora Buho, 2001.

Cohen, Robin. *Global Diasporas: An Introduction*. University College London P, 1997.

Colectivo Shampoo. "D' La Mona Plaza." *YouTube*, 13 May 2012, www.youtube.com/watch?v=cTNxctkHqgs.

Comisionado Dominicano de Cultura en Los Estados Unidos. http://www.codocul.com/.

Connor, Phillip. "The Most Common Mediterranean Migration Paths into Europe have changed since 2009." Pew Center, 18 Sept. 2018, http://www.pewresearch.org/fact-tank/2018/09/18/the-most-common-mediterranean-migration-paths-into-europe-have-changed-since-2009/.

Corniel, Zaida. "Ay Fefa, Where is the Wind?" 1994. Theatrical Script.

Coronado, Dinorah. "La mujer en el teatro dominicano." *Cielonaranja*, 2003–2004, cielonaranja.com/coronado_mujer.htm.

Coronado, Dinorah, editor. *Máscaras errantes: Antología de dramaturgos dominicanos en los Estados Unidos*. Editora Nacional, 2011.

Crichlow, Michaeline A. "Making Waves: (Dis)Placements, Entanglements, Mo(ve)ments." *Global South*, vol. 6, no. 1, Spring 2012, pp. 114–37.

Crossley, Scott. "Metaphorical Conceptions in Hip-Hop Music." *African American Review*, vol. 39, no. 4, 2005, pp. 501–12.

Cruz, Angie. *Let It Rain Coffee*. Simon & Schuster, 2005.

Cruz, Giovanny. "Inauguran Sala de Teatro Iván García Guerra en New York." *La Pasión Cultural*, 14 May 2011, lapasioncultural.blogspot.com/2011/05/sala-de-teatro-ivan-garcia-en-new-york.html.

Cuban Theater Digital Archive. http://cubantheater.org/.

Decena, Carlos Ulises. *Tacit Subjects: Belonging and Same-Sex Desire Among Dominican Immigrant Men*. Duke UP, 2011.

De Lauretis, Teresa. *Technologies of Gender: Theories on Theory, Film, and Fiction*. Indiana UP, 1987.

De Maeseneer, Rita. "Dominican Literature and Dominicanness from a European Perspective." *Reception: Texts, Readers, Audiences, History*, vol. 8, 2016, pp. 29–44.

De Moya, E. Antonio. "Power Games and Totalitarian Masculinity in the Dominican Republic." *Interrogating Caribbean Masculinities: Theoretical and Empirical Analyses*, edited by Rhoda E. Reddock, U of the West Indies P, 2004, pp. 68–102.

De Moya, E. Antonio, and Rafael García. "AIDS and the Enigma of Bisexuality in the Dominican Republic." *Bisexualities and AIDS: International Perspectives*, edited by Peter Aggleton, Taylor and Francis, 1996, pp. 121–36.

Derby, Lauren. "Gringo Chicken with Worms: Food and Nationalism in the Dominican Republic." *Close Encounters of Empire: Writing the Cultural History of U.S.-Latin American Relations*, edited by Gilbert M. Joseph et al., Duke UP, 1998, pp. 451–93.

Derby, Lauren. *The Dictator's Seduction: Politics and the Popular Imagination in the Era of Trujillo*. Durham and London: Duke UP, 2009.

Diamond, Elin, editor. *Performance and Cultural Politics*. Routledge, 1996.

"Diario Libre propone Día de Duelo Nacional por víctimas del naufragio." *Dario Libre*, 10 Feb. 2012, diariolibre.com.do/noticias/2012/02/10/i323629_diario-libre-propone-dia-duelo-nacional-por-victimas-del-naufragio.html.

Díaz, Junot. *The Brief Wondrous Life of Oscar Wao*. Riverhead Books, 2007.

Díaz, Junot. *Drown*. Riverhead Books, 1996.

Dinzey-Flores, Zaire Zenit. *Locked In, Locked Out: Gated Communities in a Puerto Rican City*. U of Pennsylvania P, 2013.

Disla, Frank. *Ascenso y caída de Andresito Reyna. Premio Teatro Letras de Ultramar 2013*. Editora Nacional, 2014.

Disla, Frank. *El Barbero de Saint Ann Street. Premios de Teatro 1999*. Casa de Teatro, 2000, pp. 11–70.

Disla, Frank. *Un Búfalo de El Paso, Texas*. Editora Nacional, 2005.

Disla, Frank. *Chicken Cordon Blue. Conjunto*, no. 116, 2000, pp. 28–38.

Disla, Frank. *Chicken Cordon Blue. Concurso Dominicano de Teatro 1997*. Casa de Teatro, 1997, pp. 75–95.

Disla, Frank. *La degradación de los agujeros negros. Máscaras Errantes: Antología de dramaturgos dominicanos en los Estados Unidos*, edited by Dinorah Coronado, Editora Nacional, 2011, pp. 119–52.

Disla, Frank. *Desarraigados (Premio Anual de Teatro Cristóbal de Llerena 1992–1993).* Secretaría de Estado de Educación, 1993.

Disla, Frank. Personal interview. New Brunswick, New Jersey, 14 Jul. 2009.

Disla, Reynaldo. "Presentación del libro: 'Ascenso y caída de Andresito Reyna' de Frank Disla." *Reynaldo Disla*, 21 Jul. 2014, reynaldodisla.blogspot.com/2014/.

Doerner, William R. "Dominican Republic Horror off Death's Head Beach." *Time*, 24 Jun. 2001, content.time.com/time/magazine/article/0,9171,145244,00.html.

"Dominican-York." https://memegenerator.net/El-Dominican-York/images/popular/alltime/page/2.

"Dominican Migrant: We Ate Flesh to Survive." *NBC News*, 4 Nov. 2008, www.nbcnews.com/id/27531105/ns/world_news-americas/t/dominican-migrant-we-ate-flesh-survive/#.WmyW5Wf3hcs.

"Dominicans Saved from Sea Tell of Attacks and Deaths of Thirst." *New York Times*, 12 Aug. 2004, www.nytimes.com/2004/08/12/world/dominicans-saved-from-sea-tell-of-attacks-and-deaths-of-thirst.html.

Duany, Jorge. *Blurred Borders: Transnational Migration between the Hispanic Caribbean and the United States.* U of North Carolina P, 2011.

Duany, Jorge, editor. *Los dominicanos en Puerto Rico: Migración en la semi-periferia.* Ediciones Huracán, 1990.

Duany, Jorge. "Los Países: Transnational Migration from the Dominican Republic to the United States." *Dominican Migration: Transnational Perspectives*, edited by Ernesto Sagás and Sintia E. Molina, UP of Florida, 2004, pp. 29–52.

Dubatti, Jorge. *Filosofía del teatro I (convivio, experiencia, subjetividad).* Atuel, 2007.

Durán Almarza, Emilia María. *Performeras de Dominicanyork: Josefina Báez y Chiqui Vicioso.* Universitat de València, 2010.

Durán, Florentino. "Faustina llegó de España cargada de obsequios." *Última hora*, 10 Jan. 2003, www.emiliopolis.net/es/int/hum/ultimahora.htm.

Epps, Brad, et al., editors. *Passing Lines: Sexuality and Immigration.* Harvard UP, 2005.

Espaillat, Rhina P. *Lapsing to Grace: Poems and Drawings.* Bennett & Kitchel, 1992.

Espaillat, Rhina P. *Where Horizons Go: Poems.* New Odyssey Press, 1998.

Euell, Kim. "Tha Playz tha Thang." *American Theatre*, vol. 19, no. 7, Sept. 2002, pp. 36–38.

Fanon, Frantz. *Black Skin, White Masks.* Translated by Richard Philcox, Grove, 2008.

"Faustina, la mujer dominicana que amamantó a 16 náufragos." *El Tiempo*, 26 Jan. 2001, www.eltiempo.com/archivo/documento/MAM-625688.

Ferrand, Loraine, director. "Ciudadano Cero en la Sala Ravelo Teatro Nacional." *YouTube*, 5 Sept. 2009, www.youtube.com/watch?v=M44iPW4wBCw.

Ferrand, Loraine. "Lo Correcto-Ciudadano Cero." *YouTube*, 24 May 2006, www.youtube.com/watch?v=ECTSXmoEqqk.

Ferrand, Loraine. "La Dramaturgia del Cuerpo en Jornada Extra." *YouTube*, 25 Aug. 2009, www.youtube.com/watch?v=aY0gwIixwfI.

"Festival Internacional de Teatro." redelae.org/fite/.

Flores, Juan. *The Diaspora Strikes Back: Caribeño Tales of Learning and Turning.* Routledge, 2009.

Flores, Juan. "Life off the Hyphen. Latino Literature and Nuyorican Traditions." *Mambo Montage: The Latinization of New York*, edited by Arlene Dávila and Agustín Laó-Montes, Columbia UP, 2001, pp. 185–206.

Flores, William V. "Citizens vs. Citizenry: Undocumented Immigrants and Latino Cultural Citizenship." *Latino Cultural Citizenship: Claiming Identity, Space, and Rights*, edited by William V. Flores and Rina Benmayor, Beacon Press, 1977, pp. 255–77.

Flores, Richard R. "Aesthetic Process and Cultural Citizenship: The Membering of a Social Body in San Antonio." *Latino Cultural Citizenship: Claiming Identity, Space, and Rights*, edited by William V. Flores and Rina Benmayor, Beacon Press, 1997, pp. 124–51.

Fortunato, René Antonio, director. *Balaguer: La herencia del tirano*. Videocine Palau, 1998.

Fortunato, René Antonio, director. *Balaguer: La violencia del poder*. Videocine Palau, 2003

Fortunato, René Antonio, director. *Trujillo: El poder del jefe I*. Videocine Palau, 1991.

Fortunato, René Antonio, director. *Trujillo: El poder del jefe II*. Videocine Palau, 1994.

Fortunato, René Antonio, director. *Trujillo: El poder del jefe III*. Videocine Palau, 1996.

Foucault, Michel. *Society Must be Defended: Lectures at the College de France, 1975–1976*. Picador, 1997.

Friedman, Susan Stanford. "Migrations, Diasporas, Borders." *Introduction to Scholarship in Modern Languages and Literatures*, edited by David. G. Nicholls, 3rd. ed., MLA, 2007, pp. 260–93.

García, Mar, and Denise Palewonsky. *Gender, Remittances and Development: The Case of Women Immigrants from Vicente Noble, Dominican Republic*. United Nations International Research and Training Institute for the Advancement of Women (UN-INSTRAW), 2006.

García-Peña, Lorgia. *The Borders of Dominicanidad: Race, Nation, and Archives of Contradiction*. Duke, UP, 2016.

Geis, Deborah R. *Postmodern Theatric(k)s: Monologue in Contemporary American Drama*. U of Michigan P, 1993.

Geirola, Gustavo. "Entrevista a Reynaldo Disla." *Arte y oficio del director teatral en América Latina. Caribe: Cuba, Puerto Rico y República Dominicana*. Argus-a, 2014, pp. 289–312.

Gilbert, Helen, and Jacqueline Lo. *Performance and Cosmopolitics: Cross-Cultural Transactions in Australasia*. Palgrave Macmillan, 2007.

Georges, Eugenia. *The Making of a Transnational Community: Migration, Development, and Cultural Change in the Dominican Republic*. Columbia UP, 1990.

Gilroy, Paul. *Between Camps: Nations, Cultures, and the Allure of Race*. Allen Lane, 2000.

Ginebra, Danilo. *Panorama del Teatro dominicano. Tomo 1*. Teatro Gratey, 1984.

Giroux, Henry A. "Reading Hurricane Katrina: Race, Class, and the Biopolitics of Disposability." *College Literature*, vol. 33, no. 3, Summer 2006, pp. 171–96.

Giroux, Henry A. *Stormy Weather: Katrina and the Politics of Disposability*. Paradigm, 2006.

Glick Schiller, Nina. "Thinking about and beyond Transnational Processes." *Caribbean Migration to Western Europe and the United States*, edited by Margarita Cervantes-Rodríguez et al., Temple UP, 2009, pp. 18–40.

Glick Schiller, Nina, and Georges Eugene Fouron. *Georges Woke up Laughing: Long-Distance Nationalism and the Search for Home*. Duke UP, 2001.

Glick Schiller, Nina, et al. "Transnationalism: A New Analytic Framework for Understanding Migration." *Towards a Transnational Perspective on Migration: Race, Class, Ethnicity Considered*, edited by Nina Glick Schiller et al., New York Academy of Sciences, 1992, pp. 1–24.

Glissant, Édouard. *Poetics of Relation*. Translated by Betsy Wing, U of Michigan P, 1997.

Goico Castro, Manuel de Jesús. "Raíz y trayectoria del teatro en la literatura nacional." *Antología literaria dominicana*, edited by Margarita Vallejo de Paredes, Instituto Tecnológico de Santo Domingo, 1981, pp. 1–34.

Górecki, Henryk M., Dawn Upshaw, and David Zinman. Symphony No. 3, Opus 36 (*Symphony of Sorrowful Songs*), Elektra Nonesuch, 1992. CD.

Graham, Pamela M. "Reimagining the Nation and Defining the District: Dominican Migration and Transnational Politics." *Caribbean Circuits: New Directions in the Study of Caribbean Migration*, edited by Patricia R. Pessar, Center for Migration Studies, 1997, pp. 91–122.

Grant, Félix. "Abren convocatoria para talleres de teatro y música folclórica dominicana." *Impacto Latino*, 10 Apr. 2015, impactolatino.com/abren-convocatoria-para-talleres-de-teatro-y-musica-folclorica-dominicana/.

Grasmuck, Sherri, and Patricia R. Pessar. *Between Two Islands: Dominican International Migration*. U of California P, 1991.

Graziano, Frank. *Undocumented Dominican Migration*. U of Texas P, 2013.

Graziano, Frank. "Why Dominicans Migrate: The Complex of Factors Conducive to Undocumented Maritime Migration." *Diaspora: A Journal of Transnational Studies*, vol. 15, no. 1, 2006, pp. 1–33.

Gregory, Steven. *The Devil Behind the Mirror: Globalization and Politics in the Dominican Republic*. U of California P, 2007.

Grieco, Elizabeth M. "The Dominican Population in the United States: Growth and Distribution." *Migration Policy Institute*, Sept. 2004, www.migrationpolicy.org/research/dominican-population-united-states-growth-and-distribution.

Griffith, Ivelaw Lloyd. *Drugs and Security in the Caribbean: Sovereignty under Siege*. Penn State UP, 1997.

Guarnizo, Luis Eduardo. "'Going Home': Class, Gender, and Household Transformation among Dominican Return Migrants." *Caribbean Circuits: New Directions in the Study of Caribbean Migration*, edited by Patricia R. Pessar, Center for Migration Studies, 1997, pp. 13–60.

Guarnizo, Luis Eduardo, and Michael Peter Smith. "The Locations of Transnationalism." *Transnationalism from Below*, edited by Guarnizo and Michael Peter Smith, Transaction Publishers, 1998, pp. 3–34.

Guerra, Juan Luis. Lyrics to "Elena." www.elyrics.net/read/j/juan-luis-guerra-lyrics/elena-lyrics.html.

Gutiérrez, Franklin. "Dedican Feria del Libro de Santo Domingo a escritores de la diáspora dominicana." *Comisionado Dominicano de Cultura en los EE.UU.*, 12 Apr. 2005, www.comisionadodecultura.com/feria.html?1109356984890.

Gutiérrez, Franklin. "Entrevista al doctor Franklin Gutiérrez." *Comisionado Dominicano de Cultura en los EE.UU.*, 2 Jan. 2006, www.comisionadodecultura.com/feria.html.

Gutiérrez, Franklin. *Literatura dominicana en los Estados Unidos: Historia y trayectoria de la diáspora intelectual.* Fundación Global Democracia y Desarrollo, 2004.

Guzmán, Manuel. "'Pa la Escuelita con mucho cuidao y por la orillita': A Journey Through the Contested Terrains of the Nation and Sexual Orientation." *Puerto Rican Jam: Rethinking Colonialism and Nationalism*, edited by Frances Negrón Muntaner and Ramón Grosfoguel, University of Minnesota Press, 1997, pp. 209–28.

Haney, Bill, director. *The Price of Sugar.* Uncommon Productions, 2007.

Hannerz, Ulf. *Transnational Connections: Culture, People, Places.* Routledge, 1996.

Hendricks, Glenn. *The Dominican Diaspora: From the Dominican Republic to New York City.* Columbia UP, 1974.

"Hermandad en el Teatro." *El Nuevo Día*, 24 Jun. 2014, www.elnuevodia.com/entretenimiento/cultura/nota/hermandadenelteatro-1799689/.

Hernández, Ramona. *The Mobility of Workers Under Advanced Capitalism: Dominican Migration to the United States.* Columbia UP, 2002.

Hernández, Ramona. "On the Age Against the Poor: Dominican Migration to the United States." *Journal of Immigrant & Refugee Services*, vol. 2, no. 1/2, 2004, pp. 87–107.

Hernández, Ramona. "On Dominicans in New York City's Garment Industry" *A Coat of Many Colors: Immigration, Globalism, and Reform in the New York City Garment Industry*, edited by Daniel Soyer, Fordham UP, 2005, pp. 169–92.

Hernández, Ramona, and Anthony Stevens-Acevedo. "Dominican Studies: A Field in its Own Right." *Camino Real*, vol. 3, no. 4, 2011, pp. 13–17.

Hilton, James, and William von Hippel. "Stereotypes." *Annual Review of Psychology*, no. 47, 1984, pp. 237–71.

Hoffnung-Garskof, Jesse. *A Tale of Two Cities: Santo Domingo and New York after 1950.* Princeton UP, 2008.

Holdsworth, Nadine. *Theatre and Nation.* Palgrave Macmillan, 2010.

"Homenajeados del Festival de Teatro del Comisionado." *Comisionado Dominicano de Cultura en los EE.UU.*, www.codocul.com/homenajeados-del-festival-de-teatro.

Horn, Maja. *Masculinity after Trujillo: The Politics of Gender in Dominican Literature.* UP of Florida, 2014.

Horn, Maja. "Passion Plays: The Dominican Diaspora in Waddys Jáquez's *P.A.R.G.O.*" *Studies in 20th and 21st Century Literature*, vol. 32, no. 2, 2008, pp. 342–58.

Hornby, Richard. *Drama, Metadrama and Perception.* Bucknell UP, 1986.

Hughes, Donna M., et al. "Dominican Republic." *The Factbook on Global Sexual Exploitation*, Coalition against Trafficking in Women, 1999, www.uri.edu/artsci/wms/hughes/domrep.htm.

Isa, Minerva, and Eladio Pichardo. "Trabas a la inmigración aumenta el tráfico de ilegales." *Hoy*, 20 Mar. 2006, hoy.com.do/migracion-causas-y-efectos-trabas-a-la-inmigracion-aumenta-el-trafico-de-ilegales/.

Itzigsohn, José. *Encountering American Faultlines: Race, Class, and the Dominican Experience in Providence*. New York: Russell Sage, 2009.

Itzigsohn, José, et al. "Mapping Dominican Transnationalism: Narrow and Broad Transnational Practices." *Ethnic and Racial Studies*, vol. 22, no. 2, 1999, pp. 316–39.

Jay, Paul. *Global Matters: The Transnational Turn in Literary Studies*. Cornell UP, 2010.

Jáquez, Waddys. "P.A.R.G.O.: Los pecados permitidos." 2001. Theatrical Script.

Jáquez, Waddys, director. *P.A.R.G.O.: Los pecados permitidos*. Deli Media Labs, 2002.

Joseph, May. *Nomadic Identities: The Performance of Citizenship*. U of Minnesota P, 1999.

Kasinitz, Philip, et al. *Inheriting the City: The Children of Immigrants Come of Age*. Russell Sage Foundation and Harvard UP, 2008.

Kearney, Michael. "Borders and Boundaries of State and Self at the End of Empire." *Journal of Historical Sociology*, vol. 4, no. 1, 1991, pp. 52–74.

Kelleher, Joe. *Theatre and Politics*. Palgrave Macmillan, 2009.

Kitwana, Bakari. *The Hip-Hop Generation: Young Blacks and the Crisis in African-American Culture*. BasicCivitas, 2002.

Kleinknecht, William. *The New Ethnic Mobs: The Changing Face of Organized Crime in America*. Free Press, 1996.

Kristeva, Julia. *The Powers of Horror: An Essay on Abjection*. Translated by Leon S. Roudiez, Columbia UP, 1982.

Krohn-Hansen, Christian. "Masculinity and the Political among Dominicans: 'The Dominican Tiger.'" *Machos, Mistresses, Madonnas*, edited by Marit Melhuus and Kristi Anne Stølen, Verso, 1996, pp. 108–33.

Krohn-Hansen, Christian. *Political Authoritarianism in the Dominican Republic*. Palgrave Macmillan, 2009.

La Fountain-Stokes, Lawrence. "Cultures of the Puerto Rican Queer Diaspora." *Passing Lines: Sexuality and Immigration*, edited by Brad Epps et al., Harvard UP and David Rockefeller Center for Latin American Studies, pp. 275–309.

La Fountain-Stokes, Lawrence. "Speaking Black Latino/a/ness: Race, Performance, and Poetry in Tato Laviera, Willie Perdomo, and Josefina Báez." *AmeRícan Poet: Essays on Tato Laviera*, edited by Stephanie Álvarez and William Luis, Centro de Estudios Puertorriqueños, Hunter College, CUNY, 2014, pp. 240–57.

La Fountain-Stokes, Lawrence. "Translocas: Migration, Homosexuality, and Transvestism in Recent Puerto Rican Performance." *E-misférica*, vol. 8, no. 1, Summer 2011.

Lehmann, Hans-Thies. *Postdramatic Theatre*. Translated by Karen Jürs-Munby, Routledge, 2006.

Lendeborg, Jorge, director. *60 millas al este*. Latin Flavor Pictures, 2008.

León de Aranoa, Fernando, director. *Princesas*. IFC First Take, 2005.

Levitt, Peggy. *The Transnational Villagers*. U of California P, 2001.

Levitt, Peggy, and Mary C. Waters. *The Changing Face of Home: The Transnational Lives of the Second Generation*. Russell Sage Foundation, 2002.

Levitt, Peggy, and Nina Glick Schiller. "Conceptualizing Simultaneity: A Transnational Social Field Perspective on Society." *International Migration Review*, vol. 38 no. 3, 2004, pp. 1002–39.

Liberato, Ana S. Q. *Joaquín Balaguer, Memory, and Diaspora. The Lasting Political Legacies of an American Protegé*. Lexington Books, 2013.

Lionnet, Françoise, and Shu-mei Shih, editors. *Minor Transnationalism*. Duke UP, 2005.

Lipsitz, George. *Dangerous Crossroads: Popular Music, Postmodernism and the Poetics of Place*. Verso, 1994.

"Lo Correcto Hip Hop Dominicano (El Documental)." *YouTube*, 20 Aug. 2009, www.youtube.com/watch?v=AEH-h1PnxfY.

Lockwood, Jaime. *Teatro dominicano: Pasado y presente*. Editorial la Nación, 1959.

Logan, John R. "The New Latinos: Who They Are, Where They Are." Lewis Mumford Center for Comparative Urban and Regional Research, 10 Sept. 2001, mumford.albany.edu/census/HispanicPop/HspReport/MumfordReport.pdf.

López, Ana M. "Greater Cuba." *The Ethinc Eye: Latino Media Arts*, edited by Chon Noriega and Ana M. López, U of Minnesota P, 1996, pp. 38–58

Lugo, A. B. "Ilka Tanya Payán Theater and the New Pregones Theater." *La Nueva Ola*, vol. 9, no. 8, 2006, www.hellohola.org/newsletter/winspr06.pdf.

Madison, Soyini D. "Forward." *Solo/Black Woman: Scripts, Interviews, and Essays*, edited by Patrick E. Johnson and Ramón Rivera-Servera, Northwestern UP, 2014, pp. xi–xiv.

"María Isabel Bosch actúa en festivales de teatro colombiano." *El Nuevo Diario*, 18 Mar. 2008, archivo.elnuevodiario.com.do/2008/03/18/maria-isabel-bosch-actua-en-festivales-de-teatro-colombiano/.

Martin, Phillip, Elizabeth Midgley, and Michael Teitelbaum. "Migration and Development: Whither the Dominican Republic and Haiti?" 15 Mar. 2002, migration.ucdavis.edu/rs/more.php?id=97.

Martin, Randy. "Artistic Citizenship." *Artistic Citizenship: A Public Voice for the Arts*, edited by Randy Martin and Mary Schmidt Campbell, Routledge, 2006, pp. 1–22.

Martínez-San Miguel, Yolanda. *Caribe Two Ways: Cultura de la migración en el Caribe insular hispánico*. Ediciones Callejón, 2003.

Martínez-San Miguel, Yolanda. "Más allá de la homonormatividad: intimidades alternativas en el Caribe hispano." *Revista Iberoamericana*, vol. 25, 2008, pp. 1039–57.

Martínez Tabares, Vivian. "Caribbean Bodies, Migrations, and Spaces of Resistance." *TDR: The Drama Review*, vol. 48, no. 2, 2004, pp. 24–32.

Martínez Tabares, Vivian. "Quince voces en busca del teatro dominicano." *Conjunto*, no. 116, 2000, pp. 2–21.

Martínez Tabares, Vivian. "Testimonio, espiritualidad y resistencia en el teatro de Chiqui Vicioso." *Latin American Theatre Review*, vol. 37, no. 2, 2004, pp. 25–40.

Mayes, April J. *The Mulatto Republic: Class, Race, and Dominican National Identity*. UP of Florida, 2014.

McLean-Hopkins, Catharine. "Performing Autologues: Citing/Siting the Self in Autobiographic Performance." *Monologues: Theatre, Performance, Subjectivity*, edited by Clare Wallace, Litteraria Pragensia, 2006, pp. 185–207.

Mejía, Ángel. "Del Partenón al foro de Colón." *Conjunto*, no. 116, 2000, pp. 22–27.

Meléndez, Agliberto, director. *Paisaje de ida*. Producciones Testimonio, 1988.

Melhuus, Marit. "Power, Value and the Ambiguous Meanings of Gender." *Machos, Mistresses, Madonnas*, edited by Marit Melhuus and Kristi Anne Stølen, Verso, 1996, pp. 230–59.

Mena, Miguel D. "Abalorios de la dominicanidad según el colectivo Shampoo." *Hoy*, 22 Oct. 2007, hoy.com.do/abalorios-de-la-dominicanidadsegun-el-colectivo%C2%93shampoo%C2%94/.

Méndez, Danny. *Narratives of Migration and Displacement in Dominican Literature*. Routledge, 2012.

Migración, prostitución y trata de mujeres dominicanas en la Argentina. International Organization for Migration, 2003, publications.iom.int/es/system/files/pdf/migracion_prostitucion_argentina.pdf.

"Millennium Development Goals." UNICEF, www.unicef.org/republicadominicana/english/overview_12559.htm.

Milleret, Margo. *Latin American Women On/In Stages*. SUNY P, 2004.

Mintz, Sidney. "The Localization of Anthropological Practice: From Area Studies to Transnationalism." *Critique of Anthropology*, vol. 18, no. 2, 1998, pp. 117–33.

Mir, Claudio. "Mondongo Scam." 1994. Theatrical Script.

Mir, Claudio, director. "Dominicanish 1st performance 1999." *YouTube*, 2 Sept. 2016, www.youtube.com/watch?v=OpFY7GM0WGU.

Miskolcze, Robin. *Women and Children First: Nineteenth-Century Sea Narratives and American Identity*. U of Nebraska P, 2007.

Molinaza, José. *Historia crítica del teatro dominicano*. Vol. 1, 1492–1844, vol. 2, 1844–1930, Editora de la UASD, 1984.

Molinaza, José. *Historia del teatro dominicano*. Editora de la UASD, 1998.

Molinaza, José. "1863–1987: Del indigenismo a la dramaturgia de los ochenta." *Escenarios de dos mundos: Inventario teatral de Iberoamérica. Escenarios de dos mundos. Tomo 4. Portugal, Puerto Rico, República Dominicana, Uruguay, Venezuela*, edited by Moisés Pérez Coterillo, Centro de Documentación Teatral, 1988, pp. 147-63.

Morón Espinosa, Antonio César. "El teatro escrito en español en la Ciudad de Nueva York: búsqueda y generación de identidad(es) desde la dramaturgia." *Latin American Theatre Review*, vol. 48, no. 2, 2015, pp. 87–105.

Mota, Carlos Rafael. *Antología del teatro dominicano del siglo XX*. 2006.

Mota, Carlos Rafael. *Corrientes renovadoras del teatro dominicano del siglo XX*. 2003.

Moya Pons, Frank. *The Dominican Republic: A National History*. Marcus Wiener, 1998.

Mroué, Rabih. "Introduction." *Theatre and Human Rights*, by Paul Rae, Palgrave Macmillan, 2009, pp. ix–xii.

Muñiz, Ángel, director. *Nueba Yol*. Venevision, 1995.

"Netherlands Antilles." *Migration Policy Institute*, Migration Information Source, 16 Oct. 2006, www.migrationinformation.org/datahub/countrydata.cfm?ID=464.

Nevins, Joseph. "A Tale of Two Voyages." *Nacla*, 19 Feb. 2012, nacla.org/blog/2012/2/19/tale-two-voyages-and-global-color-line.

Ngai, Mae M. *Impossible Subjects: Illegal Aliens and the Making of Modern America*. Princeton UP, 2004.

"Nuestros socios y sus obras. Paco Chanona." *SACM Sociedad de Autores y Compositores de México*, www.sacm.org.mx/biografias/biografias-interior.asp?txtSocio=00587.

Nwosu, Chiamaka, and Jeanne Batalova. "Immigrants from the Dominican Republic in the United States." *Migration Policy Institute*, 18 Jul. 2014, www.migrationpolicy.org/article/immigrants-dominican-republic-united-states.

Olwig, Karen Fog, and Ninna Nyberg Sørensen. *Work and Migration: Life and Livelihoods in a Globalizing World.* Routledge, 2002.

Ong, Aihwa. *Flexible Citizenship: The Cultural Logics of Transnationality.* Duke UP, 1999.

Ortiz, Fernando. "Del fenómeno social de la 'transculturación' y de su importancia en Cuba." *Contrapunteo cubano del tabaco y el azúcar.* Ariel, 1973, pp. 129–35.

Ortiz, Fernando. "Los factores humanos de la cubanidad." *Etnia y sociedad*, edited by Isaac Barreal Fernández, Editorial de ciencias sociales, 1993, pp. 1–20.

Ovalle, Elizabeth. *Por hora y a* Piece-Work. *Teatro: Obras premiadas.* Casa de Teatro, 1993, pp. 15–38.

Ovalle, Elizabeth. *Por hora y a* Piece-Work. *La mujer frente al espejo (Antología anotada de dramaturgas dominicanas contemporáneas).* BYU and La Trinitaria, 2007, pp. 244–62.

Pacini Hernandez, Deborah. *Oye como va: Hybridity and Identity in Latino Popular Music.* Temple UP, 2010.

Paravisini-Gebert, Lizabeth, and Consuelo López Springfield. "Introduction." *Callaloo: A Journal of African Diaspora Arts and Letters*, vol. 23, no. 3, 2000, pp. 819–20.

Paravisini-Gebert, Lizabeth, and Consuelo López Springfield, editors. *Dominican Republic Literature and Culture.* Special issue of *Callaloo: A Journal of African Diaspora Arts and Letters*, vol. 23, no. 3, 2000, pp. 819–1161.

Passerin d'Entrèves Maurizio. "Hannah Arendt and the Idea of Citizenship." *Dimensions of Radical Democracy*, edited by C. Mouffe, Routledge, pp. 145–68.

Pérez, Guillermo. "Culpables pagarían hasta 20 años de prisión." *Listín Diario*, 9 Feb. 2012, www.listindiario.com/la-republica/2012/02/09/221051/culpables-pagarian-hasta-20-anos-de-prision.

Pérez, Loida Maritza. *Geographies of Home: A Novel.* Viking, 1999.

Pérez Rosario, Vanessa. *Hispanic Caribbean Literature of Migration: Narratives of Displacement.* Palgrave, 2010.

Pessar, Patricia R. "Transnationalism and Racialization within Contemporary United States Immigration." *Problematizing Blackness: Self-Ethnographies by Black Immigrants to the United States*, edited by Percy C. Hintzen and Jean Muteba Rahier, Routledge, 2003, pp. 21–34.

Pessar, Patricia R. *A Visa for a Dream: Dominicans in the United States.* Allyn and Bacon, 1995.

Peterson, Michael. *Straight White Male: Performance Art Monologues.* UP of Mississippi, 1997.

"Pocas posibilidades de más sobrevivientes." *Diario Libre*, 7 Feb. 2012, www.diariolibre.com/noticias/pocas-posibilidades-de-ms-sobrevivientes-IJDL323209.

Portes, Alejandro, and Min Zhou. "The New Second Generation: Segmented Assimilation and Its Variants." *Annals of the American Academy of Political and Social Science*, no. 530, 1993, pp. 74–96.

Quackenbush, Howard, L. *Antología del teatro dominicano contemporáneo.* BYU and La Trinitaria, 2004.

Quackenbush, Howard, L. "Los lectores del ático." *Antología del Teatro dominicano.* Vol. 1, edited by Howard Quackenbush, BYU and La Trinitaria, 2004, pp. 95–100.

Rae, Paul. *Theatre and Human Rights.* Palgrave Macmillan, 2009.

Ramírez, Dixa. *Colonial Phantoms: Belonging and Refusal in the Dominican Americas, from the 19th Century to the Present.* New York UP, 2018.

Ramos-García, Luis A., editor. *The State of Latino Theater in the United States: Hybridity, Transculturation, and Identity.* Routledge, 2002.

Repertorio Español. "Plays Produced by Repertorio Español since Its Founding in 1968." https://www.repertorio.org/#/repertorio-espanol.

Ricourt, Milagros. *Dominicans in New York City: Power from the Margins.* Routledge, 2002.

Ridout, Nicholas. *Theater and Ethics.* Palgrave Macmillan, 2009.

Rivera Céspedes, Julissa. *Miches: Ponle Esperanza.* ¿Quién se atreve con un entremés de Cristóbal de Llerena? *Premio Internacional de Teatro 2005.* Casa de Teatro, 2005, pp. 191–241.

Rizk, Beatriz J. "Una crónica no anunciada: El 'otro' latino en el ámbito teatral de Estados Unidos." *Aisthesis*, no. 45, 2009, pp. 39–55.

Rodríguez, Marco Antonio. *Ashes of Light.* NoPassport, 2012.

Rodríguez, Marco Antonio. *Barceló on the Rocks/Barceló con hielo.* NoPassport, 2016.

Rodríguez, Marco Antonio. *La luz de un cigarrillo.* NoPassport, 2012.

Rodríguez, Marco Antonio. "Re: Ashes of Light." Received by Camilla Stevens, 24 Aug. 2018.

Rodríguez, Marco Antonio. www.marcoantoniorodriguez.com/.

Rodríguez, Néstor E. *Divergent Dictions: Contemporary Dominican Literature.* Translated by Kersten Oloff, Caribbean Studies Press, 2011.

Rodríguez, Yolanny. "Los ATI demostraron que vale la pena vernos también." *Vetas*, 19 Jan. 2012, agendagraficadiaria.blogspot.com/2012/01/los-ati-demostraron-que-vale-la-pena.html.

Rodríguez de León, Francisco. *El furioso merengue del norte: Una historia de la comunidad dominicana en los Estados Unidos.* Editorial Sitel, 1998.

Romero, Simon. "Nightmare at Sea Shatters Dreams in a Dominican Town." *New York Times*, 16 Aug. 2004, www.nytimes.com/2004/08/16/world/nightmare-at-sea-shatters-dreams-in-a-dominican-town.html.

Ronzino, Maickel. "La soledad me da tiempo de crear." *Clave Digital,* 14 Sept. 2005, www.clavedigital.com.

Rosario, Nelly. *Song of the Water Saints.* Vintage Books, 2003.

Rose, Tricia. *Black Noise: Rap Music and Black Culture in Contemporary America.* Wesleyan UP, 1994.

Rossini, Jon D. *Contemporary Latino/a Theater: Wrighting Ethnicity.* Southern Illinois UP: 2008.

Sagás, Ernesto. *Race and Politics in the Dominican Republic.* UP of Florida, 2000.

Sagás, Ernesto, and Sintia E. Molina. "Introduction: Dominican Transnational Migration." *Dominican Migration: Transnational Perspectives*, edited by Sagás and Sintia E. Molina, UP of Florida, 2004, pp. 1–28.

Sánchez, Luis Rafael. *Quíntuples.* Ediciones del Norte, 1985.

Sandín, Lyn Di Iorio, and Richard Perez, editors. *Contemporary U.S. Latino/a Literary Criticism.* Palgrave Macmillan, 2007.

Sandoval-Sánchez, Alberto. *José Can You See? Latinos On and Off Broadway.* U of Wisconsin P, 1999.

Sandoval-Sánchez, Alberto. "Politicizing Abjection: Towards the Articulation of a Latino AIDS Queer Identity." *Passing Lines: Sexuality and Immigration*, edited by Brad Epps et al., Harvard UP and David Rockefeller Center for Latin American Studies, pp. 311–19.

Sandoval-Sánchez, Alberto, editor. *Sirena Selena vestida de pena.* Special issue of *Centro Journal*, vol. 15, no. 2, 2003, pp. 1–283.

Sandoval-Sánchez, Alberto, and Nancy Saporta Sternbach. *Stages of Life: Transcultural Performance and Identity in U.S. Latina Theater.* U of Arizona P, 2001.

Sassen, Saskia. "Global Cities and Survival Circuits." *Global Woman: Nannies, Maids, and Sex Workers in the New Economy*, edited by Barbara Ehrenreich and Arlie Russell Hochschild, Metropolitan Books, 2002, pp. 254–74.

Sención, Viriato. *Los que falsificaron la firma de Dios.* Taller, 1992.

Sención, Viriato. "Viriato Sención, 18 años después del Premio Nacional de Novela." Interview by José Carvajal, *José Carvajal*, 7 Aug. 2010, escritorjosecarvajal.blogspot.com/2010/08/viriato-sencion-18-anos-despues-del.html.

Sención, Viriato, and Asa Zatz. *They Forged the Signature of God.* Curbstone Press, 1995.

"60 millas al este." *La Esquina Dominicana*, laesquinadominicana.com/2008/05/60-millas-al-este/.

Shafir, Gershon, and Alison Brysk. "The Globalization of Rights: From Citizenship to Human Rights." *Citizenship Studies*, vol. 10, no. 3, 2006, pp. 275–87.

Smith, Andrew. "Migrancy, Hybridity, and Postcolonial Literary Studies." *The Cambridge Companion to Postcolonial Literary Studies*, edited by Neil Lazarus, Cambridge UP, 2004, pp. 241–61.

Smith, Michael Peter. "Transnationalism and Citizenship." *Approaching Transnationalisms: Studies on Transnational Societies, Multicultural Contacts, and Imaginings of Home*, edited by Brenda S. A. Yeoh, Michael W. Charney, and Tong Chee Kiong, Kluwer Academic, 2003, pp. 15–39.

Sørensen, Ninna Nyberg. "Narratives of Longing, Belonging, and Caring in the Dominican Diaspora." *Caribbean Narratives of Belonging: Fields of Relations, Sites of Identity*, edited by Jean Besson and Karen Fog Olwig, Macmillan Caribbean, 2005, pp. 222–41.

Stavans Ilan, and Edna Acosta Belén, editors. *The Norton Anthology of Latino Literature.* W. W. Norton, 2011.

Stefansson, Anders H. "Homecomings to the Future: From Diasporic Mythographies to Social Projects of Return." *Homecomings: Unsettling Paths of Return*, edited by Fran Markowitz and Anders Stefansson, Lexington Books, 2004, pp. 2–20.

Stephens, Tom. *Dictionary of Latin American Racial and Ethnic Terms. Part 1: Spanish American Terms*. UP of Florida, 1999.

Stevens, Camilla. *Family and Identity in Contemporary Cuban and Puerto Rican Drama*. UP of Florida, 2004.

Stevens, Camilla. "Hispanic Caribbean Theatre on the Move: Crossing Borders, Redefining Boundaries." *Latin American Theatre Review*, vol. 50, no. 1, 2016, pp. 11–27.

Suárez, Lucía M. *The Tears of Hispaniola*. UP of Florida, 2006.

Svich, Caridad, and María Teresa Marrero, editors. *Out of the Fringe: Contemporary Latina/o Theater and Performance*. Theatre Communications Group, 2000.

Taylor, Diana. *The Archive and the Repertoire: Performing Cultural Memory in the Americas*. Duke UP, 2003.

Teátrica. http://www.teatrica.org/.

Tölölyan, Khachig. "Rethinking Diaspora(s): Stateless Power in the Transnational Moment." *Diaspora: A Journal of Transnational Studies*, vol. 5, no. 1, 1996, pp. 3–36.

Toney, Joyce. "The West Indians: A Century of Living in New York City." *Social Science Docket*, vol. 9, no. 2, 2009, pp. 52–54.

Torres-Saillant, Silvio. "Antelación: Sobre la perspectiva diaspórica." *El retorno de las yolas: Ensayos sobre diáspora, democracia y dominicanidad*. Ediciones Librería La Trinitaria/Editorial Manatí, 1999, pp. 393–404.

Torres-Saillant, Silvio. "Diasporic Disquisitions, Dominicanists, Transnationalism, and the Community." *Dominican Studies Working Papers I*. Dominican Studies Institute, 2000.

Torres-Saillant, Silvio. "Epílogo: Contrapunteo de la diáspora y el Estado." *El retorno de las yolas: Ensayos sobre diáspora, democracia y dominicanidad*. Ediciones Librería La Trinitaria/Editorial Manatí, 1999, pp. 405–24.

Torres-Saillant, Silvio. *An Intellectual History of the Caribbean*. Palgrave Macmillan, 2006.

Torres-Saillant, Silvio. *Introduction to Dominican Blackness*. CUNY Dominican Studies Institute, City College of New York, 2010.

Torres-Saillant, Silvio. "Problematic Paradigms: Racial Diversity and Corporate Identity in the Latino Community." *Latinos: Remaking America*. 2nd ed., edited by Marcelo M. Suárez-Orozco and Mariela M. Páez, U of California P, 2009, pp. 435–55.

Torres-Saillant, Silvio. "Redimir la utopía en el reino del cinismo: salutación de un libro." *El retorno de las yolas: Ensayos sobre diáspora, democracia y dominicanidad*. Ediciones Librería La Trinitaria/Editorial Manatí, 1999, pp. 227–35.

Torres-Saillant, Silvio. *El retorno de las yolas: Ensayos sobre diáspora, democracia y dominicanidad*. Ediciones Librería La Trinitaria/Editorial Manatí, 1999.

Torres-Saillant, Silvio. "El retorno de las yolas." *El retorno de las yolas: Ensayos sobre diáspora, democracia y dominicanidad*. Ediciones Librería La Trinitaria/Editorial Manatí, 1999, pp. 15–98.

Torres-Saillant, Silvio. "Similitudes y un ancho mar de diferencia: La experiencia literaria aquí y allá." *El retorno de las yolas: Ensayos sobre diáspora, democracia y dominicanidad.* Ediciones Librería La Trinitaria/Editorial Manatí, 1999, pp. 99–108.

Torres-Saillant, Silvio. "The Tribulations of Blackness: Stages in Dominican Racial Identity. *Callaloo: A Journal of African Diaspora Arts and Letters*, vol. 23, no. 3, 2000, pp. 1086–111.

Torres-Saillant, Silvio, and Ramona Hernández. *The Dominican Americans.* Greenwood, 1998.

Torres-Saillant, Silvio, and Ramona Hernández. "Editors' Preface: Dominican Quiddities in the U.S. Academy." *Punto 7 Review: A Journal of Marginal Discourse*, vol. 3, no. 1, 1996, pp. 1–10.

Torres-Saillant, Silvio, et al. *Desde la Orilla: hacia una nacionalidad sin desalojos.* Editora Manatí, 2004.

Trochimczyk, Maja. "*Mater Dolorosa* and Maternal Love in the Music of Henryk Górecki." *Polish Music Journal*, vol. 6, no. 2, 2003, polishmusic.usc.edu/research/publications/polish-music-journal/vol6no2/mater-dolorosa-and-maternal-love-in-goreckis-music/.

Trubowitz, Rachel. "'Nourish-Milke': Breast-Feeding and the Crisis of Englishness, 1600–1660." *Journal of English and Germanic Philology*, vol. 99, no. 1, Jan. 2000, pp. 29–49.

United Nations. "Universal Declaration of Human Rights." www.un.org/en/universal-declaration-human-rights/.

Valdez, Elena. "Masculinities in Crisis: A Tíguere, a Military Figure, and a *Sanky-Panky* as Three Models of Being a Man in the Dominican Republic." *Queering Iberia: Iberian Masculinities at the Margins*, edited by Josep M. Armengol-Carrera. Peter Lang, 2012, pp. 113–31.

Valdez, Pedro Antonio. "Paradise." *Reciclaje (flor de textos teatrales).* Isla Negra Editores, 2006, pp. 12–29.

Valdez, Pedro Antonio. "Writing in New York." *Literatura en los Estados Unidos: Historia y trayectoria de la diáspora intelectual*, edited by Franklin Gutiérrez, Fundación Global Democracia y Desarrollo, 2001, pp. 95–105.

Valencia, Sayak. *Gore Capitalism.* Translated by John Pluecker, Semiotext(e), 2018.

Van Hear, Nicholas. *New Diasporas: The Mass Exodus, Dispersal and Regrouping of Migrant Communities.* U of Washington P, 1998.

Vargas, Wilfrido. "La Yola." *El Funcionario*, Karen, 1994. CD.

Vargas, Wilfrido. "La Yola (1983)." *YouTube*, 12 Apr. 2017, www.youtube.com/watch?v=dQrrWKqcoHM.

Vásquez Escaño, Álex. *Yoleros. Palabras acentuadas: Antología de cuatro dramaturgos latinos en la ciudad de Nueva York.* La Ovejita Ebooks, 2014, pp. 72–119.

Vega, Manuel A. "Suman 48 los muertos por la yola que zozobró en Samaná." *Listín Diario*, 9 Feb. 2012, www.listindiario.com/la-republica/2012/2/8/221050/Suman-48-las-personas-muertas-por-yola-que-zozobro-en-Samana.

Veloz Maggiolo, Marcio. *Cultura, Teatro y relatos en Santo Domingo.* Universidad Católica Madre y Maestra, 1972.

Vergés, Pedro. "Un memorial de fracasos." *Escenarios de dos mundos: Inventario Teatral de Iberoamérica*. Vol. 4, edited by Moisés Pérez Coterillo and Carlos Espinosa Domínguez, Centro de documentación teatral, 1989, pp. 145–56.

Vertovec, Steven. *Transnationalism*. Routledge, 2009.

Vicioso, Luisa Sherezada. "My Dominican food: Chiqui Vicioso-Writer." *Dominican Cooking*, 7 Dec. 2012, www.dominicancooking.com/11131-my-dominican-food-chiqui-vicioso-writer.html.

Vicioso, Luisa Sherezada. *Nuyor/Islas. Aquí me tocó escribir. Antología de escritor@as latin@as en Nueva York*, edited by Paquita Suárez Coalla, Trabe, 2006, pp. 66–78.

Vicioso, Luisa Sherezada. "An Oral History (Testimonio)." Translated by Nina M. Scott. *Daughers of the Diaspora: Afra-Hispanic Writers*, edited by Miriam De Costa-Williams, Ian Randle Publishers, 2003, pp. 313–18.

Volonteri, Mónica. "Pargo o la irrupción de la verdad." *Conjunto*, no. 123, Oct.-Nov. 2001, pp. 70–73.

Wallace, Clare. "Monologue Theatre, Solo Performance and Self as Spectacle." *Monologues: Theatre, Performance, Subjectivity*, edited by Clare Wallace, Litteraria Pragensia, 2006, pp. 1–16.

"Weekend Update with Jane Curtin and Bill Murray." *Saturday Night Live*, created by Lorne Michaels, season 4, episode 8, NBC, 1978, http://snltranscripts.jt.org/78/78hupdate.phtml.

Wijers, Marjan. "Women, Labor, and Migration: The Position of Trafficked Women and Strategies for Support." *Global Sex Workers: Rights, Resistance, and Redefinition*, edited by Kamala Kempadoo and Jo Doezema, Routledge, 1998, pp. 69–78.

Ybarra, Patricia. *Latinx Theater in the Times of Neoliberalism*. Northwestern UP, 2017.

"Yoleros at Bushwick Starr Theater." https://www.indiegogo.com/projects/yoleros-at-bushwick-starr-theater#/.

Index

Note: Page numbers in *italics* refer to figures.